WARLORDS, INC.

Black Markets, Broken States, and the Rise of the Warlord Entrepreneur

Edited by **NOAH RAFORD** and **ANDREW TRABULSI**

Foreword by **ROBERT J. BUNKER**

North Atlantic Books
Berkeley, California

Published by
North Atlantic Books
P.O. Box 12327
Berkeley, California 94712

Cover and book design by Mary Ann Casler
Printed in the United States of America

Warlords, Inc.: Black Markets, Broken States, and the Rise of the Warlord Entrepreneur is sponsored and published by the Society for the Study of Native Arts and Sciences (dba North Atlantic Books), an educational nonprofit based in Berkeley, California, that collaborates with partners to develop cross-cultural perspectives, nurture holistic views of art, science, the humanities, and healing, and seed personal and global transformation by publishing work on the relationship of body, spirit, and nature.

North Atlantic Books' publications are available through most bookstores. For further information, visit our website at www.northatlanticbooks.com or call 800-733-3000.

An older and—in parts—more detailed version of Chapter 6 previously appeared as "The (Un)bearable Lightness of Violence: Warlords as an Alternative Form of Governance in the 'Westphalian Periphery,'" in *State Failure Revisited II: Actors of Violence and Alternative Forms of Governance*, edited by Tobias Debiel and Daniel Lambach (7–49), Institute for Development and Peace, University of Duisburg-Essen (INEF Report, 89/2007).

A version of Chapter 10 was published as "Green Social Democracy or Barbarism: Climate Change and the End of High Modernism," in Craig Calhoun and Georgi Derluguian, eds., *The Deepening Crisis: Governance Challenges after Neoliberalism, Volume 2* in the Social Science Research Council's series *Possible Futures*, NYU Press, June 2011.

A version of Chapter 13 was previously published as "Beyond Survival: A Short Course in Pioneering in Response to the Current Crisis," Triarchy Press, 2009.

Library of Congress Cataloging-in-Publication Data
Warlords, Inc. : black markets, broken states, and the rise of the warlord entrepreneur / edited by Noah Raford and Andrew Trabulsi ; foreword by Robert J. Bunker.
pages cm
Summary: "A cutting-edge examination of new types of political actors who emerge in a world of drug cartels and transnational criminal organizations. Leading experts chart the changing geopolitical landscape as the world's elaborate but fragile political systems become increasingly vulnerable to breakdown and deliberate disruption" — Provided by publisher.
ISBN 978-1-58394-901-6 (paperback) — ISBN 978-1-58394-902-3 (ebook)
1. Warlordism. 2. Political stability. 3. Organized crime--Political aspects. 4. Transnational crime--Political aspects. 5. Political corruption. I. Trabulsi, Andrew. II. Raford, Noah.
JZ1317.2.W374 2014
364.1'3--dc23
2014032400

1 2 3 4 5 6 7 SHERIDAN 19 18 17 16 15
Printed on recycled paper

To Napier Collyns

Contents

Foreword

Violent Entrepreneurs and Techno Warlords ... All Edge

Robert J. Bunker

Two Vignettes

When Frederick VI of Nuremberg called in his loan marker with Emperor Sigismund of the Holy Roman Empire in 1411, times got downright nasty in the old fief of Brandenburg. Sigismund, perennially short of hard cash, had put up the fief as collateral—when he couldn't cover his marker, Frederick VI foreclosed, like any self-respecting strongman would do. Sigismund didn't care, since the lands had helped him become emperor, and he had no real control over the fief anyway—it belonged to the Quitzow and other landed knightly families and now would be Frederick VI's headache. Undaunted, Frederick VI worked a deal to contract a siege train—composed of what was then high-tech cannon like "Lazy Greta"—from Thuringia to blast the local Quitzows and the other knights out of their strongholds and make the foreclosure complete. It took only a few hundred years and quite a few suppressed rebellions, but the Hohenzollern family, of which Frederick VI was a part, became secure in their rule and the legitimate rulers of the fief. In time, Prussia and many other lands were added to the family holdings, with their Hohenzollern descendants eventually gaining the titles of kings and emperors. Not a bad run for a royal family that can trace back its origins to a medieval mafioso out of Nuremberg who made a killing—and killed with impunity—to get his principal and a tidy profit back from that fateful marker owed to him by a Holy Roman emperor.

Joaquín "El Chapo" (Shorty) Guzmán grew up a poor child of Sinaloa, Mexico, mostly in the 1960s. He was extremely ambitious, climbing up the trafficking ranks to become a member of the Guadalajara cartel while still in his twenties. With the split up of that cartel, due to the torture killing of U.S. Drug Enforcement Administration (DEA) agent "Kiki" Camarena and the creation of the plaza system, El Chapo went on to form the Sinaloa cartel with a triumvirate of other hardened traffickers. As a brilliant criminal mastermind, El Chapo thought strategically, only killed when necessary, and would rather corrupt his way into gaining influence than get into an all-out shooting war. "Shorty" at one time even made it to the Forbes list of richest individuals in world. Still, he is responsible for a number of invasions of plazas in Mexico controlled by opposing cartels, has sent his forces into Central and South America, and has readily terrorized entire cities with broken and tortured bodies dumped on the streets and hung from bridges to get his sanguine points across. Unlike the progeny of Frederick VI, though, those of El Chapo will probably not ascend to dynastic greatness as a legacy of the little man's violent entrepreneurial tendencies. But then the narco wars in Mexico are far from over. While El Chapo's family has taken a hit with his 2014 arrest—he has gotten away from prison once before—his kids are still alive and ultimately the Sinaloa cartel has plenty of gunmen, territory, and illicit profits at its disposal, making it the most powerful criminal organization in all of Mexico.

All Edge

The above vignettes illustrate how historical patterns can and do repeat themselves. A Central American peasant's fatalistic complaints of "La misma mierda, solamente las moscas son diferente" (The same shit, only the flies are different) about the Sandinistas pretty much nails part of this process.[1] The insights offered by a science-fiction writer like William Gibson, on the other hand, are more focused with his take on conflict and entrepreneurship in cyberspace. We only have to look at the slogan of one of the predatory biotechnology corporations found in *Burning Chrome:* "Maas. Small, fast, ruthless. All Edge," for that to become self-evident.[2] Still, take away about 650 years of technological advances from his writings and the actions of Frederick VI of Nuremberg in the first vignette appear remarkably similar to those of Maas Biolabs GmbH. Strip away even fewer years of civilizational evolution—half-a-century or so—and, at its core, the vignette of "Shorty" also provides us with the same edgy and dangerous entrepreneurship vibe.

A more scholarly perspective identifies a four-stage process of human social and political organization that exists related to weapons systems and coercive-extraction mechanisms. This process, linked to the evolving economic and political systems of civilizations, not surprisingly underlies the key observation identified in this book's introduction, "that, over time, the line between black, gray, and white markets blurs, and warlord enterprises become indistinguishable from other forms of legal enterprise or, indeed, even the state itself." This process can be readily observed in the historical evolution of the knight—the rise and fall of a fundamental component of the medieval age.

The first stage of this process is that of entrepreneurism and experimentalism. A weapons system was required to contend with the barbarian raiders that had plagued Western Europe for centuries. These raiders were greatly responsible for the destruction of the Roman Empire and precipitated the shift from the classical to the medieval age. By the Battle of Tours, it was apparent that heavy cavalry was the solution to this threat. This required taking infantry and mounting them on horseback. The Carolingians and other empires of the era—essentially lead by local warlords and strongmen who had seized power—had to go through a trial-and-error process to make this new system work. The entire arms and armor, training and organization, and logistical support system (like the mass breeding and sustaining of warhorses) had to be created from the ground up. As this system was established, heavy cavalry forces grew increasingly deadly.

The second stage in this process is institutionalization. In this stage, not only have "things been worked out" but also standard operating procedures have developed. Mounted cavalrymen not only became the first line of defense for western Christendom but also gained position and privilege on their way to legitimacy within the new civilization that had formed. Lands were won, castles erected, and ultimately the knight allowed the empire and kingdoms of the West to go on the offensive in what were essentially crusades in eastern Europe and the Holy Lands.

Ritualism characterizes the third stage of this process. The effectiveness of the knight on the battlefield began to be severely degraded as technological threats matured. Dogma and oppressive bureaucracy set in, with armor becoming heavier and heavier and with cumbersome ornamentation beginning to appear. In this stage, things are done because that is the way they have always been done; process becomes more important than progress. Further, a climate of zero tolerance and risk aversion exists. Questions about the efficacy and logic of directives are suppressed while new and creative ideas are stifled.

The final and fourth stage of this historical process is satirical in nature. That visionary brute with a hunger in his eyes, quite willing to kill quickly and without remorse, who existed in the first stage has now been fully neutered. Strong arms and armor and a stout warhorse have given way to orders based on fluff, the wearing of gaudy dress, and cushy saddles. Once heroic figures, embodied in images such as St. George the Dragon Slayer, devolved into old men on broken-down mounts fighting monsters made out of windmills. The time of knights had passed and to field them now in battle would be blatantly suicidal.

In fact, the knight had been stalked for some time by a new visionary businessman and killer, one wielding early firearms and siege cannon. This warlord entrepreneur was not of polite society and was not an agent of the state; in fact, he was considered little better than a common criminal—if not worse, as his weapons smelled of fire and brimstone and suggested that dark and demonic forces were at play. His weapons were strange and disruptive, he had no stake in the prevailing status quo, and he would readily kill if disrespected or if the contract was lucrative enough. Against such entrepreneurs and their brethren, the technologically inferior knight was no more than prey and was eventually hunted into extinction.

So the process began anew, and another social and political life cycle was born as history passed from the medieval to the modern age. Mercenary captains and master gunners linked up with dynastic entrepreneurs who connived and fought their way to legitimacy. In the process, economies, warfare, and states changed. Proto-capitalism and mercantilism evolved into free-market economies; standing armies were formed and divisional elements added; crude firearms and cannons gave way to armored formations, air forces, and ballistic missiles. In fact, civilization itself was recast as the modern age advanced, with the early dynastic states of Europe evolving into the present system of Westphalian states within our current international system.

Contrary to some earlier allegations, history has by no means come to an end. Social and political organizational change is constant—it is how human civilization advances. As this book will attest, this four-stage process has begun anew. Charles Tilly's prosaic statement that organized crime is inherently linked to war making and state making cannot be denied.[3] El Chapo's story in Mexico, and the stories of millions of his lesser contemporaries across the globe—such as computer hackers, nihilist terrorists, or Chinese triad members—represent the emerging techno-warlords of our era. This is a new type of warlord, who is increasingly exploiting the deviant and dark forms of globalization and illicit economies that have appeared, ranging from narcotics to organ harvesting to cyber crime and beyond. These are the violent entrepreneurs of which Martin van Creveld has said, "In the future, war will not be waged by armies but by groups whom today we call terrorists, guerrillas, bandits and robbers, but who will undoubtedly hit upon more formal titles to describe themselves."[4]

And so, with their onslaught, comes the transition from the modern to the postmodern age, and with it, a rise in political instability, black markets, and transnational crime. This book, at a visceral level—analogous to the

Central American peasants with their mutterings about shit and flies—examines such a future as it exists today, yesterday, and tomorrow. It is not a pretty one for the Westphalian state and its social and political form of organization. While it might be easy to overlook in the buzz of our daily lives, once you see, you can't un-see. Dark swarms are massing on the horizon.

Introduction

Warlords, Inc.—A Portrait

Andrew Trabulsi

On a rainy night in 1994, a squad of counternarcotics troops surrounded the first floor of a condominium complex in a wealthy suburb in Cali, Colombia, the country's third largest city. The agents, prepared to uncover a stash of cocaine and automatic weapons, instead discovered something more menacing: a large and sophisticated computer center.

Owned by a front man for the godfather of the Cali cartel, José Santacruz Londoño, the complex housed a $1.5 million IBM AS400 mainframe networked to a half-dozen computer terminals and monitors, staffed by up to six technicians twenty-four hours a day.[1] Loaded with custom-written data-mining software, the mainframe gathered intelligence that would otherwise have been available only to government agencies—the addresses and telephone numbers of U.S. diplomats and agents based in the country; the entire call log for the local phone company, leaked after threats of violence against employees; shipping and distribution information for deliveries being made around the country and abroad; and a detailed record of complex money transfers through proxy off-shore bank accounts, via clients whose interests lay in everything from money laundering in Tel Aviv to counterfeit pharmaceutical sales in Lima.[2] This was the kind of technology that many sophisticated Fortune 500 companies dreamed of, but for the Cali families, it was just a small piece of a much larger puzzle that kept operations humming everywhere from Bogotá to Madrid.

To international authorities, the Cali cartel was public enemy number one, having drawn fire from the U.S. State Department, Scotland Yard, and Interpol. Yet to their supporters, the Cali bosses epitomized the kind of rags-to-riches fame one could otherwise find only in a Hollywood movie. Jose Santacruz Londoño, a one-time delinquent, studied engineering and went into construction, emerging years later as "El Estudiante," a sagacious real estate tycoon whose marble *narquitectura* mansion loomed high above the sugarcane fields of Cali. His business partner, Gilberto Rodríguez Orejuela, earned his epithet, the "Chess Player," as an operational mastermind, growing up impoverished only to parlay youthful jobs—as a drugstore clerk by day and a kidnapper by night—into a vast network of enterprises, including a pharmacy chain, office and apartment buildings, banks, car dealerships, radio stations, and Cali's coveted América soccer team. His younger brother Miguel, a handsome socialite known as "El Señor," became a fixture on the local scene, owning nightclubs and restaurants throughout the country. Their children, privately educated in the United States and Europe, held an esteem in the country comparable to that of the Rockefellers or Kennedys—a name not only respected but also aspired to by fellow Colombians.

Having escaped the backwater slums of Colombia's Cauca River Valley, they came to rule Cali, a city starved for investment and security. While the cartels in Medellin, two hundred miles to the north, kept the media's attention, Cali quietly produced more cocaine than any other city on the planet, up to 70 percent of the substance in the United States, and, according to the U.S. Drug Enforcement Agency, as much as 90 percent of the drug in Europe.[3] With bank accounts as far afield as Hungary and Israel, the Cali families managed a global distribution network with hubs in Antwerp, New York, Los Angeles, and Tokyo.

While perhaps surprising, the story of the Cali cartel is by no means unique. In the sphere of international development and security, such vignettes represent a pattern of growth and opportunism found again and again around the world. From the oligarchs of Russia to the yakuza in Japan, ambitious non-state actors operating under weakened regulatory or flexible security environments follow similar paths.

Beginning as small-time operators, they can grow to become significant forces in the economy, both preying upon and playing a part in the mechanics of the state and traditional markets. As their influence grows, especially in economically depressed locales, they can become market makers and market shapers, rivaling and often exceeding traditional economic development enterprises. Having captured existing markets and made new ones, they can diversify into established legal trades, financing these efforts with cash from a network of globalized criminal syndicates. Then, armed with wealth and power, these deviant economic agents eventually become political actors themselves, often assuming leadership roles in the same state organizations and institutions upon which they originally preyed.

We trace the evolution of this phenomenon by following the footsteps of an identity designed for an allegorical purpose, finding it manifest across the world from the streets of Bangalore to the White Mountains: the warlord entrepreneur.

Warlord entrepreneurs are the impresarios of black markets, managing an array of illicit activity that generates untold trillions of dollars in the global economy each year. They exist in a world that is both divergent from and linked to legitimate state and private administrative apparatuses, a world dependent on the infrastructures of a globalized society, such as shipping lanes and IT networks, but cut off from the intent such systems were designed with. Warlord entrepreneurs both depend upon and persistently weaken the world's legal and market frameworks.

With the unique position outside of and between the worlds of conventional market and government actors, warlord entrepreneurs are able to outmaneuver and outrun the orthodox administrative capacities of the state and private economies. As a result, they usurp and even define power structures inside the conventional political-economic machine itself, by bribing, threatening, killing, provoking, blackmailing, and otherwise subverting traditional political-economic actors. Warlord entrepreneurs are therefore powerfully positioned to both work with and exploit their legal economic counterparts, particularly in emerging markets and developing countries, where the scaling of traditional businesses can largely depend on a degree of cooperation between illicit economic parties, who frequently control territorial resources through use of coercion or force, wagging the tail of the conventional economic dogs looking to sustain, develop, or penetrate new markets around the world.

Our book focuses not only on the individual behavior of these actors but also on what happens as an effect of their organization, adaptation, and growth in political economies globally, as they rise to become a preponderant force, the warlord enterprise.

The term *warlord enterprise*—an intimation of our book's title—describes the broader organizational dimension of the business of warlord entrepreneurialism, the dimension at which an element of scale is required to succeed. Through this lens, we examine transnational criminal activity as more than just independent, stand-alone operations serving small market segments or demographics, like the neighborhood meth house or basement cannabis grower—although those may be nodes inside a much larger illicit network. Instead, we look at the warlord enterprise as a large, interconnected, and highly adaptive organization that plays a deeper, more foundational role in the development of political-economic systems, while simultaneously serving the interests of black markets. These shadowy actors, as we will show, fill in the gaps and round out the edges of the global political economy, frequently—though not exclusively—in places where the rule of law is up for grabs and the faculties of the state are loosely held, creating an incorporated set of warlords—*Warlords, Inc.*

The key observation of this book is that, over time, the line between black, gray, and white markets blurs, and warlord enterprises become indistinguishable from other forms of legal enterprise or, indeed, even the state itself. In the sphere of international affairs, this creates additional friction between nation-states seeking to enhance diplomatic efforts and strengthen foreign policy, and in turn, it becomes a means through which diplomatic efforts and foreign policies are pursued.

For those caught in the crossfire of such economic deviance, the allure of participation in the illicit economy, at least on the production and labor side, is more complicated than simply a matter of immoral decision making. Rather, it is a survival strategy for those without easy access to legitimate, sustainable market opportunities—the poor and undereducated, as well as those in locations with ineffective or corrupt institutional support for mainstream business.

In this respect, the world of transnational crime and the corollary mechanics of warlord entrepreneurialism is, in many cases, a story of the stark realities of life in developing countries—and one that benefits those already in the developed world. Whether the transport of drugs, harvesting of organs, extralegal extraction of commodities, deployment of weapons to insurgencies and rebel groups, or movement of laundered money into anonymous bank accounts in Switzerland, the consequences of such behavior continue to position those already well positioned in the economic value chain against those perpetually struggling to make it.

The consequences of the rise of such insidious forces are at once both staggering and, unfortunately, remarkably foreseeable. As the tensions of globalization mount, the world's complex but fragile political systems are becoming increasingly vulnerable to breakdown and deliberate disruption. Modern states are at elevated risk of partial failure or even collapse as the infrastructure—networks, supply chains, trade routes—grows more tenuous, resources become more contested, and normative authority becomes difficult to maintain.

Crisis, when it occurs, will open new arenas of competition for political and economic control and new opportunities for innovation and reorganization. It will also test the resilience of a citizenry that has grown used to unusually high levels of security and prosperity.

Successful pioneers and opportunists in this new world will prosper by competing to establish new directions and approaches in a rapidly changing environment. Examples of current organizations that succeed include transnational gangs, ideological insurgencies, and organized criminal groups. Most established organizations—whether in government, business, or civil society—are poorly positioned to adapt. Their legitimacy and competitive advantage will erode as the world becomes less stable and shocks become more common. Increasingly, deviant actors will compete for legitimacy and influence by playing a role in markets and services currently provided by the state or mainstream business.

How will civil society and underfunded governments compete against ideologically driven groups intent on working outside the law? How will government and commerce function in a world where contracts cannot be enforced and regulations are selectively applied? What state services and economic functions might such deviant actors compete to provide? And finally, how might existing organizations prepare for the tensions that will ensue?

Warlords, Inc. brings together a team of writers to explore challenges like these that societies—both developing and developed—will face in such environments. In particular, it looks at the competitive dynamics of deviant and violent actors in post-state and weakened state politics and public administrations, as well as the forces that constrain or compete with them for influence.

We developed *Warlords, Inc.* as an anthology in an attempt to holistically capture the breadth and complexities of a subject of interminable nuance. Our goal, modestly, is to elevate the dialogue on issues concerning international security, human rights, cross-border conflicts, urban warfare, child immigration, terrorism, the mafia, state failure, and transitional crime. We want both to shed light on traditionally opaque subjects, illustrating the real and growing threats of transitional crime, and to give readers the information they need to effectively analyze potentially grave scenarios, should they arise. We also aim to provide clarity on what actions citizens and policymakers alike may take to combat and peacefully ameliorate legitimate threats to sovereignty and human security.

To accomplish this, we amassed a team of international experts whose background and specialties range from advisory roles to heads of state and consultants for the intelligence community to award-winning academics and career law-enforcement professionals. These contributors provide varied and thought-provoking perspectives on the structure, dynamics, and implications of warlord entrepreneurs as a global force to be reckoned with. We hope to illustrate the unique ways that such actors are shaping our world of tomorrow and provide inspiration for further discussion of our collective role in it.

The focus of this book is not just to highlight the immediate effects that such actors have on economic development, politics, state building, and the evolution of international relations. We also seek to draw attention to the long-term threats and opportunities that such trends will bring to global citizenry in decades to come. To accomplish this goal, we have divided the book into three parts, using the metaphor of "black market, black governance" and "light markets, light governance" to explore the spectrum of "gray markets, gray governance" between them.

In our first part, we uncover the dark side of warlord entrepreneurialism, asking, "What happens when nothing works?" Egypt, Libya, Syria, Mali, Tunisia, Mexico, Honduras, Brazil, Tibet, India, Pakistan, Iraq, Afghanistan, Myanmar, Somalia, Nigeria, Sudan, Ukraine, Lebanon … Russia, China, Britain, Japan, the United States. Are the difficulties faced by the West and its developed-world counterparts to effectually maintain their power in the first fifteen years of the twenty-first century a pattern or an outlier?

As we demonstrate, those actors managing the subtleties of the world's underground economy are better positioned than governments to take advantage of a planet driven by disarray. Whether by manipulating the flow of drugs (or humans) or by placing a hit on a political leader, black-market economic actors have a capacity that very few are able to use—and even fewer have had to master.

In the second part, we explore the middle ground: the world of semi-legal trade and state building. This part, drawing on case studies from around the world, identifies the many ways that warlord entrepreneurs add value—and even provide social services—to the communities they are nestled in. In doing so, we hope to demonstrate that the dynamics of deviant economics are anything but simple and that frequently such actors maintain—and even scale—their capacity by providing services that the state and legal enterprises cannot support.

Finally, in our last part, we provide stories and case studies that illustrate the positive steps that we can take to mitigate the worst impact that warlord entrepreneurs might have and to learn from the best that they have to offer. As we will show, in the face of such looming crises as resource shortages and climate change, there are still paths we can choose that will avoid some of the most negative effects that the world of black-market entrepreneurship brings to the table.

Twenty years after the bust of the Cali cartel's high-tech computer center, Cali, like much of Central and South America, still struggles to lift itself out of continuous threat of violence and widespread poverty.[4] Boasting a homicide rate of more than 85 per 100,000 residents—roughly four times that of Chicago—the city is torn apart by warring neo-paramilitary groups and other warlord entrepreneurial forces, even as it makes improvements. While the country receives praise in international media for recent booms in its mining and oil industries, little attention is paid to the persistent inequalities levied upon many of the country's citizens, those still left out of much of the nation's economic progress and still vulnerable to survival-driven participation in the country's never-ending dance with illicit trade.

Such examples serve as stark images of the world we may inherit. As the long journey of civilization continues, we find it important to look toward the periphery of human endeavors to identify the possibilities that may lie ahead. Our intent is not only to present alternative points of view as to what that future could be but also to offer narratives of hope, ways that society can adapt to the impacts warlord entrepreneurs will have on our global political economy.

Part 1

THE DARK SIDE

1 Of Warlords and Rodeos

Why Nothing Works

Vinay Gupta

When a stream of revenue large enough to finance an armed group cannot be extracted by any legitimate nonviolent enterprise, the businessmen who rise are by their very nature violent and illicit: they are warlord entrepreneurs.

It would be easy to dismiss these actors as phenomena of the edges, like cracks in neglected sidewalks, but they are really phenomena of failure, and failure is everywhere, once you let yourself see it. The cracked sidewalks are not only far away in countries with UN missions, they are in wealthy countries too, in those pockets where old industries died, leaving deskilled wastelands. In a stable, competitive environment, business eats the lunch of prospective warlord entrepreneurs. Vast capital assets, high trust networks, and deep human resources will always win against the comparatively small and disorganized warlord entrepreneur's tenacious little businesses. But things fall apart, the center cannot hold, and a certain somebody and friends do business where the state, IBM, and Walmart have all failed. Just as scrub comes in shortly after great oaks are felled, so our warlords are first through any available gap.

What is it that fails, giving the warlord entrepreneurs room for maneuver? Some say rule of law. Others, property rights or the state itself. I say it is accountability that fails: when nobody is willing to go to the wall for what is right, the failure that counts has started. The gap between

3

no profit for business and loss of state legitimacy is filled with corrupt authorities. A warlord entrepreneur's customers were first turned away by regular service providers, then alienated from the state. A customer should be able to get a legitimate visa, but the office is closed—except for bribes. A container ship is leaving on Thursday, but the available space is unavailable because there is nobody to inspect the shipment for arms until Monday. This area is meant to have regular police patrols, but after nine in the evening they are hardly seen.... The warlord entrepreneur is always last. It is the place you go when there is nobody else—the loan shark, the protection racket, the forged travel papers.

America's past warlord entrepreneurs are lionized. The Mafia and Vegas, baby, their town. During Vegas's heyday, the Rat Pack fluidly bridged acting, music, politics, activism on race issues, and organized crime. Nobody doubted that Frank Sinatra was tight with the mob; it was part of his charm, all part of the glamour. To this day, Vegas provides a service: vice. Once, that vice included alcohol, but now it is just drugs and prostitution. For Vegas to exist, the state had to turn a blind eye to warlord entrepreneur operations there—not just for a few years, but for decades. In this crisis—a failure of values—comes the inevitable transfer of legitimacy from the state to warlord entrepreneurs. In your mind's eye, meet Big Joe, who could be from anywhere. He genuinely cares about your problem, as he is personally responsible for your money and for the merchandise. He will take personal responsibility for outcomes, unlike all other actors involved in the situation, who hide behind job titles, policies, and badges. Everybody else has a policy. Warlord entrepreneurs have obligations. Everybody else has a hierarchy. Warlord entrepreneurs are accountable to the situation. Our bureaucracies create an enormous gap between the laudable goals and the public-relations front and the actual dysfunction and callousness of front-line operations. Dragons grow in this gap.

Every place a promise is made and then broken, the state loses legitimacy. Everywhere legitimate business will not do business, black-market business thrives. Cannot get a wire transfer from Guyana to Ghana to pay for your website, because the banks charge a fortune or simply will not send the money? That is just fine—use bitcoin like normal people. Cannot get a MasterCard in Liberia? Use a prepaid debit card from a foreign bank through your cousin in New York—and refill it by acting as a smurf for structured payments when they are laundering money. Every barrier to normalized business, to the smooth and effective functioning of business as usual, creates a shadow. In the deep shade, those dragons mature.

The little man who fixes visas sprouts teeth and becomes the criminal logistics magnate of a war-torn city. His protection racket works, because this is not Iowa and his men are accountable. Five AK-47s and an old Toyota become civilization's darning needle, holding together enough to let life go on just one more day. Everybody knows it's wrong, but in these times, what else to do? The budding warlord entrepreneur delivers when nobody else can. Pretty soon there's a vehicle fleet and a pool of capital and an operations base with a small training and recruitment program. If the guy's smart, he'll clean up a little and sign on with the State Department after the army leaves, providing logistics and security for programs with lax oversight. How often has this happened in Iraq and Afghanistan already? The answer is: always. Once the social fabric is torn, the warlord entrepreneur is like the clotting blood, the scab forming over the wound. It is a messy healing process, and infections can be terminal to the rule of law. But without the clean, smooth function of the legitimate system—without unbroken skin—these problems are inevitable. And once a situation has mostly scabbed over? The smart, logical thing to do is to mainstream the previously warlord entrepreneurs as businessmen who did rather well during the crisis period. That's the right thing to do, isn't it? I mean ... sure, we all know this guy had a past, but we can leave him out there in the cold, running a criminal syndicate, or we can get him to focus on his legitimate businesses ... the least bad of the bunch ... and pretty soon this kind of thinking puts the Taliban back in charge, because, you know, they're tough on opium production.

How did we wind up in this mess? The answer is disturbingly simple: we lost our legitimacy at the goat rodeo.

The Goat Rodeo Index

		goals				
		same	different	I	a divorce	
				II	a commune	
players	same	cartel	competition	III	a dying industry	
				IV	a toxic watershed	
				V	NATO / EU	
				VI	UN	
	different	cooperation	goat rodeo*	VII	the bank crises	
				VIII	a pandemic	
				IX	climate, MDGs	
				X	nanobio regulation	

Figure 1.1 Left, players versus goals in goat rodeo; right, levels of goat rodeo complexity.

The term *goat rodeo* is taken from aviation, where it means a situation in which several impossibly difficult things have to simultaneously go correctly for there to be any realistic chance of survival. The term also refers to the messy Texas practice of having small children practice their lasso skills on goats, as a safer alternative to full-sized cattle. For our purposes, a goat rodeo occurs when a committee sets out to solve a problem but is composed of individuals with different goals who are representing different classes of organization or agency. A typical post-disaster goat rodeo might include a couple of people from State Department or another government agency, some NGO reps, a few local partner organizations, and a few people from national monopolies for water and electricity, plus the host-state representatives, of course. Lacking a shared competitive framework or genuinely shared goals, the situation inevitably devolves into failure. Cooperation is impossible, because people want different things, and competition is implausible because the actors involved have entirely different rule sets. For larger problems, increase the size and diversity of the group until no action is possible at all. The size of the failure can be estimated using the scale above.

Again and again, chains of command and responsibility are abrogated in complex, shared governance arrangements that produce no responsible parties when failure comes. From no-fault divorce through to Kyoto, Copenhagen, Cancun, and the Millennium Development Goals, we plead that none of us are responsible, because all of us are. Warlord entrepreneurs eat this for breakfast. Every time the world of the white picket fences or the blue helmets of peace and justice fail to deliver on their promises, every time they burn people in internecine bickering over different priorities in the crisis, legitimacy bleeds out. Every time the bureaucrats do the wrong thing for the right reasons—or, more commonly, simply fail to do anything at all—a little more of the lifeblood of our civilization leaks out.

That's where the warlord entrepreneurs are coming from: it's us, screwing up one day at a time. American drug policy burns half of South America. European immigration policy ensures human trafficking remains intensely lucrative. Uneasy collusion in Africa is good for business, but that's not just legitimate business, it's every dirty scam going—from diamond mining to over-advertising breast-milk substitutes in places where we know there's no clean water.

You have to wonder how the world runs at all when we, the people who are supposed to be governing, supposed to be helping, cannot get our acts together. Every time we quietly complain about the bureaucracy, about lax decision making, about human resources, about inadequate briefings and vague political goals, that's your reminder that we are part of the problem, not just vendors of the solution.

My advice is to prevent goat rodeos: permit only a single class of player to participate, or fix the goal and bar those with alternative objectives.

2 Social and Economic Collapse

Lessons from History and Complexity

Peter Taylor and Noah Raford

The Potential for Societal Collapse and Reshaping of Society in the Next Twenty Years

There is now a substantial body of evidence—from studies of both historical and contemporary cases—that human societies and their economies are prone to rapid collapse at the peak of their prosperity.[1] Why is this the case? The evidence argues that the cause of collapse can be attributed to a mixture of external factors, such as the loss of critical resources like fuel or water, and internal political and economic stresses, which combine to exceed the system's ability to cope with change. But often it is not clear what triggered the decline. Almost all such rapid declines were unforeseen at the time, though in hindsight we may rationalize them as inevitable bubbles where demand outruns supply. Complexity theorists and punctuated equilibrium studies suggest that such rapid "phase transitions" may be endemic to all classes of complex systems but are particularly prevalent in those experiencing certain combinations of internal and external strain.

Could such a rapid phase transition—that is, social collapse—happen to our civilization? And if so, what might trigger it, and how can we best mitigate its effects? Commentators from a wide range of fields suggest that we may face serious threats to civilization in this century.[2] While there may be many risks associated with many resources—food, water, information networks, the environment, and climate—and the knock-on effect of their failure on financial systems, economies, and social institutions would be severe—the greatest immediate threat may come from energy.[3] With a rapidly increasing population in the majority of the world, studies suggest that demand will remorselessly exceed supply even if oil discovery continues at current levels. Technological innovation and cheap energy sources have allowed us to build a world in which our food, energy, goods, and services are more likely to be remotely sourced than locally produced. Longer, more efficient "just-in-time" supply chains may deliver goods and services to our doorstep from across the world, but any rupture to the links in these chains can propagate failures throughout the global network, and, in turn, precipitate other failures in other supply chains.

Other external shock factors increase the risk of such disruption. Rapid developments at the nano-scale in biological systems, computers, and materials make it likely that not only will further threats emerge to humanity and the environment, but that rogue groups, including terrorists and unsupervised tinkerers, will find it increasingly easy to use these technologies, as we have seen with computer viruses propagated through the Internet. Some authors see technology as a potential solution to these problems—that, as these technologies begin to be used against us, technological fixes will be developed to counter them. While technologies will undoubtedly keep moving the goalposts of the discussion, the time they take to come to maturity makes their immaturity potentially more of a threat than a solution in our time frame, especially in bioterrorism, which requires much less investment than, say, nuclear weapons.

The combination of external shocks and decreased internal resiliency is exactly the formula found before past phase transitions in complex civilizations. Credible scholars and leaders in positions of influence are beginning to look seriously at the threat of systemic failures and social collapse as a result. What many of them have not stated explicitly, however, is the imminence of the threat.[4]

A threat in 2050 is someone else's problem, and, as with climate change, it may be that we can do little but wring our hands and sound the alarm. But a threat in 2025 is rightly ours and should be addressed directly and vigorously while we still enjoy the advantages of a fully functioning global supply system.

Why are decision makers beginning to get worried? Even if stresses reach a breaking point, why should they lead to "collapse" and not just a cascade of small failures or, at worst, a gentle decline into the sunset of civilization's years? Empirical evidence from ecosystems to economics suggests that when a transition occurs in interlinked, networked systems, it is sharp and dramatic. Thinking of human society as a "complex system" shows why this might be so. As connections within systems develop in time, they typically move from one state of dynamical equilibrium to another—and do so very rapidly, as seen in examples from phase transitions in liquids to crashes in financial markets. The argument is that the system itself becomes more prone to collapse as its connectedness increases. Simple computer models illustrate this behavior clearly and offer explanations of catastrophic change in many areas of the natural, financial, and social world. However, these models are primarily explanatory rather than predictive. Even networks we thought were robust, such as the Internet, turn out to be fragile.

If Western society continues to develop in response to economic demands, as it has done to date, it will further lengthen our supply-chain networks and increase our interdependence and fragility in the event of major failure. A recent comparison of the effect of an actual economic collapse in Russia and a hypothesized collapse in the United States highlighted the massive exposure coming from the Western lifestyles. In Russia, nationalized power utilities and transport systems kept running during the collapse, people could not be dispossessed of their homes, and people lived near to their places of work. After fifty years of cheap transport, most of these conditions are no longer true in the United States and industrialized West. One of the ironies, then, of highly interconnected structures is that they make us more—not less—prone to collapse.

What Responses Are Effective
in Post-Collapse Environments?

The argument is simple—unfettered growth and interconnectedness makes human society more, not less, susceptible to collapse. Many foresee the crisis yet offer little in the way of practical answers, other than hopes for technical progress, a move to sustainability, or hitherto unseen forms of inter-governmental cooperation. Unfortunately, we expect neither a technological white knight nor some new form of socially responsible humanity to occur. Instead, we fear that it is far more likely that the current trend of self-interested economic growth will continue until it literally reaches a breaking point.

Let us suppose, then, that failure will happen and that it will be abrupt. What then? In the absence of other measures, should we presume that we will rely on martial law to see us through a crisis? A sobering prospect, given that the track record of such measures has been poor (see chapter 7 in this volume). Shouldn't we instead look to the way people naturally behave under the pressure of collapse? We have good evidence that in the immediate aftermath of a catastrophe, people behave well, often waiting for assistance and offering each other mutual support until it arrives. But such behavior does not last forever. Other research indicates that although communities often support themselves in the immediate aftermath of a collapse, without the intervention of outside institutions, there is often a breakdown into scavenging, self-defense, and far less reasoned, communitarian behavior. History has shown that, indeed, we are just "nine meals from anarchy" in these conditions.

Playing this forward, the final breakdown in historical cases often occurs when stocks of plunderable resources are exhausted, after which local militias coalesce into small administrative or tribal groups that either destroy or are destroyed. We have seen such cycles on a small scale in natural disasters such as hurricanes and earthquakes, on a medium scale with the aftermath of wars and plagues, and on a large scale with the failure of entire civilizations. In many cases, most notably when resources are exhausted, the social order does not recover in its original form. There is a lot we can and should learn from human and social response to real-life disasters. *A key action is to review and maintain "best-practice" measures for post-disaster recovery and keep these measures up to date.*

In business, we are used to problems like this and are required to have "business continuity"—also known as DR (disaster recovery)—plans in place and to test them regularly. They came to the fore in London following the IRA terrorist attacks and in New York following the 9/11 attacks. Such DR measures are not cheap to implement, and to rehearse, adding significant costs to running a business, but they are now mandatory in some circles. *A second action is to produce scenarios and "continuity plans" for all relevant institutional elements of our society, such as local councils.*

Given the recognized link between increased connectedness and to socioeconomic fragility, it is surprising there is so little active research into structural resilience. The authors of this chapter and others have developed "toy models" that allow simple dynamics of collapse and response to be tested. More complex models, such as the large-scale agent-based models created by Sandia Labs to test disruptions to the U.S. supply chain, offer more analytical power. Further research into such models is necessary, however, as long as it does not cause us to fall into the trap of believing the models are actually predictive (however explanatory they may be). Bridging the gap between massive, empirically tuned mathematical models run on supercomputers and the simple toy models explored above will help policy makers assess a variety of combinations and contingencies for local "continuity," social resilience, economic response, and policy and policing options. *A third action is to analyze and model socioeconomic systems to see what measures might be most effective and then, where possible, to compare these measures with what happened in actual cases of collapse.*

Without such actions (and barring some deus ex machina intervention, such as the discovery of vast new resources or a technological breakthrough like nuclear fusion or space colonization), we believe that the "probable future" for many parts of the developed world will look surprisingly similar to its origins: violent, decentralized, inefficient, and uncontrolled, with islands of stability in an otherwise vast sea of law-lessness. Under these conditions, the strengths and tactics of unconventional actors will come to the fore, suggesting that the second half of the twenty-first century may indeed be dominated by non-state and para-state economic actors operating under the auspices of a new organization: the warlord enterprise.

3 Innovation, Deviation, and Development

Warlords and Proto-State Provision

Nils Gilman, Jesse Goldhammer, and Steven Weber

Development between the Cracks

Warlord entrepreneurs are some of the most audacious experimenters, risk-takers, and innovators in today's global economy. In their relentless search for competitive advantage, they engage in just about all of the activities that other entrepreneurs do—marketing, strategy, organizational design, product innovation, information management, logistics, financial analysis....

Hidden and powerful, this underground movement of human trafficking, drug dealing, gun running, cross-border waste disposal, organ trading, sex tourism, money laundering, and transnational gangs—a movement we call *deviant globalization*—is growing at twice the rate of the legal economy.

In many cases, warlord entrepreneurs create enormous profits while extruding inefficiencies from huge markets. And they often go to extreme lengths to drive new business ventures to success, placing their economic livelihood and sometimes their lives at risk. Talk about "animal spirits" (Adam Smith) or "disruptive innovation" (Clayton Christensen) or "creative destruction" (Joseph Schumpeter)—it is all here. Just because these markets feature goods and services that may disgust us, does not mean we can't learn a great deal from deviant globalization's "success stories" and "best practices."

15

Deviant globalization is, in many crucial respects, about unsavory things happening in the Global South for the apparent benefit and pleasure of those in the Global North. Whether the harvesting of organs, extralegal extraction of commodities, deployment of weapons to insurgencies and rebel groups, or movement of laundered money into numbered Swiss bank accounts—these would all seem to indicate that deviant globalization represents yet another instance of the global rich oppressing the global poor. This classical view, shared by liberals and Marxists alike, holds that the sorts of illicit economies encompassed by deviant globalization represent a form of economic parasitism that diverts developmental energy, capital accumulation, human assets, and other valuable resources away from more "productive" uses. Instead of providing a platform for self-sustained growth, such deviant markets appear merely to line the pockets of gangsters.

But the role of the warlord entrepreneur in the "development" of the Global South is more complicated than this view would suggest. Nations, institutions, and NGOs from the Global North dedicate huge amounts of time and immense sums of money trying to help nations of the Global South modernize, diversify, and grow their economies. Liberal proponents of mainstream globalization view these efforts as a set of market-building steps toward delivering on the promise of capitalism. Marxist opponents criticize these "development" practices for fostering dependency and, paradoxically, a permanent state of (at least relative) poverty. What both sides fail to appreciate is that many people living in poor nations in the Global South are already engaged in radical experiments in actual development through deviant globalization. Behind the backs of—and often despite—all those corporations and development NGOs, as well as the World Bank and the International Monetary Fund, the poor are renting their bodies, selling their organs, stealing energy, stripping their natural environments of critical minerals and chemicals, manufacturing drugs, and accepting toxic waste—not because they are evil, but in order to make a living. Thus, deviant globalization is a form of economic development.

Participating in the production side of deviant globalization—hopefully as an entrepreneur, but at least as a worker—is a survival strategy for those without easy access to legitimate, sustainable market opportunities, which is to say the poor, the uneducated, and those in locations with ineffective or corrupt institutional support for mainstream business. People sell their organs, become drug mules, process toxic garbage, or offer sex to middle-aged foreigners because these jobs are often the fastest, best, easiest, and even, in some cases, the most sustainable way to make money. Even for the line workers in deviant industries, the money accumulated over a few years can often form a nest egg of capital to start more legitimate businesses. To paraphrase John Lennon, deviant globalization is an important part of how development happens while the official development agencies "are busy making other plans."

To make the claim that deviant globalization is a form of development is not to deny the awfulness and oppressiveness of many deviant industries the significant social and environmental externalities that deviant globalization often imposes, or the fact that many of the participants in deviant globalization are coerced into their working roles. No doubt there are better and worse ways to improve one's lot in life, but it's rare that participating in deviant globalization is the worst available choice. Mining coal in China, for example, may be a more legitimate profession than pirating ships off of the coast of Somalia, but it is debatable whether the former is a better job than the latter. Most importantly, like them or not, both professions contribute to a kind of development.

Considering deviant globalization as a form of development challenges cherished views of the relationship between economic growth, transnational crime, and illicit behavior. Rather than representing a divergence from the liberal norm of licit growth in the formal economy, deviant globalization might better be conceived as a way for the globally excluded to find a space to be innovative, a space in which the rules of the game have not already been stacked against them. At the same time, however, this is not a subversively heroic Robin Hood morality tale. Today's deviant globalizers are not proto-revolutionaries, aiming to remake society in an inclusive and collectively progressive fashion. Rather, they are opportunistic parasites whose public personae and brands are built around unbridled capitalist spirits—living fast, dying hard, and letting the rest of the world go to hell. The form of development they are enacting, in other words, is in many respects an ultra-libertarian one—one that tacitly rejects what the liberal political economy defines as "the public good."

Challenging the State

Why does this matter? Even if one grants that state-led development has mostly failed (with a few very large but still uncommon exceptions) and been widely replaced, or at least backfilled, by illiberal forms of self-empowerment, does that matter for the larger geopolitical system? Some argue that deviant globalization is just an annoying side effect of mainstream globalization, one that saps a small amount of cash from each of these mainstream processes as a kind of persistent tax but that doesn't affect the larger functioning of the system. From this perspective, deviant globalization might be worth commenting on, but not worth taking all that seriously, compared to the big things that "really matter" in international politics.

We disagree. Our argument is that deviant globalization has profound geopolitical implications, because it is degrading state power, eroding state capacity, corroding state legitimacy, and, ultimately, undermining the foundations of mainstream globalization. More specifically, deviant globalization is creating a new type of political actor whose geopolitical importance will only grow in the coming decades. What makes these political actors unique is the fact that they thrive in weak state environments and their activities reinforce the conditions of this weakness. In his many essays, John Robb refers to these new players as "global guerrillas."[1]

Warlord enterprises wield political power in three distinct ways. First, they have money. As we have seen, deviant entrepreneurs control huge, growing swathes of the global economy, operating most prominently in places where the state is hollowed or hollowing out. State corruption fueled by drug money on both sides of the U.S.-Mexico border exemplifies this point. Second, many deviant entrepreneurs control and deploy a significant quota of violence—an occupational hazard for people working in extralegal industries, who cannot count on the state to adjudicate their contractual disputes. This use of violence brings deviant entrepreneurs into primal conflict with one of the state's central sources of legitimacy, namely its monopoly (in principle) over the socially sanctioned use of force. Finally, and most controversially, in some cases, these warlord entrepreneurs are also emerging as private providers of security, health care, and infrastructure—that is, precisely the kind of goods that functional states are supposed to provide to the public. Hezbollah in Lebanon, the Movement for the Emancipation of the Niger Delta (MEND) in Nigeria, the narco-traffickers in Mexico, the criminal syndicates in the favelas of Brazil—all are warlord entrepreneurs who not only have demonstrated that they can shut down their host states' basic functional capacity, thereby upsetting global markets half a world away, but who are also increasingly providing social services to local constituencies.

Warlord entrepreneurs generally do not start out as political actors in the sense of actors who wish to control or usurp the state. In the first iteration, as we saw in earlier, deviant globalization represents a response to the failure of development and the hollowing out of the state. Once these deviant industries take off, however, they begin to take on a political life of their own. The state weakness that was a condition of deviant globalization's initial emergence becomes something that the now empowered warlord entrepreneurs seek to perpetuate and even exacerbate. They siphon off money, loyalty, and sometimes territory; they increase corruption; and they undermine the rule of law. They also force well-functioning states in the global system to spend an inordinate amount of time, energy, and attention trying to control what comes in and out of their borders. Although deviant globalization may initially have flowered as a result of state hollowing out, as it develops, it becomes a positive feedback loop in much the same way that many successful animal and plant species, as they invade a natural ecosystem, reshape that ecosystem in ways that improve their ability to exclude competitors.

What's new in this dynamic is that many of these "political actors" only rarely develop an interest in actually taking control of the formal institutions of the state. Warlord enterprises have developed market niches in which extractable returns are more profitable—and frankly easier—than anything they could get by "owning" enough of the state functions to extract rents from those instead. Organizations such as the First Command of the Capital in Brazil, the 'Ndrangheta in Italy, or the drug cartels in Mexico have no interest in taking over the states in which they operate. Why would they want that? This would only mean that they would be expected to provide a much broader menu of services to everyone, including ungrateful and low-profit clients, those so-called citizens. None of these organizations plan to declare sovereign independence and file for membership of the United Nations. What they want, simply, is to carve out autonomous spaces where they can do their business without state intervention. This underscores a crucial point about deviant globalization: it does not thrive in truly "failed" states—that is, in places where the state has completely disappeared—but rather in weak but well-connected states, in which the warlord entrepreneur can establish a zone of autonomy while continuing to rely on the state for some of the vestigial services it continues to furnish.

Alas, states and warlord entrepreneurs are unlikely to find a sustainable equilibrium. On the one hand, the more deviant industries grow, the more damage they do to the political legitimacy of the states within which the warlord entrepreneurs operate, thus undermining the capacity of the state to provide the infrastructure and services that the warlord entrepreneurs want to catch a free ride on. On the other hand, the people living in the semiautonomous zones controlled by deviant entrepreneurs increasingly recognize those entrepreneurs rather than the hollowed-out state as the real source of power and authority—if for no other reason than the recognition that if you can't beat them, you should join them. As these groups take over functions that would have been expected of the state, their stakeholders increasingly lose interest in the hollowed-out formal state institutions. Thus, even though warlord entrepreneurs hardly want to kill their host state, they may end up precipitating a process whereby the state implodes catastrophically. Something like this took place in

Colombia in the 1980s and in Zaire/Congo since the 1990s and may be taking place in Mexico today.

Blurring the Lines: Security, Economy, and Regulation in a Post-Collapse Environment

The unavoidable truth is that both mainstream globalization and its deviant twin present difficult choices and trade-offs for everyone who either analyzes or experiences their processes. And that is now almost everyone. To see these choices and trade-offs for what they are, not what we might wish they might be, is an absolute prerequisite for constructing policies that governments, businesses, transnational organizations, and anyone else would seek to use to ensure that the benefits of globalization, broadly understood, are maximized and its horrors minimized.

But what happens if globalization fails and the systems that support it crumble? The implications of this volume are that deviant entrepreneurs in post-collapse environments are likely to emerge explosively. Nor will they be marginal players. Rather, through a variety of innovative and entrepreneurial means, they may assume dominance through hybrid state, market, and ideological functions. Their ability to establish authority and stability will depend first on their martial might, second on their organizational prowess, and third on their ability to stabilize their gains and provide para-statal services to those upon which they prey, depend, and support. Our ability to understand the dynamics of this transition and help nurture its progress from anarchic violence to established fiefdoms and, possibly, markets and para-statal institutions, could make the difference between a world of repeated episodes of Rwandan-style horrors and pockets of relatively mutualistic, resilient communities.

4 Sovereignty, Criminal Insurgency, and Drug Cartels

The Rise of a Post-State Society

John P. Sullivan

State change and shifts in sovereignty are a potential consequence of the erosion of state authority, legitimacy, and capacity. Possible outcomes of such shifts could include failed states, the capture of state authority by transnational criminals, and potentially the emergence of new state-forms. Insurgencies, high-intensity crime, and criminal insurgencies that challenge state legitimacy and inhibit governance are a key national and global security issue.

State failure is one potential outcome of insolvent governance and extreme instability. This issue has been a concern to the global security and intelligence communities for several years, specifically since the implosion of the Somalian state. *State failure* refers to the complete or partial collapse of state authority. Failed states have governments with little political authority or ability to impose the rule of law. They are usually associated with widespread crime, violent conflict, or severe humanitarian crises, and they may threaten the stability of neighboring countries.[1] Understanding this issue has led to some very good work on the dynamics of state erosion. For example, the State Failure Task Force—now the Political Instability Task Force (PITF)—a CIA-funded academic research initiative, was established in 1994 to examine Somalia. Its mandate includes assessing general political instability, including revolutionary or ethnic war, adverse regime change, genocide, and politicide. After 9/11, it added the relationships between states and terrorists to its scope of inquiry.

Among the powerful research presented by the PITF is a global model for forecasting political instability.[2] That model is simple. It uses a few variables and has achieved a reliable degree of accuracy for forecasting conventional changes of political states—including violent civil wars and nonviolent democratic reversals. This suggests common factors are at play in both situations. The four independent variables incorporated in the PITF model are regime change, infant mortality, conflict-ridden neighborhood indicators, and state-led discrimination.

This robust work looks at state failure from a conventional or political vantage point, but what about nontraditional or irregular drivers like transnational crime?

Transnational Crime as a Driver of State Failure, Transition, or Change

Two United Nations Office on Drugs and Crime reports that highlight the impact of transnational crime on states are: "Threat of Narco-Trafficking in the Americas"[3] and "The Globalization Of Crime: A Transnational Organized Crime Threat Assessment."[4] According to the reports, both states and communities are caught in the crossfire of drug-related crime and the violence that it fuels in the Americas and across the Atlantic to Europe and Africa. According to Antonio Maria Costa, executive director of the United Nations Office on Drugs and Crime, "Narco-trafficking is also posing a threat to urban security, from Toronto to Tierra del Fuego. Gang violence and gun-related crime are on the rise. Some neighborhoods have become combat zones."[5]

Transnational criminal enterprises appear to be the early beneficiaries of the knowledge society. Manuel Castells outlined the rise of the networked, information society in the trilogy *The Information Age: Economy, Society, and Culture*.[6] In that work, Castells envisioned the emergence of powerful global criminal networks as one facet of the shift to a new state/

sovereignty structure in which the state no longer controlled all facets of the economy and society. The conflict and security dimensions of networks have given rise to the concept of netwar[7] and criminal netwarriors.[8]

The shift of government authority from the state to "para-states" or non-state actors/non-state armed groups or criminal netwarriors is a consequence of globalization, networked organization, and the exploitation of regional economic circuits to create a new base of power. These new power configurations may result in the decline of the state,[9] new forms of sovereignty, or new state forms such as the "network state"[10] or "market state."[11] As such, criminal gangs and cartels may be acting as new state-making entities.[12]

The capture, control, or disruption of strategic nodes in the global system and the intersections between them by criminal actors can have cascade effects.[13] The result is a state of flux, resulting in a structural "hollowing" of many state functions while bolstering the state's executive branch and its emphasis on internal security. This hollowing-out of state function is accompanied by an extra-national stratification of state function with a variety of structures or fora for allocating territory, authority, and rights.

These fora—including border zones and global cities—are increasingly contested, with states and criminal enterprises seeking their own "market share." As a result, global insurgents, terrorists, and networked criminal enterprises can create "lawless zones,"[14] "feral cities,"[15] and "parallel states."[16] Figure 4.1 describes the local through global geospatial distribution of these potentials, ranging from failed communities (or neighborhoods) to failed or feral cities through failed states or regions.

Local   **Global**

Failed Communities   Failed/Feral Cities   Failed States/Regions

Figure 4.1. Governance (State) Failure Continuum

The result has been characterized as a battle for information and real power.[17] These state challengers—irregular warriors or non-state combatants (i.e., criminal netwarriors)—increasingly employ barbarization and high-order violence, combined with information operations, to seize the initiative and embrace the mantle of social bandit[18] and confer legitimacy on themselves and their enterprises. Sovereignty is potentially shifting or morphing as a result of these challenges. This shift could result in a New Middle Ages, with fragmented authority, competing governmental structures, and a proliferation of chaos and violent non-state (and state) competition and conflict that challenges the primacy of the Westphalian state.[19] Power and sovereignty are challenged by globalization and may result in new state formulations.[20]

Mexico and Latin America as a Laboratory for State Transition

Mexico and Latin America are currently experiencing a onslaught from organized crime (cartels and gangs/*maras*) that challenges and erodes state capacity to govern, negates the rule of law through endemic impunity, and drives humanitarian crises through high-intensity violence and barbarization. In Mexico, over sixty thousand persons were killed in the crime wars between 2006 and 2012, along with an estimated twenty thousand in 2013. This extreme violence is concentrated in four of Mexico's thirty-two states: Chihuahua, Sinaloa, Guerrero, and Baja California.

The situation is not constrained to Mexico. Guatemala, Honduras, and El Salvador are also particularly challenged.[21] The spillover of the cartel war in Guatemala threatens institutional collapse, as cartels align with already virulent gangs and strike out with impunity. As a result, Guatemala City is subject to the brutal murders of bus drivers who refuse to pay extortion taxes to the *maras,* and the Zetas have invaded Guatemala's northern departments, which caused the government to declare a "state of exception" to bring martial forces to bear against the criminal incursion. The alliances of cartels and gangs are hollowing out the state, controlling turf and roads and establishing training camps. In addition, they are starting to provide social goods to the communities where they operate. The cartels are also actively pursuing information operations (info ops) to secure their freedom to operate.[22]

According to the UN Office on Drugs and Crime, organized crime has diversified, gone global, and reached macroeconomic proportions: illicit goods are sourced from one continent, as the report neatly puts it, trafficked across another, and marketed in a third.[23] Mafias today are truly a transnational problem, and they are a threat to security, especially in poor and conflict-ridden countries. Crime is fueling corruption, infiltrating business and politics, and hindering development. Essentially, transnational organized crime and gangs are undermining governance by empowering those who operate outside the law:

- Drug cartels are spreading violence in Central America, the Caribbean, and West Africa.
- Collusion between insurgents and criminal groups in central Africa, the Sahel, and Southeast Asia fuels terrorism and plunders natural resources.
- The smuggling of migrants and modern slavery have spread in eastern Europe as much as in Southeast Asia and Latin America.
- In many urban centers, authorities have lost control to organized gangs.
- Cyber crime threatens vital infrastructure and state security, steals identities, and commits fraud.
- Pirates from the world's poorest countries (the Horn of Africa) hold ships from the richest nations for ransom.
- Counterfeit goods undermine licit trade and endanger lives.
- Money-laundering in rogue jurisdictions and uncontrolled economic sectors corrupts the banking sector worldwide.

These criminals are more than simple brigands; they are challenging the fabric of the state and civil society within the areas they operate in. This phenomenon is described in the essay "Criminal Insurgencies in the Americas."[24]

Transnational criminal organizations and gangs are threatening state institutions throughout the Americas. In extreme circumstances, cartels, gangs or *maras*, drug trafficking organizations, and their paramilitary enforcers are waging de facto criminal insurgencies to free themselves from the influence of the state.

A wide variety of criminal gangs are waging war amongst themselves and against the state. Rampant criminal violence enabled by corruption and weak state institutions has allowed some criminal enterprises to develop virtual or parallel states. These contested or "temporary autonomous" zones create what theorist John Robb calls "hollow states" with areas where the legitimacy of the state is severely challenged. These fragile, sometimes lawless zones (or criminal enclaves) cover territory ranging from individual neighborhoods, *favelas* or *colonias* to entire cities—such as Ciudad Juárez—to large segments of exurban terrain in Guatemala's Petén province, and sparsely policed areas on the Atlantic Coast of Nicaragua.

As a consequence, the Americas are increasingly besieged by the violence and corrupting influences of criminal actors exploiting stateless territories (criminal enclaves and mafia-dominated municipalities) linked to the global criminal economy to build economic muscle and, potentially, political might.

Criminal Enclaves/Other Governed Areas

These criminal gangsters are removing themselves from the control of the state. Essentially, many areas in Mexico and Central America are experiencing the creation of para-states and lawless or contested zones within and across their borders. Understanding this situation is essential to recognizing the key factors in developing an understanding of the dynamics of non-state armed groups (criminal soldiers) and their impact on the state. These criminal soldiers are forging their own operational space. According to Sullivan and Weston:

> Criminal-soldiers come in many guises. They may be members of a street gang or *mara*, members of a mafia or organized criminal enterprise, terrorists, insurgents, pirates, or warlords. In all cases, they challenge the traditional state monopoly on violence and political control. They may co-exist within stable states, dominate ungovernable, lawless zones, slums, or "no-go" zones, or be the de facto rulers of criminal enclaves or free-states. Likewise, the "criminal state" may range from a street gang's narrow gang-controlled turf of a few blocks or segments of blighted housing estates to larger uncontested neighborhoods in a *barrio, favela, gecekondu, chawl,* slum or mega-slum. Alternately, they can exist as "para-states," "statelets" or "virtual states" in a combination of physical and increasingly networked terrain.[25]

The cartels and gangs are not only criminal actors, but they have several political dimensions. As recently stated by Sullivan and Rosales: "The cartels may not seek a social or political agenda, but once they control turf and territory and effectively displace the state they have no choice—they become 'accidental insurgents.'"[26]

Criminal Insurgencies

Criminal insurgencies is one way to characterize these activities. Figure 4.2 shows a continuum of instability that embraces the types of state-challenging violence that may be experienced. This figure, adapted from a table in "Terrorism, Crime, and Private Armies,"[27] places criminal insurgencies in context to other forms of civil war and strife. Criminal insurgencies challenge the state by generating high-intensity criminal violence that erodes the legitimacy and solvency of state institutions.[28] Criminal insurgencies can exist at several levels:

- **Local Insurgencies:** First, criminal insurgencies may exist as "local insurgencies" in a single neighborhood or "failed community" where gangs dominate local turf and political, economic, and social life. These areas may be "no-go zones" avoided by the police. The criminal enterprise collects taxes and exercises a near-monopoly on violence. A large segment of the extreme violence in Mexico is the result of local insurgencies. Municipalities like Ciudad Juárez or portions of some states, like Michoacán, are under siege. The cartels and other gangs dominate these areas through a careful combination of symbolic violence, attacks on the police, and corruption and by fostering a perception that they are community protectors (i.e., "social bandits"). Here the criminal gang is seeking to develop a criminal enclave or criminal free state. Since the nominal state is never fully supplanted, development of a parallel state is the goal.

- **Battle for the Parallel State:** Second, criminal insurgencies may be battles for control of the "parallel state." These occur within the parallel state's governance space but also spill over to affect the public at large and the police and military forces that seek to contain the violence and curb the erosion of governmental legitimacy and solvency that results. In this case, the gangs or cartels battle each other for domination or control of the criminal enclave or criminal enterprise. The battle between cartels and their enforcer gangs to dominate the "plazas" is an insurgency where one cartel seeks to replace the other in the parallel state.

- **Combating the State:** Third, criminal insurgencies may result when the criminal enterprise directly engages the state itself to secure or sustain its independent range of action. This occurs when the state cracks down and takes action to dismantle or contain the criminal gang or cartel, and the cartel attacks back. This is the situation seen in Michoacán, where La Familia retaliates against the Mexican military and intelligence services in counterattacks. Here the cartels are active belligerents against the state.

• **The State Implodes:** Fourth, criminal insurgency may result when high-intensity criminal violence spirals out of control. Essentially, this would be the cumulative effect of sustained, unchecked criminal violence and criminal subversion of state legitimacy through endemic corruption and co-option. Here the state simply loses the capacity to respond. This variant has not yet occurred in Mexico or Central America but is arguably the situation in Guinea-Bissau, where criminal entities have transitioned the state into a virtual narco-state. This could occur in other fragile zones if cartel and gangs violence is left to fester and grow.

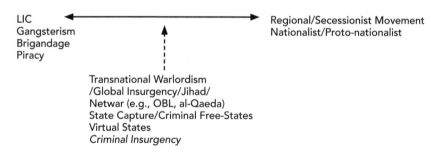

Figure 4.2. Warlord Continuum of Instability

Assessing the Situation

Traditional measures that may inform understanding of the situation include the work of the PITF, while data sets from the World Bank (and

World Bank Institute) on indicators of "governance" aid the assessment of the impact on the state—that is, state capacity and governability. The World Bank Worldwide Governance Indicators assesses six "governance" dimensions: (1) voice and accountability; (2) political stability and lack of violence/terrorism; (3) government effectiveness; (4) regulatory quality; (5) rule of law; and (6) control of corruption.[29]

Pertinent units of analysis are the cartels and the Mexican state—the government of Mexico and its constituent states and municipalities—as well as the Mexican public. In a broad sense, the variables are violence, corruption, intimidation, and state capacity.

Specific variables and indicators that are germane to developing intelligence and an analytical framework include violence (assassinations of police and public officials, beheadings, etc.)—specifically, violence among cartels (criminals) and violence directed toward state officials (including armed engagements between the cartel and the police or military)—corruption; the degree of transparency; the reach of the cartel or gang; the effectiveness of governance and policing; community stability; the effectiveness of economic regulation; and the degree of territorial control (loss or gain by the state versus the cartels).

The impact of warlord enterprises on state capacity, control of territory, and legitimacy is critical. All of these activities occur across time. Some changes are slow moving; some are rapid.

Moving forward, it's important that such activity is explored through a variety of lenses, not just through the lens of state failure or atrophy, but also, as we explore in upcoming chapters, through the lens of the management and sustenance of the state itself.

5 From Patronage Politics to Predatory States

Crime and Governance in Africa

Tuesday Reitano

Big Man in Malibu

It is perhaps fitting that the case that finally put an end to the impunity of Equatorial Guinea's second vice president, Teodoro Nguema Obiang Mangue, in the United States would have such a bizarre name. On October 10, 2014, the United States Department of Justice made public the settlement of the case of *United States v. One Michael Jackson Signed Thriller Jacket and Other Michael Jackson Memorabilia; Real Property Located on Sweetwater Mesa Road in Malibu, California; One 2011 Ferrari 599 GTO.*[1] One might ask how a former minister of environment of a tiny West African nation, whose official salary was less than $5,000 a month, might end up in possession of a $35 million house in Malibu, a Gulfstream business jet, and a crystal-covered white glove used by Michael Jackson on his *Bad* tour. You could equally inquire how his father, Equatoguinean president Teodoro Nguema Obiang Mbasogo, had stockpiled, by 2004, a $700 million fortune in U.S. bank accounts when, up until then, the GDP of his entire country was a mere $330 million a year. Or how he could spend public money to purchase a $180 million luxury building on the exclusive Avenue Foch in Paris—and furnish it with $50 million in furniture[2]—when more than half his population has no access to clean water.[3]

33

Regrettably, the scurrilous stories of the Obiangs's shameless self-enrichment are by no means unique in global politics. There are countless stories, from all continents, of leaders who abuse power to amass private fortunes and massive shoe collections while their citizens suffer in poverty. One of the key observations of this book is that, over time, warlord enterprises can become indistinguishable from the state itself. Examples of this phenomenon cluster with particular frequency in Africa, where we hear appalling stories of corruption and crime by heads of states and their cronies. This distinctive style of governance has resulted in the coining of *kleptocracy* to describe the limitless pillaging of state resources and the culture of nepotism and corruption that accompanies it.[4]

African states are characterized by political tribalism and patronage systems that became ingrained as a system of governance in the colonial period and in the years following independence. Over subsequent decades, these systems were transformed first into authoritarian regimes and then into weak multiparty democracies dominated, in each case, by a series of "Big Men." It is this structure, which can be seen in all corners of the continent, that has lead to the development of what are arguably warlord states, where the entire resources of the nation, both licit and illicit, are held hostage by the most potent of kingpins while the majority of the population remains mired in poverty and beleaguered by repression, human-rights abuses, and conflict. The analysis of warlord states reveals two uncomfortable truths, which earn this chapter its place rounding out the bleak picture presented in "The Dark Side."

The first uncomfortable truth is that international community holds its share of culpability for enabling and perpetuating warlord states: an over-reliance on elite pacts to end conflict has created a vicious cycle of fragility. Moreover, the failure of the international financial regime to prevent or prosecute major capital flight allows African resources to be diverted from development objectives. The second truth comes in recognizing the role that patronage governance has played in fostering the growth of terrorist movements (with both domestic and international agendas) from what might otherwise have been, arguably, legitimate insurgent movements.

There are few, if any, obvious fixes to this Gordian knot, though later chapters will highlight some glimmers of hope that can be seen, Pollyanna-esque, in the grim status quo. As this chapter morbidly concludes, how-ever, there is little evidence that there are either the structural conditions or the political will to take the steps necessary not only to demand higher standards of accountability from these warlord states but also to achieve them ourselves.

Patronage Politics and Pacts of the Elite

There is a longstanding body of literature, covering multiple African states, that describes how the political order is shaped by a framework of patronage, also known as clientelism, whereby leaders purchase support by dispensing largesse: opponents are bought off; allies are rewarded. The ability to allocate resources at will is considered the entitlement of the vic-tor, not theft from ordinary citizens. President Obiang has long used this argument in defense of his son's playboy lifestyle: "He earned money in accordance with the laws of Equatorial Guinea, even if those don't com-ply with international standards."[5] A recent continental study of the use of Chinese foreign development assistance to Africa, which, unlike assis-tance from Organisation for Economic Co-operation and Development countries, comes entirely without earmarking, found that the birthplace of the head of state receives 270 percent more than other regions.[6]

Some locate the roots of this governance style in the colonial period, where colonizing states sought alliances with local big men in order to control territory. These territories were frequently organized along ethnic lines, and the administrative localities were organized accordingly, which increased the warlord's territorial dominance.[7] It was a significant chal-lenge to transform these former colonies—whose primary objective had been the generation of resources for the colonizing states—into effec-tive, independent entities that focused on equitable delivery of services to geographically and ethnically dispersed populations. Under colonialism, the formation of cities was not organic; urban areas were formed to serve as transport hubs for colonizers extracting resources.[8] The postcolonial legacy to Africa featured sharp rural-urban divides—elite-centric governance in urban hubs and borderland populations who saw little or no evidence of the state. Those who could find no compelling means by which to ally themselves to the state elite found themselves quickly marginalized.

The key characteristic to note is that in these patronage arrangements, the big men do not generally control followers, but rather, it is in the interest of the followers to maintain ties with a big man, because he provides economic possibilities, political and physical protection, and social security.[9] The gathering of power and its maintenance are built on reciprocity, and if the big man does not distribute enough largesse, he will eventually lose his supporters. This style of governance has also been described as "factional politics" and is based more on transaction than issues of principle. "That Big Men constantly have to demonstrate their power through displays of wealth and force is not indicative of their strength but of the very fragility and negotiability of their status ... in the business of winning not votes but clients; not spearheading a party but a political network."[10] Societies that rely on this constant negotiation—a combination of patronage, coercion, and fragile pacts between elites—are far from stable. Any stresses that affect the status quo—such as the death of a leader, external security threats, or economic and demographic pressures—will shift the balance of power, cause a realignment of networks, and frequently trigger violence or conflict. As the UN secretary general concluded in 1998, "The nature of political power in many African States, together with the real and perceived consequences of capturing and maintaining power, is a key source of conflict across the continent. It is frequently the case that political victory assumes a 'winner-takes-all' form with respect to wealth and resources, patronage, and the prestige and prerogatives of office."[11]

Regrettably, the default method of resolving these conflicts has been through the negotiation of another elite pact rather than a transformation of state-society institutions. A 2009 study found that the average number of cabinet posts in African democracies has grown by nearly 25 percent over thirty years, as leaders seek to accommodate potential dissenters by bringing them into government. The study further observed that when leaders are required to hand over the reins of power, they will reduce the number of cabinet posts before the transition, thereby hamstringing their successor by forcing him to make more uncomfortable power-sharing negotiations.[12] The challenge is that societies that rely on patronage to find stability without broader and deeper institutional transformation risk a vicious cycle. Furthermore, each bout of violence further weakens institutions and destroys social capital, making it a trap that becomes increasingly difficult to escape from.[13]

The events in Mali following the coup in 2012 demonstrate this very well. Amadou Toumani Touré (commonly known as ATT) was overthrown by a seemingly spontaneous putsch lead by junior military offers frustrated at the lack of investment and equipment in the national army, which had to fight a growing separatist movement in the north. ATT had governed since 2002 through "a loose network of personal, clientelistic, even mafia-style alliances with regional elites with reversible loyalties rather than on robust democratic institutions."[14] That the coup came only a few weeks before a democratic presidential election was scheduled—in which ATT had clearly indicated his intention not to seek another term—was a clear signal that there something deeply rotten in the state of governance. Following international stabilization efforts, a new government was elected a mere four months later. It was headed by Ibrahim Boubacar Keïta (often known as IBK), a veteran career politician who had little in the way of a substantive political platform but had excellent relations with the international community. His party conspicuously backed a number key Tuaregs, who were linked with armed groups in the north, which raised concerns that this was business-as-usual clientelist politics.[15]

Criticisms of this hurried election proved to be well founded. IBK's government has been beset by corruption scandals, the majority of which are linked directly to the president himself, and IBK shows little indication that he plans to uphold the pledge he made at his inauguration: "Restoring state authority will coincide with a tireless fight against corruption.... Let no one enrich themselves illicitly at the expense of the Malian people."[16]

Government spending remains under the control of the International Monetary Fund (IMF) following an investigation into a no-bid defense contract worth an estimated $136 million that was awarded to a crony of the president, including an alleged $14 million overhead payment to his private company.[17] While defense-related purchases do not require public tender, for reasons of national security, the IMF investigation found that the overwhelming majority of the contract was for nonmilitary items such as trucks, cars, and clothing. This was shortly followed by a greater scandal—the purchase of a new $40 million presidential jet, again without a tender process and again with a multimillion-dollar kickback to a presidential crony. Not only did the president already have a jet at his disposal from the previous regime (unlike the Malian military, which has no air capacity), but the purchase also coincided with a renewed humanitarian appeal by the United Nations for an estimated 1.4 million Malians who were in need of food assistance.[18]

Elites and Illicit Flows

If patronage politics is based on the accumulation and distribution of resources, governance is easier when resources are plentiful. In times of economic stress, however, the pressure to continuously pump income down patronage networks can become a strain, resulting in fragmentation, competition, and again, conflict.

During the 1980s and 1990s, structural adjustment policies imposed by the World Bank and the IMF created widespread economic hardship for newly independent African states, severely taxing state institutions, and in many ways, reinforcing clientelism over good governance. Attempting to meet the World Bank and IMF conditions required a radical realignment of the region's economies to make them internationally competitive in those fields where they were thought to have productive capacity, chiefly agriculture. This often meant replacing subsistence landholdings with huge state-run or privately run agricultural enterprises, the contracts for which were distributed to preferred partners of the incumbent heads of state. It also meant a renewed—and almost neocolonial—focus on catering to international development partners to secure continued support. Throughout the decade of structural adjustment, some thirty-six governments in sub-Saharan Africa entered into stabilization agreements; 243 loan agreements were issued, worth more than $200 billion. Foreign aid and loans became crucial components of African economies, but most of these governments made few institutional reforms—economic, social, or political—as the primary concerns of political leaders were the maintenance of their political power and the accumulation of wealth for themselves and their supporters. By 1990, thirty of the thirty-six countries had negotiated the rescheduling of 120 foreign loans, as Africa's debt soared to $160 billion.[19] Almost ironically, despite being referred to as "stabilization packages," every country where IMF- and World Bank-style adjustment was set in motion was plagued by waves of unrest and instability.[20]

In this period, the need for funds began to be trumped by the legitimacy of the source of those resources, as leaders increasingly signed agreements that would mortgage the future of their nations to unethical corporations. For example, in 1992, to fund his re-election campaign, Pascal Lissouba, the first democratically elected president of the Democratic Republic of the Congo, arranged an oil-backed loan from the U.S. oil company Occidental Petroleum (Oxy), which agreed that Congo's share of oil production was to be sold at a mere $3 per barrel. Market price at the time was $22. With the help of the Oxy loan, however, Lissouba won the elections soon after.[21] President Mugabe has long defended his thirty-four-year tenure in Zimbabwe against accusations that he accepts foreign investment from a shady Chinese corporate group known as the Queensway syndicate to secure off-record contributions for running his secret police, a critical arm of his coercive patronage network. Reportedly, these investments have secured the Queensway syndicate rights to a number of mineral resources, as well as Zimbabwe's sanctioned diamonds, with no payments coming through the state budget.[22]

These are but a few examples of many that can be found across the continent, and the scale of funds that have been diverted is staggering.

African economies have been riding the crest of a global commodity wave that could transform the continent's prospects, but very little of these resources are benefitting those who need them most. According to a current study, between 1970 to 2010, illicit capital flight from Africa increased from about $2.6 billion to more than $1.7 trillion, an increase of over 650 times.[23] This was made possible through embezzlement of natural-resource exports, tax evasion, corruption, transfer pricing, and the outright smuggling of capital. By contrast, as emphasized by the African Progress Panel, the subcontinent's total outstanding external debt was barely a third of that figure, estimated at $293.8 billion at end of December 2010.[24]

While fingers are pointed regularly at the corruption and kleptocracy of African leaders, since the publication of an Oxfam report in 2000, more attention is also being directed at the way that international financial systems, including offshore corporations and tax havens, have enabled capital flight. It is estimated that developing nations lose at least $50 billion a year due to aggressive tax avoidance by private corporations, and more recently, the Tax Justice Network has estimated that a pool of 139 lower-income countries had squirreled away between $7.3 and $9.3 trillion in offshore accounts, which, had it been subject to even modest tax in a legitimate state, would have generated $189 billion per year that could have been spent on development.[25]

Without the anonymity provided by international tax havens, and without the assistance of the enablers of these illicit financial flows, including some of the world's largest and most reputable financial and legal institutions, it would be significantly more difficult for money to leave a country illicitly in the first place. There is little evidence, however, that the will to address these financial transparency requirements exists. At the 2014 G8 Summit, the issue of addressing trade secrecy was put high on the agenda, particularly by the Africa group, but reaching an agreement that would actually compel North American and European jurisdictions to reveal their corporate structures and tax-haven registrations remained a long way off. Similarly, at the first U.S.-Africa Summit, which took place in December 2014, demands for addressing the frameworks facilitating illicit trade remained secondary to presidential pleasantries between Presidents Obama, Obiang, Kabila, and others.

Cocaine Politics and Organized Crime

While some African states were able to exploit discoveries of oil or minerals, a number of other warlord states also came to welcome overtures from criminal enterprises. With the prevailing need for funds to support patronage systems, affiliation or control over criminal flows (arms, drugs and, people) became an alternative means of securing rents. The most infamous example of this phenomenon is Guinea-Bissau, where heads of state and senior members of the armed forces became deeply entrenched in the cocaine trade, but that case is by no means unique.[26] The temptations of criminal groups are compelling and have corrupted leaders of countries and organizations. In 2010, the nephew of the then president of Mauritania, and a former officer for Interpol, was sentenced to seven years in jail for his involvement in a drug-trafficking ring.[27] Sidi Mohamed Ould Haidallah, the son of former president Khouna Ould Haidallah, was arrested in Morocco in 2007 in possession of eighteen kilos of cocaine. In 2004, in his inaugural speech as Interpol secretary-general, Jackie Selebi, a former national police commissioner of South Africa, made it a priority "to find systems to make sure that our borders and border control are on a firm footing." A mere four years later he resigned in shame, mired in a corruption scandal that saw him sentenced to fifteen years in jail for accepting bribes from drug traffickers.[28]

Former president Blaise Compaoré, who had lead Burkina Faso under a semi-authoritarian regime from 1987 until his unseating in a popular coup in 2014, was a powerbroker not afraid to dabble in illicit affairs. For a long time, Burkina Faso—and particularly its president—was a regional pariah, deeply involved in the trafficking of conflict diamonds while providing arms and mercenaries for civil wars in the region, thus breaking international embargoes. And while, in recent years, he has repeatedly served as a mediator in regional conflicts (including in the Malian crisis, where Compaoré was the official mediator for the Economic Community of West African States [ECOWAS]), he is also commonly known to have enriched himself by aiding ransom negotiations for the many kidnappings that have occurred in the region. These ransoms are reported to have netted terrorist groups upward of $100 million, of which he would have taken a cut.[29]

Turning a blind eye to, or relinquishing control over, illicit flows is another strategy to provide dividends in an elite pact, in particular where the capacity for the state to exercise control over remote borderlands is limited. During his forty-four-year rule of Libya, Muammar Gaddafi frequently used control over territory and illicit resources as a bargaining chip in ethnic conflict and to pacify the peripheries.[30] Similarly, during his tenure as president of Mali, Amadou Toumani Touré created a new administrative region in northern Mali to allow overt control over trafficking routes and access to the state, and then selected which local actors would be in control of illicit trade, while also ensuring a cut for those in the capital, Bamako. This policy by the Malian state "exacerbated rivalries by operating an arm's length policy that selected favorites, rewarded them with illicit revenues, and did nothing to control losers' grievances over exclusion from local circuits of power."[31]

One of the key conclusions of the 2014 West Africa Commission on Drugs (WACD) was that corruption at the top is facilitating drug trafficking across the subcontinent. They found that traffickers were easily able to connect with people of influence, both utilizing and creating informal social networks that would allow them to access or co-opt the formal security apparatus. One key point where states are most vulnerable to the infiltration of illicit funds—though one that is by no means exclusive to Africa—appears to be during elections. The majority of African nations have limited or no restrictions on campaign financing or mechanisms for monitoring elections, which makes them susceptible to illicit offers. Furthermore, "in many cases, candidates tend to 'own' parties, funding them from their private resources or raising support from friends, regional allies, or from their ethnic base."[32] In Kenya, it is recognized that professional drug traffickers and criminal groups have infiltrated politics to the extent that they have formed a distinct block in the national parliament.[33]

Warlord states that include significant criminal elements, or in which the head of state is protecting criminal interests, present a significant challenge to the international community and its multilateral frameworks. The state has crucial importance for social order and for the delivery of political, social, and economic goods. A state that is not working in the interests of its people but instead enriches individuals or protects criminal interests makes a mockery of multilateral decision-making processes.[34] State collusion with organized crime also has implications for community dynamics, as the breakdown of the rule of law and the perception of impunity for elites has widespread deleterious effects. Citizens are more likely to themselves operate in the illegal economy if they see their government as kleptocratic, and protection economies develop as criminal groups stand as regulators within the local community. And, as Biró's chapter in part 2 discusses, when criminal groups provide services in the absence of the state, these groups can command legitimacy and loyalty from the local populations.[35]

The Antistate

One of the by-products of warlord states built on clientelist patronage networks is a spectrum of disenchanted groups. At best, these are marginalized groups who have been ignored or overlooked entirely by the state, who have little or no access to social services, justice, or employment—some of the worst development indicators on the planet. At worst, these groups form virulent opposition groups with active grievances against the state that can manifest in separatist or terrorist goals. While some consider the emergence of terrorism in Africa to be a relatively recent phenomenon—something that has come to prominence only in the last five years—longstanding watchers of Africa have argued that "Africa is the continent most affected by domestic or sub-national terrorism," and that the root causes of this brand of terrorism, in which armed groups with political motives enact acts of violence against nonmilitary targets to provoke terror, is "partly a hangover of the process of decolonization, but is more intimately linked to the failure to effect sustained development and to consolidate accountable and effective governance."[36]

Absence of the central state, however, does not equate to absence of governance. Communities that have been cut off from effective state authority—whether out of government indifference or because of protracted warfare or vested local and external interests in perpetuating conditions of state failure—consistently seek to provide for themselves the functions that the missing state is supposed to assume, especially basic security. In that vacuum, local big men will consolidate their own networks, and with the right conditions, they may gather enough resources to challenge the state. Due to the state controlling legitimate resources, it is often the case that antistate groups will lean to illicit resources to sustain themselves. In West Africa, political conflict that began in Liberia and spread to Sierra Leone and the Ivory Coast later gave way to more organized crime across the region, as warring factions pillaged natural resources to buy arms and pay fighters. With that chaos, drug-trafficking networks penetrated the region, and what had begun as a means for financing war became a successful business model for trafficking drugs, diamonds, timber, arms, and humans. Charles Taylor, first a rebel, then Liberian president from 1997 until 2003, was accused in his indictment by the Special Court of Sierra Leone of amassing a fortune of $105 to 450 million through "a joint criminal enterprise ... [to exercise] control over the territory of Sierra Leone ... and the population ... [by] unlawful killings, abductions, forced labour, physical and sexual violence." At the height of the conflict in Sierra Leone, Taylor was reportedly facilitating a trade in illegal diamonds worth more than $200 million, resources that helped him consolidate the political support needed to secure the presidency.[37]

One characteristic of the insurgent conflict triggered by patronage politics is that it is typically asymmetric, because the state commands the majority of resources and has a monopoly on power. Challengers, resourced by illicit flows, will use terror tactics to have a greater impact against the state. Thus is born the dangerous complicity of crime and terror. At a briefing to the security council in 2013, Téte António, permanent observer for the African Union, reported that " 'narco-terrorism' had given rise to new forms of 'mercenarism' in Africa, with fighters motivated more by financial gain than ideological persuasion."[38] And while analysts a decade ago frequently asserted that terrorist groups and drug traffickers had diametrically opposing motivations—the first seeking attention, the other requiring secrecy—the DEA now estimates that upwards of 60 percent of terrorist groups globally have links to drug trafficking.[39]

The war on terror has arguably polarized the nature of insurgent conflict in Africa. By affiliating with international terrorist groups, domestic insurgencies can attract fighters and additional resources. While the Somali terrorist group al-Shabaab nominally shares the same goals as al-Qaeda—namely, global jihad—al-Shabaab's leaders have almost exclusively focused their efforts on Somali priorities and protests.[40] Similarly, al-Qaeda in the Islamic Maghreb (AQIM), which evolved from a hardline Salafist organization, the Algerian Group for Preaching and Combat (GSPC), began the process of alignment with al-Qaeda in 2003, officially affiliating with them and changing its name in 2006. Apart from the name, however, the group showed little practical attachment to the global organization before 2011, and even their subsequent expansion beyond national borders has been confined largely to the immediate subregion, without any designs on international targets in other theaters.[41] It is also worthy of note that Boko Haram, which is possibly the most virulent of the domestic terror groups, with estimates that it has killed over ten thousand civilians in the last ten years, was largely ignored by the international community (until very recently), as its targets have remained domestic, and it has not indicated any international intensions or affiliations.[42]

The linkages made to transnational terrorist movements not only drew international attention but also changed the nature of domestic interaction. African governments have embraced foreign assistance in strengthening their security capacity, and a number of examples exist where countering terrorism has been used as the justification to violate human rights, quell political opposition, and suppress dissent. In Mauritania in 2003, for example, the then-president used the war on terror to justify arresting twenty-one people, including the militant activist Hamada Ould Mohamed Kheirou, who would later rise to prominence as a leader in the groups that continue to terrorize Mali's north. Mauritania's move, which was described more as an opportunistic attempt to remove political opponents than as an interest in combatting global terror, resulted in Kheirou's move to join al-Qaeda training camps in Iraq followed shortly thereafter. As the *Economist* succinctly expressed it, "In many cases such men do not move from country to country voluntarily, but one step ahead of the security forces."[43]

Putting Patronage in Its Place?

The perpetuation of warlord statehood has serious ramifications, and not only for African states and their citizens. Local political conflicts interlinked with organized crime in a context of globalization has consequences in both northern and southern hemispheres, and these consequences are becoming increasingly visible. The extraordinary growth in conflict- and crime-driven displacement, both in Africa and in Central America, has had enormous humanitarian and financial consequences. Predation by armed groups on commodities in vulnerable states imposes costs throughout the global market: in 2009, an attack by insurgents on an oil facility in the Niger Delta raised the price of oil by $2.33 per barrel, increasing costs for around the globe.[44]

There is an urgent need to strengthen governance and institutions in these warlord states. But it is frankly hard to see much reason to be optimistic. Successful indictments, like the U.S. case against the Obiangs, are mere glimmers of hope in an otherwise bleak picture. Even when individual states find themselves with a leader genuinely committed to the greater good and sustainable development of his people, the structural conditions make it broadly unlikely. These states need significant reforms of electoral politics and constitutions, and they need strengthened state institutions staffed by capable individuals of integrity. Instead, democratic reforms have largely reinforced patronage political frameworks. Diplomatic and civil-service appointments are offered as rewards; capacity-building opportunities are offered to a favored ally as a chance for international travel and some donor-sponsored shopping trips. Resources that should be spent on health-care, educational, and infrastructure development that could facilitate livelihoods or trade are squandered or squirreled away into an international financial system that offers far too many opportunities to hide resources. Popular uprisings and crises are often heralded as a "new dawn," an unprecedented opportunity to achieve change. Regrettably, all too often, they fall quickly into business as usual, as international diplomacy offers insufficient time or space for genuinely inclusive dialogue, and financial austerity reduces the capacity for external support. Furthermore, as multilateral frameworks become increasingly hamstrung by warlord states determined to filibuster action or veto change, the possibility for genuine reform recedes still further.

Reversing this paradigm will require extraordinary political will and a shared accountability framework by which both nation-states and their international partners agree to hold themselves (rather than each other) accountable for the woeful state of affairs. There is precious little evidence that these conditions exist, and thus the status quo of the warlord state will continue to sit heavily on the shoulders of the poorest and most vulnerable in society.

Part 2

SHADES OF GRAY

6 Warlord Governance

Transition Toward—or Coexistence with —the State?

Daniel Biró

Given the persistent caricatured and demonizing portrayal of warlords in the media and in scholarship dedicated to so-called failed states, the core objective of this chapter is to correct, to a certain extent, this tendency toward oversimplification and sensationalizing. By delineating a governance space within the particular social context of warlordism, it is my intention to describe the phenomenon of warlordism as an alternative form of organizing political communities outside and beyond the classical state's centralized monopoly over violence. In doing so, this chapter argues that warlordism is neither just "the opposite of the state" nor an anachronistic remnant of feudalism, but instead it represents a modern hybrid form of *state/market* economy that privileges decisive action—preponderantly, but not exclusively, military action—together with low-level administrative control.

In describing the phenomenon of warlordism as another way of organizing political communities beyond the state, this chapter is structured around two axes. First, alongside the "governance" aspect, it is important to collect some historical and contemporary evidence that shows that, under specific circumstances, warlords have—and to some degree still do—performed important social functions supporting religion, culture, and other basic aspects of a civil society. These include, in some instances, maintaining some kind of societal order, if not law; adjudicating disputes; building infrastructure (road and bridge construction, for example); as well as, to some extent and in specific circumstances, health and education provision, albeit in unconventional forms. It must be emphasized that warlords are not the only non-state armed actors involved in the provision of social services in conflict zones in general or in the so-called failed states in particular. While there are still debates regarding their motivations, there seems to be a consensus that, particularly in recent times, these groups do provide some social services.[1] Having the widest range of services delivered, Hezbollah and Hamas are probably the most prominent non-state armed groups that provide services, but they are clearly not exceptions. Among other examples, "the Revolutionary Armed Forces (FARC) in Colombia supply medical services, the Tamil Tigers in Sri Lanka maintained mail delivery (among other services), and the Communist Party of the Philippines (New People's Army) supports literacy programs and performs marriage ceremonies for their supporters. The IRA provided transportation services within Republican neighborhoods during the Troubles and even smaller Loyalist groups delivered milk for new mothers living in their communities"[2]

Second, and deriving from this diversity of motivations and services, it is important to touch upon the specific circumstances under which this alternative form of governance can occur, distinguishing between the warlords' source of income, their relationship to other local or regional powers, and their relationship to foreign institutions such as NGOs and aid agencies. The suggestion put forward as a result of this inquiry is that, far from being isolated from the state or society, the position of the warlord is enhanced by and is dependent on the links with both. In this regard, the zero-sum game analyzing the warlords in terms of an absence of the state is misguided. I suggest that these entrepreneurial controllers of organized violence (warlords) obtain their autonomy from both state and society by situating themselves in a nodal position in the network of various providers of social services (states, NGOs, INGOs, and IGOs). Through these two axes, it becomes clear that the view of the warlord as simply a bandit is overly simplistic and ignores his—invariably in my research the warlord is a man—position as complex entrepreneur and provider of governance.

In the public perception, popularized by the media at large, the warlord is associated with feudalism, and this is used as an explanatory device to explore the causes and effects of state failure. In contrast, a scholarly understanding of the phenomenon of warlordism must move toward a more sophisticated perspective. Specifically, it is important to understand that in its contemporary incarnation, the warlord stands outside the model of the modern state and (despite what is sometimes claimed) also outside feudal societies;[3] nevertheless, the warlord shares selected characteristics with and appropriates functions from both. This understanding allows us to avoid the error of ignoring the public goods that—intentionally or inadvertently—may be delivered as part of warlord governance. It also allows the examination of cases of long-term resilience, despite the widespread expectations of warlordism either disintegrating or transitioning (sooner rather than later) into some form of state or state-like governance. In Afghanistan, for instance, even though the country has gone through several regimes in the last three decades, one constant has remained: the presence of warlords such as Ismail Khan and Abdul Rashid Dostum, both still prominent actors in Afghan politics.[4]

Before addressing these points in detail, it is useful to offer a précis of the ways in which warlords provide social services. The literature on the "economy of war" has developed, since the early 1990s, as a result of the emphasis on how globalization and transnational economic dynamics have facilitated the thriving of the warlords (though it has never fully accounted for their appearance in the first place). This literature focuses on the motives and rational strategies employed by warlords to promote their personal interests, unveiling the "modern warlord" as an integral part of a contemporary globalized international economy. Despite the substantial contribution of this "economic" paradigm to the development of a sophisticated perspective on the study of warlordism, predictably, the description of non-state armed groups in the process of "building authority through commerce" in a violent environment most often ignores their provision of social services. The positioning of the warlord in strict op-position to the institutions and functions of the state—a view held by most analysts—partly justifies this tendency. As one prominent scholar argued, the strategy of building authority through commerce rather than insti-tutions "obviates the need to build bureaucracies, since warlord political authority that fails to replace the state would make no pretension of car-rying out state-like functions."[5] Furthermore, it is suggested that the war-lord's reluctance to carry out state-like functions derives from systemic constraints—warlords risk losing their advantage over their competitors in the market of violence if they consume scarce resources by providing social services.

The case of contemporary Afghanistan, however, points toward some limitations of a perspective depicting warlords as driven strictly by the pursuit of their individual economic interests and reluctant to perform any social functions. Based on his extensive research, Antonio Giustozzi argued for a long time that, at least in the particular case of Afghanistan, "social status derives from the control of security rather than of money.... These warlords are more akin to politicians than to businessmen, in that what they are looking for is power rather than money as an end in itself."[6] This being said, it is true that, in their attempt to introduce develop and maintain a degree of social order, the prime social function that armed groups provide is in the area of security and protection (jut like the state itself).

Moving beyond Afghanistan, research has shown that as late as the 2000s, in significant areas of Colombian territory, some paramilitary units and guerrilla insurgents—in particular, FARC—were the major if not the only agents that had both the capability and the will to limit the spread of some forms of local crime and violence by repressing petty criminals.[7] To be sure, the strengthening of the Colombian state institutions, the expan-sion and modernization of the state armed forces (between 2002 and 2012, the size of the military and national police almost doubled), the changes at the international level (with both the United States and the European Union including FARC on their lists of terrorist organizations), and the

decapitation of its leadership, the stature of FARC had significantly di-
minished, and with this, FARC's legitimacy and its capacity to provide social services, including security, has atrophied. However, as Garry Leech
has shown, without ignoring its involvement in illicit drug trafficking or
the use of terrorism and human rights violations, for a significant period,
FARC acted as a de facto authority in the area under its control, most im-
pressive in the department of Meta, introducing a "revolutionary" judicial
system and building electrical grids, roads, bridges, schools, and so on.[8]

Following an investigation of the social content of the interaction
between the paramilitary, their social constituency, and the state in Colombia, some scholars have warned against too strict an interpretation of
the conflict as fuelled solely by economic considerations, concluding that
it "cannot be reduced to rent-seeking."[9] Not only did Colombian armed
groups try to legitimize their control by providing some social functions,
offering, for instance, security against petty thieves, but, due to a complex
relation with the state, "they [were] intent on inviting both state agencies,
and investment, and on guaranteeing a stable economic environment."[10]
Evidence of similar activities in the "establishment and maintenance of
basic law and order, and re-enforcement of mechanisms of survival in a
particular area or among a particular section of the populace" is reported
from research on Tajikistan,[11] as well as on Sierra Leone, where, at least
initially, the Kamajors militias were "providing security to communities
and enforcing social norms that most people considered legitimate."[12]

It is important to note the existence of a small number of studies that
not only approach warlordism as a violent form of predation or primitive
"racketeering" but also emphasize the potential—by no means ubiqui-
tous—provision of some social services. To be certain, the vast majority of these services appear to develop in close relation to the necessities
of military confrontations and, in particular, appear to be subordinated
to the objective of satisfying the necessity of supplying war factions. For
instance, returning to the case of Afghanistan, during the long years of
civil war, in areas otherwise far too remote from the government control
to benefit from state infrastructure projects, war was the environment that

led to the development of a new and patchy infrastructure. Some areas gained a limited "new infrastructure including roads, hotels and bazaars due to the need for secure supply routes for the resistance."[13] Giustozzi reminds us, however, that prolonged conflicts can sometimes lead to the development of "political complexes" in which military aspects are intrinsically linked with economic, political, and social dimensions: "a more sophisticated type of warlord may develop some form of partial legitimacy and transform his dominion into a 'proto-state',... a structure featuring some sort of civilian administration and providing at least some services, such as education, policing, electricity and other supplies, public transport, etc."[14]

Afghanistan is a powerful illustration of a case in which, not being able to penetrate society beyond the capital, the structures of the modern state were and still are complemented by what some scholars define as traditional "networks of solidarities."[15] In such a social configuration, with the state present but weakened, traditional clan-based khans and warlords, who benefit from the additional apparatus of armed forces, function as a surrogate for the state in supporting at least some segments of the population by "re-distribution of wealth through patronage" and by using accumulated wealth to create "public goods like irrigation [and] influence with or protection from outside powers." Thus, in some regions under warlord control, the conventional depiction of warlords acting in an environment void of any form of governance does not correspond to the reality on the ground.

In 1992, at the end of President Mohamed Najibullah's grip on power, the majority of Afghan provinces were under the direct control of various military commanders. Among those, the most substantial substitute systems of governance in face of the atrophy of central authority were the ones founded by Ahmad Shah Massoud and Ismail Khan. In the eastern provinces under his control—due to energetic support from a mixture of sources such as USAID or NGOs such as the Swedish Committee for Afghanistan and the United Kingdom's Afghan AID—Massoud was involved in social provision ranging from engineering projects to education and health projects (building clinics and attracting doctors).[16] Working toward the creating what Barnett Rubin considers to have been "the most extensive proto-state in Afghanistan", Massoud's Shura-yi Nazar-i Shamali (Supervisory Council of the North) grew as an administrative system that incorporated committees dealing with "judicial and military affairs, civil administration, finances and economy, culture and education, health, political affairs, intelligence and Kabul affairs."[17] Similar reports show that, while the northern province of Balkh was run "almost totally separated from the central government,... basic services such as schools and health centers [were] funded by a combination of resources from regional leaders and international aid."[18]

A third important military commander, Ahmed Rashid Dostum, controlled the northern part of Afghanistan and, during the most important part of the 1980s, managed to prevent the region, including the major city of Mazar-i-Sharif, from becoming a battleground, like the rest of the country. Furthermore, following the fall of the Soviet-supported regime of Najibullah, the preservation of some liberties—including the presence of unveiled women, the selling of alcohol, cinemas, and the like—led one author to proclaim the territory under the control of Dostum, the Autonomous Northern Zone, as "the glittering jewel in Afghanistan's battered crown." Similarly, Brian Glyn Williams has written recently that, "by [the] Afghan standards of the 1990s, Dostum's realm was a true sanctuary from the fundamentalism and warfare that had swept over much of the country. With financial and military support coming from the neighboring Uzbekistan, Dostum's fiefdom thrived. Dostum ran his own airlines—*Balkh Air* [and] protected the only university in Afghanistan that women could still attend—*University of Balkh*."[19]

Another spectacular case is that of the self-titled "Amir of Western Afghanistan," Ismail Khan. Situated in western Afghanistan, bordering Iran, the province of Herat was dominated by the charismatic military commander Ismail Khan for about twenty years until his replacement as governor by President Hamid Karzai. During this time, essential public services functioned in Herat, unlike in the vast majority of Afghanistan's other provinces, with relatively large numbers of women having access to education and opium cultivation maintaining a low profile.[20] A large part of the significant domestic extraction in the province of Herat was spent on public projects, once again privileging infrastructural works. Thus, following agreements at the highest level with officials from Pakistan, he was actively involved in the regional project to open a secure route from Quetta to Kandahar to Herat and reaching Ashkhabad in Turkmenistan.[21] It is not unjustified to speculate that, had it not been for the centralizing movement of the Taliban, which eventually conquered Herat and imprisoned Khan, the trade growth on that route would have significantly increased the revenues of Khan's system and would have propelled Herat even more toward being a regional trade hub. Further demonstration of the diversity of his financial and political sources is that he started work—with Iranian support—on rebuilding the road linking Herat with the Iranian border city of Qala at the same time that he initiated work to restore important regional irrigation canals to functionality.[22]

How can one account for the longevity of these military commanders and the relative stability, security, and development within the realms under their control? To the extent that it refers to direct means of delivery, it may be true that "warlords did not re-distribute [the entire] part of the resources accumulated to the population in the territory they control."[23] The networks of solidarity were—and continued for a long time to be—more open to the traditional bearers of authority, be they clan or village elders ("white beards"), khans, mullahs, or *pirs*. Yet the comparative advantage of the warlord whose authority—founded as it is on military force—extends beyond one particular group of solidarity, can be found precisely in aspects that are an intrinsic part of its modernity: its connectivity to the globalized markets and its de-territorialized nature. It is this global connectivity that enables warlords to "act locally but think globally."[24] The clearest expression of this connectivity is provided by the numerous linkages that the top military commanders had with "institutions beyond the traditional localized continuum: [transnational] Islamic parties, foreign countries, [NGOs,] and international organizations."[25]

The importance of warlords in contemporary Afghanistan clearly originated in their military strength, but their strength was maintained and reinforced by their capacity to attract resources to be redistributed through
patronage, via traditional groups of solidarity.

Access to this variety of sources of resources, by virtue of his prominence in the economy of war, allowed the warlord to surpass and, in many
cases, to replace the traditional local leadership in his capacity to attract
and distribute resources. In a sense, the warlord came to occupy a position
in the tradition of the local notable "who not only is able to secure [his]
group's autonomy in relation with the state, but one who can attract and
canalize the maximum aid from the state or other sources toward [his]
own group, simultaneous with the capacity to maintain a certain degree
of autonomy in [his] domestic affairs."[26] But as his power is based neither on a given territory nor on direct administration, the warlord needs
the cooperation of various solidarity groups, be they secular (tribal or
clan-dominated) or religious. Warlordism, as developed in Afghanistan,
is definitely a form of patrimonialism, sharing with the Weberian ideal the
fundamentally personal nature of power. Yet it departs from the ideal in
that the power of the military leader, beyond his charisma and his foundation in the control over the means of organized violence, depends on a dynamic process of bargaining with various local solidarity networks whose
channels are vitally important for the distribution of resources. This is essentially a different configuration of social control than the one imagined
by a patrimonial leader controlling the military means in isolation from
other social forces.

Warlord, State, and Society

The samples of warlordism used for illustration thus far are circumscribed
to a political context defined by the formal existence of a state (Afghanistan
or Colombia) with limited capacity in all arenas of governance, including the military, political, economic, and social spheres. Is this evidence
enough to conclude that warlords indiscriminately "seek to overthrow

[the state] in order to secure their own form of military autocratic rule," as the conventional view on warlordism seems to assume?[27] A cursory look at the paradigmatic case of warlordism in China seems to signal a negative answer. There seems to be a general consensus that supports and extends the assertion that Guangdong's "residential warlord" from 1929 to 1936, General Chen Jitang, and other military leaders at the time did not have ambitions to expand their rule beyond the provinces under their control and definitely had no ambitions to overtake the state, despite providing significant public services such as health care and education and despite building large-scale infrastructure projects such as bridges and roads. While these warlords had no intention of expanding their power to the entire state, they did seize power in the provinces no longer under state control and organized a de facto autonomous governance, serving their own private interests with little or no contact with the central government.[28]

If that was the situation in the historical Chinese case, is that still the case today? In the post–Cold War era, scholars refer to the challenges to central authority in collapsed/failed states in terms of "several battles [that] take place *within* the state, not [just] against it."[29] Dr. Kirill Nourzhanov is one of the rare voices to introduce a radical departure from the traditional view on warlordism as necessarily opposed to the state. In particular, he mentions the rise of a particular category of warlords "who not so much confront or tolerate the state, but work in partnership with it."[30] Cases as diverse as Sierra Leone, Colombia, and Afghanistan point in the same direction, since local warlords, while involved in a military confrontation against the central authorities' attempt to bring their fiefdoms under control, do benefit from the presence of the state in its weakened condition.

Thus, for instance, Colombia contains a complex relationship between the state and the paramilitary, who are tied together through a multitude of contradictory relationships, being simultaneously linked "as all[ies], as competitor[s] in an oligopolistic market for the provision of security, as parasite[s], and as military adversar[ies]."[31] In Africa, a common denominator seems to be the importance that warlords capture the state—or at least be able to use its globally recognized sovereignty in order to increase their ability to secure external patronage.[32] In Afghanistan, in line with traditional political forces, the warlords have, in fact, "a need for a distant and benevolent state, whose existence they do not challenge."[33] An expression of this connection between the warlord and an unobtrusive state is the ease with which the government of President Karzai was able to incorporate into its structures powerful regional controllers of organized violence, such as generals Fahim and Dostum, as well as Ismail Khan.

The common denominator of all these cases seems to be the concept of an "oligopoly of violence." The concept of an oligopoly of violence was devised as an analytical tool to apply to postcolonial Africa, but it appears to be applicable to various crisis regions in which the European model of a state monopoly over violence has limited empirical value. Inspired by economists' understanding of an oligopoly as an imperfect form of competition in which there are only a few providers of a product or a service for which there are multiple buyers, oligopolies of violence are described as a particular arrangement between security providers, comprising "a fluctuating number of partly competing, partly co-operating actors of violence of different quality."[34] Of course, within these parameters, there is no single type of oligopoly, the markets of violence being no less homogeneous than the economic markets, with the specific characteristic being given exactly by "the mixture of competition and complementarities of rules, claims and authorities."[35]

Warlordism thus described emerges as a form of governance defined by the concept of an oligopoly of violence, in which the state remains an important actor on the market of violence but is not alone any more. Warlords can be seen as autonomous actors whose power and autonomy derive from their possession of an efficient military force, but who cannot exist in isolation from both society and the state (be it his own state or other, usually neighboring states). The warlord is a significant actor in a situation characterized by an asymmetry between a previously "strong society" and a "weak state."[36] He is autonomous in the sense that, although active in the territory (or territories) nominally under the control of a state, there is no higher authority (including the state) capable of regulating or dictating his actions. Thus the warlord coexists with both the state and various communal networks of the society but is not within the military reach of any of them.

However, while born from the strength of his military force, the warlord's autonomy is maintained and perpetuated not by ignoring the society or the state, but by installing himself in a nodal position between the society he controls, the targeted state, and other actors, such as other states, international organizations, international NGOs, and transnational corporations, among others. There are numerous instances in which those actors have cooperated in one way or another with warlords: the United States support for the burgeoning warlords-to-be in the Afghan-Soviet war, for instance, and their cooperation in the campaign against Taliban is well publicized. In other examples, Liberia under the control of Charles Taylor's National Patriotic Front of Liberia (NPFL) became France's "third largest African supplier of logs,"[37] and both Pakistan and, in particular, Iran were allegedly heavily involved in supporting one or another of the Afghan warlords, as were NGOs such as the Swedish Committee for Afghanistan and Oxfam. Moreover, certain religious groups continue to cooperate with warlords in varying parts of the world, as do corporations, such as Shell Oil in Nigeria, Executive Outcomes and its offsprings on the African continent, and the like.

Far from being cut off from relations with either state or society, the autonomy of the warlord, founded as it is on his military strength, depends on his successful bid for a central place in a network with most of these actors. In this way, he maintains a parasitic relation with both state and society, while breaking from a unique dependency on either of them. As long as the warlord is capable of manipulating the flow of resources *within* the weak institutional edifice of the state, he has no incentive in the further development of state structures. In a sense, the warlord does not govern directly, as most of the time, he is not directly involved in the provision of public goods, but rather, he oversees the provision of these functions by other actors. If Afghanistan is to serve as an example, the functions of governance in areas as diverse as education, training, agriculture, and irrigation systems, were transferred or outsourced to various NGOs by both central government (like the Taliban) and the local warlords.[38] The warlords, though, were active in attracting resources to allow public goods to be provided, as well as in setting up the conditions under which NGOs or other external actors were able to operate. Accordingly, the nature of governance for the communities under a warlord's control depends on his actions and on his manipulation of the network of actors capable of providing social services.

Regardless of the position one takes in identifying the structural causes underlying the appearance of warlordism and its consequential development of "markets for violence" (economic or noneconomic in nature), it is hard to deny that the "continuation of violence is based on economic motives or unconscious economic behavior."[39] Underscoring the importance of the economic dimension should not impede the recognition that warlords, deliberately or simply as an unintended consequence of their newly acquired status, can and sometimes do play a significant role in supplementing those social functions underperformed by an atrophied central state.

Analysis: Warlord Entrepreneurship as Governance

From the above analysis, we can summarize a few characteristics of warlords as entrepreneurs and the polities they control. First, the warlord appears in those parts of the world in which formal state institutions crumble under the combined pressures of traditional loci of political authority and the melting down of Cold War support for the central authorities. Without a doubt, the warlord's primary source of power is located in his private possession of military might, which he is forced to exhibit periodically and to eagerly defend against any attempt of dispossession coming either from a central authority, fellow warlords, or external intervention. To compensate for the weak political authority deriving from his autonomous use of violence, the warlord becomes a central player on the market of violence, using his position in the global economy of war to attract various resources, while at the same time avoiding locking himself into dependency on a single source. While the central asset that raises the interest of the warlord remains procurement of weapons, these resources cover a wider range, from channeling aid to attracting foreign NGOs in the provision of basic services such as food, health, or education. His political position depends not only on his military prowess but also on his ability in securing those resources, as well as on the extent to which he is embedded in various solidarity networks capable of redistributing those resources in his name.

Second, far from being a homogenous phenomenon, warlordism is highly heterogeneous. Although it may be possible that some of its existing forms will develop into stable alternative forms of governance in an oligopoly of violence, this is likely to occur in only a few instances. It is impossible to avoid the fact that the provision of social services is rarely characteristic of the warlord order. However rare it is, though, it is legitimate to investigate the circumstances under which warlords can move beyond the purely predatory behavior of ordinary bandits and advance toward partial forms of governance in the absence of efficient state mechanisms of redistribution.

Third, it may be argued that the contemporary warlord, given the circumstances in which he acts (globalized economies, both legal and illegal, and state and non-state competitive actors), is not dependent on domestic extraction. He does not control the population, as much as he keeps it captive. The participation of foreign humanitarian intervention (NGOs, IGOs, and the like) might be thus explored as a form of ransom. Some existent public services (such as health and education) are not performed by warlords; instead, these functions are performed by external actors from which the warlord extracts resources. In this way, we may have a semblance of an answer to why some services are performed. Important as it may be, the warlord is interested not so much in his domestic legitimation function deriving from this performance as in negotiating with the actors interested in performing those functions.

Finally, the necessity of dealing with failed states, dysfunctional institutions, and a lack of good governance at the periphery of international law has pushed the process of state building to the core of current scholarly interests, and even more so to the attention of political decision makers. Organized violence outside the control of the state characterizes contemporary life in a significant number of societies, and it seems to be a fact that many now take as inherent to many of the conflicts plaguing the world. The burgeoning literature on state failure, however, is founded on a negative logic, one triggered by the analyses of what is missing in polities at the periphery of the Westphalian system—in particular, the absence of the centralized monopoly over violence. Building on this negative logic, the solutions widely offered revolve around the recentralization of the control over organized violence in a manner reminiscent of early state-formation theories. In contrast, by acknowledging the provision of social services such as infrastructural networks, health care, and education in at least some of the areas outside the central government's control over violence, we find that a positive, inductive logic—one centered on identifying what is already in place in those political units—may be better equipped to explain the circumstances that lead to the weakening of the state and that allow warlords to thrive locally as entrepreneurs on the market of violence and to prosper at a national, regional, and international level.[40]

7 5GW

Into the Heart of Darkness

Mark Safranski

Fifth-generation warfare (5GW) has been a controversial concept among military theorists, analysts, and bloggers ever since it was proposed as a successor to fourth-generation warfare (4GW), a strategic theory originally put forward by defense intellectual William Lind and subsequently expanded by others. The 4GW school posited a succession of generations of historical warfare paradigms rising and falling—1GW (close-order musket drill), 2GW (massed firepower and mass armies in entrenched defenses), 3GW (fast combined arms maneuver warfare), and finally 4GW (irregular, antistate conflict focused on the moral level of war). The problems posed by transnational terrorist organizations like Hezbollah or al-Qaeda, the robust, decentralized insurgencies in Iraq and Afghanistan, and chaotic failed states like Somalia gave traction to the arguments of 4GW thinkers and caused some analysts to look for a kind of future warfare that might defeat 4GW fighters or replace them as a more urgent threat.

These speculations, loosely grouped under the rubric *5GW,* while often creative, share little in common with one another and have faced a critical reception in the defense community. Many orthodox military strategists rejected the entire 4GW theoretical construct as deeply flawed and ahistorical. In the 4GW school itself, William Lind dismissed claims for

5GW as premature and has said that the signs thought to be pointing to 5GW are merely new aspects of 4GW—as 4GW has yet to fully unfold. Some "XGW" theorists, like those in this book, discarded chronological linearity in articulating a model of 5GW based upon secrecy and deception, while grand strategist Thomas Barnett and futurist John Robb have used 5GW to describe elements of their own well-developed strategic theories. On the subject of 5GW, there is not a chorus of voices but a cacophony.

A better definition is that 5GW will be whatever mode of warfare successfully counters the threat of the decentralized, networked, irregular warfare of the kind seen in Afghanistan, Iraq, Mexico, and the Horn of Africa. 5GW is not here now, which makes categorical definition elusive, but it will be the great counteroffensive, the iron response of the state to crush its 4GW enemies. The reason for the conceptual resilience that 5GW enjoys—despite a broad lack of consensus regarding its very existence, much less a satisfactory working definition—is that the chaotic and fast-evolving conditions of postmodern warfare have defied the attempts of the best military minds to provide a simple, explanatory, strategic narrative.[1]

Instead, the disorderliness of the battlespace has invaded the realm of ideas and even familiar terms like *conventional* and *irregular* are now in question, as nation-states struggle to adapt to warfare that includes a wide range of unpredictable, adversarial, evolving non-state actors operating at multiple levels of conflict, under conditions of globalized connectivity that William Lind and others call 4GW.[2] 4GW—whether we accept the terminology or substitute another explanation—brings higher levels of uncertainty and unmanageable complexity in war. It is forcing states, armies, and societies into corners where their survival will depend on their ability to adapt.

This is a path of grave danger. States will either successfully adapt, or they will fail. Many will fail, lacking either sufficient political resilience to weather protracted civil conflict or an economic base from which to wage it. Those that manage to adapt will be most likely to do so by either

(a) adjusting their response to complex, decentralized insurgencies down to a granular level of society with intelligence, counterinsurgency (COIN), information operations, and economic development—states, in essence, becoming more complex themselves—or (b) savagely ratcheting back the systemic level of complexity by a sustained application of extreme violence to disrupt the social fabric and simplify it by atomizing social networks deemed to be enemies of the state.

The first option involves counterinsurgency warfare and skillfully selective political and economic concessions by the state to separate the people from insurgents and to strengthen the legitimacy of the state in their eyes by displaying competence in providing physical security, desired public goods, civic engagement, and appropriate reactions to insurgency attacks. This is a sophisticated and exceptionally difficult policy to carry out and requires governmental elites to consider long-term national interest over their own immediate interests. This usually proves to be the sticking point.

The French lost politically in Indochina and Algeria—long before they lost on the battlefield—due to deeply exploitative and punitive colonial regimes that they could not bring themselves to reform. The United States, in turn, never succeeded in convincing the Saigon governments to reduce corruption or enact meaningful reforms that might appeal to South Vietnam's rural peasantry, even when the regime was facing collapse. This contrasts with the more positive COIN experiences of the Malayan Emergency, El Salvador, and most recently, Iraq, where a more nuanced and concessionary approach, coupled with more precise uses of force, enlisted the population as allies (or as armed paramilitaries) against the insurgency. Even in El Salvador, where COIN was far more "kinetic" than it is today, it involved major political concessions by the Forty Families oligarchy in establishing genuine democratic government.

Unfortunately, because of the difficulty of finding or persuading sufficiently enlightened elites to reform in their own self-interest—and the challenges of navigating old-fashioned Maoist insurgency, to say nothing of today's 4GW environments—most efforts at prosecuting COIN warfare have failed.[3] We can expect that in the future, while some will succeed brilliantly, many states will likewise fail—especially those without a great power patron, as in the recent case of the deposed royal government of Nepal. These kinds of states—unpopular, authoritarian, relatively backward, corrupt, and isolated—are exceedingly poor candidates for bootstrapping a COIN strategy on their own. Or even with considerable outside help.

This brings us to the probability that for the aforementioned states, the actual options for their ruling elites for adapting to the threat of 4GW will be between accepting varying degrees of failure—conceding temporary autonomous zones (TAZ) to rebels, being overthrown, or imploding into anarchy as insurgents encroach—or taking the gloves off and using the indiscriminate, unrestricted violence of genocide to annihilate real and potential enemies before the international community can mobilize to prevent it. History suggests they might well succeed.

The Soviet Union

The Stalinist Soviet Union had, since the publication of Conquest's *The Great Terror: A Reassessment* (1991), been one of the major examples of state democide—comparable to the great ethno-racial-sectarian genocide of European Jewry by the Nazis or of the Armenians by the Ottoman Turks. What is less well understood about Stalin's crimes are that the apparently random terror, with quotas for arrests issued to branches of the secret police in every Soviet oblast, which swept up millions of Soviet citizens in the 1930s, contained a far more targeted campaign against specific and readily identifiable networks that Stalin considered especially problematic potential enemies.

Though small compared to the victims of the Great Terror at large, these networks compose a formidable list that included Old Bolsheviks; former Left Socialist Revolutionaries; the Jewish Socialist Bund; Trotskyites (real followers of Leon Trotsky, not those sentenced under Article 58), former Mensheviks; Ukrainian Communist Party leaders; most senior officials of the Soviet secret police agencies prior to Nikolai Yezhov assuming control of the NKVD (the more powerful forerunner of the KGB); Leningrad Communist Party leadership under Kirov; the Red Army officer corps, especially general officers; Comintern agents, especially those who went to Spain and China; Soviet military intelligence (GRU) officers; and foreign communists resident in the USSR.

The methodical nature of Stalin's "inner terror" can be seen by looking at a few examples. The Polish Communist Party, in Soviet exile from the Pilsudski dictatorship, had its entire leadership arrested, along with 50,000 followers and relatives, of whom 10,000 were shot outright. In 1938, the effectively defunct Polish Party was formally dissolved.[4] The Ukrainian Communist Party—and Kosior, who was the Soviet satrap in Kiev—particularly irritated Stalin, because of their Ukrainian "nationalism" and paid a heavy price when Nikita Khrushchev was dispatched to deal with them. Khrushchev personally ordered the shooting 55,741 Ukrainian party officials, including thirty-five out of thirty-eight provincial secretaries. Lavrenty Beria, who would succeed Yezhov as NKVD boss and oversee his predecessor's murder, had a staggering 268,950 Transcaucasian Communists and their family members arrested and liquidated 10 percent of the Georgian Communist Party.[5] Approximately 90 percent of the Red Navy officers were killed in 1937–1938, and in the Red Army, though less thoroughly savaged at the lower ranks, lost 154 out of its 186 division commanders and almost every army commander and army corps commander, along with their political commissars.

A frequent Stalinist purge technique was to liquidate not only the holder of an important post in an organization, but his immediate replacement as well (and not infrequently, the replacement's replacement). They not only atomized existing social networks but also terminated institutional memory, as the documentary records were purged with the same severity as the staff. This permitted a complete reshaping of organizations in any fashion the dictator desired, and Stalin could be sure the "new blood" was completely loyal to him and untainted by previous "enemies." Soviet society had been so thoroughly terrorized by the end of the Yezhovschina

("Yezhov's time"—the Soviets' name for the great terror of 1937–1938) that no effective opposition of any kind existed to Stalin's will. Neither the Soviet government nor the Communist Party nor the general staff of the Red Army retained any independent functionality after 1938, and after 1948 the politburo itself fell into gradual disuse under Stalin's paranoid eye, as he arrested the wives and families of his closest collaborators.

Cambodia

Despite being a secretive, almost cult-like, ultra-Maoist movement, Cambodia's Khmer Rouge leadership aped Stalin's bureaucratic, totalitarian regime in conducting a two-tiered auto-genocide designed to exterminate specific networks, even as it is deconstructed Cambodian society as a whole. Submerged within the most radical and terrifying democidal expression of Marxist-Leninism in history was a sinister racial and religious subtext that would have warmed the heart of Heinrich Himmler. And like Stalin's Great Terror, Pol Pot's "Year Zero" left Cambodian society completely prostrate and incapable of even conceiving of resistance. "They treated us like dogs; we dared not protest" recalled one ethnic Chinese Cambodian peasant who was doubly suspect, not only for his ethnicity, but also for having converted to Protestant Christianity.[6] As Khmer Rouge cadres would say, "To keep you is no gain; to kill you is no loss."[7]

The Khmer Rouge idealized a peasant Communist utopia and followed revolutionary tradition in targeting the "bourgeoisie," a category the Khmer Rouge radically expanded to embrace all urban dwellers all those with an education, famously killing those who wore eyeglasses on the presumption that they could read. Like other Marxists, the Khmer Rouge sought an atheistic state and targeted the Buddhist clergy for liquidation, along with those Cambodians who had been converted to foreign religions like Islam or Christianity. But the Khmer Rouge leadership also had deep pseudo-racialist antipathy for Muslim Chams, ethnic Vietnamese, and ethnic Chinese, all of whom—as non-Khmers—were slated for destruction, though to appease Beijing's sensibilities, ethnic Chinese were always classed as "bourgeois" and not killed specifically for their ethnicity, unlike the Vietnamese minority.

As with Stalin's purges of the Communist Party of the Soviet Union and the Polish and Ukrainian Communist Parties, the Khmer Rouge achieved a chilling thoroughness in their elimination of leadership networks in "traitorous" or "enemy" groups. Of the Islamic leaders in Cambodia categorized as "community leaders," "deputies," "Haji," and "teachers," the death toll was approximately 90 percent. The primary political vehicle of the Chams, the Islamic Central Organization, was killed off to almost the last man.[8] Islam and the Cham language were banned.

An innovation in genocide, if it can be called that, instituted by the Khmer Rouge and later perfected by the Interahamwe militias of Rwanda, was the devolution of state-sanctioned mass murder from being the job of the elite to that of a granular social level. Unlike the Nazi Gestapo and the special Totenkopf SS division that ran Hitler's death camps or Stalin's NKVD, which executed political prisoners in secret or in faraway gulags, Pol Pot ordered that village officials, ordinary soldiers, peasants, or even children be enlisted to execute enemies, hacking them to death with farm implements in order to save bullets. One former Khmer Rouge official confessed to personally killing five thousand people by wielding a pickaxe.[9]

This downward dissemination of responsibility for genocide created situations where victims were frequently compelled to become perpetrators, demonstrating their loyalty by slaughtering neighbors, friends, spouses, parents, or children. These survivors under the Khmer Rouge regime were left with their social relations atomized, unable to reconstruct new social networks, as forming bonds of trust was impossible so long as the rule of Pol Pot endured.

Rwanda

The most "granular" genocide in history occurred in Rwanda in 1994, where between eight hundred thousand and one million Tutsis and "moderate" Hutus were systematically murdered over the course of just one hundred days by radical Hutu mobs mobilized and directed by Interahamwe and Impuzamugambi militiamen and the Rwandan government, possibly abetted by French military intelligence officers—France was formally accused of complicity in the Rwanda Genocide in 2008 by an investigatory commission of the Rwandan government.[10] One of the most publicized genocides in real time, the Rwandan genocide is notable for the recruitment of enormous numbers of participants—every Hutu citizen was expected to play the role of an enthusiastic SS officer—and for the failure of the genocide to affect the military capabilities of the Tutsi rebel Rwandan Patriotic Front, which ultimately overthrew the Hutu government in Kigali.

Philip Gourevitch, author of *We Wish to Inform You That Tomorrow We Will Be Killed with Our Families*, described the unique character of the genocide in Rwanda in an interview with PBS Frontline.

What distinguishes Rwanda is a clear, programmatic effort to eliminate everybody in the Tutsi minority group because they were Tutsis. The logic was to kill everybody. Not to allow anybody to get away. Not to allow anybody to continue. And the logic, as Rwandans call it, the genocidal logic, was very much akin to that of an ideology very similar to that of the Nazism vis-à-vis the Jews in Europe, which is all of them must be gotten rid of to purify in a sense the people. There›s a utopian element in genocide that›s perplexing. But it is an effort to create community in the most strict sense of «us versus them,» by literally eliminating them and bonding all of us in complicity, in the course of that elimination. The idea was that all Hutus should participate in killing of Tutsis. And there have been cases of mass political murder, there have been cases of massacres and genocidal massacres, but never a country and a society so completely and totally convulsed by an effort at pure, unambiguous genocide since the end of World War

II, since the passage of the Genocide Convention by the United Nations in the aftermath of the Holocaust.[11]

As with the genocide of Communist regimes, the radical Hutu state was targeting latent social networks of potential opposition in trying to destroy the Tutsi population, but unlike Stalin or Pol Pot, Hutu generals also faced an active military opponent in the Rwandan Patriotic Front (RPF), with which they were locked in a civil war, "Note that in 1991 Rwandan Major General Augustin Ndindiliyimana originally proposed creating the self-defense militias that became monstrous killing machines over the next three years. That same general as commander of the National Gendarmerie was a member of the 'Zero Network' used by the conspirators of the genocide. His case is hardly unusual; there was nothing spontaneous about the Rwandan genocide. Even as the interim government of Rwanda crossed to safety in Zaire in July 1994, Melvern quotes Prime Minister Kambanda proclaiming, 'We have lost the military battle but the war is by no means over because we have the people behind us.' "[12]

That statement, hundreds of pages of government records, testimony at the International Criminal Tribunal for Rwanda, and countless first-person accounts from the genocidal killers document what the genocide was all about: continued Hutu political domination of Rwanda.

The genocide failed to stabilize the radical Hutu government and, instead, led directly to its overthrow by its Tutsi rebel enemies. The RPF rebels were based in Uganda, and unlike most insurgents, they did not lose their military effectiveness because of the Hutu destruction of their civilian Tutsi base. By contrast, Rwandan society and the machinery of the government were severely disrupted by the genocide, both by the loss of Tutsi personnel throughout the private and public sector and by the mobilization of the Hutu population and prioritization of genocidal killings over their normal activities. The regime was less able to field effective military resistance to the RPF during the genocide than during the civil war, and it collapsed in July of 1994.

Analysis: Genocide as Statecraft

These historical case studies point not only to the persistence of genocide as a historical tragedy but its perceived utility as a tool of statecraft by regimes of a paranoid character that consider themselves surrounded by enemies, real or imagined. The siege mentality that is an inherent characteristic of governmental elites in states like Burma, Algeria, North Korea, Zimbabwe, and Sudan are like gasoline waiting to be ignited by the spark of 4GW into a monstrous conflagration.

4GW entities like Hezbollah, like the complex, decentralized insurgencies seen in Iraq, or like the narco-insurgency raging in Mexico operate at what strategist John Boyd refers to as the mental and moral levels of war, seeking to erode the legitimacy of the state and win over the primary loyalty of the population—or a segment of it—to itself. It would be hard to conceive of a more antagonizing type of opponent for a paranoid, statist elite than a 4GW group whose existence and successes tend to inflame the worst kind of conspiracy theorizing. For elites of this kind, a democidal response to the challenge or the potential of 4GW conflict offers pragmatic and psychological benefits.

The pragmatic benefit is that genocide is often, though not always, effective at decimating the capacity of a targeted population to resist while terrorizing observers within the society into passivity or even active complicity. Algeria in the 1990s, Iraq in the 1980s, Guatemala in the 1970s, and Indonesia in the 1960s all successfully used death squads on a massive scale and in conjunction with regular military and security forces to brutally put down targeted groups: Islamist terrorists, Communist guerillas, or restive minority populations. Genocide does not require the sophisticated and expensive state security apparatus fielded by the Nazis. As Rwanda and Cambodia demonstrated, political mobilization and recruitment of a "perpetrator population" is enough; Rwandan Hutu militiamen actually murdered more efficiently with their machetes than the SS did with Auschwitz.

Psychologically, a regime that opts for so extreme a policy as genocide to crush an insurgency is akin to Cortez burning his boats before assaulting the Aztec empire. The state backs itself into a moral corner, and the only sure path for safety for its high-level apparatchiks is to prevail and retain power indefinitely. The bonds between members of the regime are tightened by mutual guilt and a common enemy (or perhaps by the enmity of the whole civilized world), as well as, frequently, by an increasingly distorted worldview, as the need to minimize the genocide or rationalize it as justifiable becomes an imperative, when the genocide is discovered by other states.

For many illiberal and less than legitimate states in the twenty-first century, embarking down the path of unspeakable crimes will become a likely adaption to the challenges of a 4GW threat. Their 5GW will be entering into the heart of darkness.

8 Weaponizing Capitalism

The Naxals of India

Shlok Vaidya

I have said in the past that left-wing extremism is the single biggest security challenge to the Indian state. It continues to be so.

—Prime Minister Manmohan Singh

Despite the attention potential conflict with Pakistan, Kashmir, and the menace of radical Islam receive, there is another, more immediate threat to India's existence. In 2005, the government estimated that the Naxals are responsible for 89 percent of violent deaths. In 2012, Naxals conducted over 1,500 violent acts. Their influence spans two hundred districts, up from seventy-five just five years ago. Over the same time period, the Naxals have murdered thousands of civilians, killed hundreds of security forces, and lost many of their own.1 The once-suppressed Naxalite insurgency is siphoning the flows of globalization and inhibiting the economic expansion of almost half the country.

From Ideology to Warfare

The insurgency takes its name from the village where it originated, Naxalbari, in West Bengal. There, in March 1967, a generation of college-educated Maoist ideologues was given purpose when it united to free the peasant class from the bonds of servitude. By May, this cadre had recruited some two thousand villages and more than fifteen thousand residents as activists. In short order, these ragtag forces, armed with crude bows, arrows, and farming implements, had claimed some three hundred square miles of territory. Within this "liberated zone" the cadre set up a governing body that canceled debt, destroyed ownership records, and fixed wages as well as commodity prices. A focus on delivering on ideology resulted in a lack of emphasis on security, and soon a combination of poor tactical skills, lack of modern weaponry, and the overwhelming force of state police put an end to this insurrection. Five thousand attempts to reignite the flames of revolution over the next three years failed, and by 1972, some forty thousand members and leaders of the insurgency languished in jail.[2] For the next decade, the Naxals lay mostly dormant. A handful of highly fragmented groups focused on energizing their rural population base and conducting sporadic guerrilla operations. When the violence began to gain intensity and speed, it faced ruthless opposition, particularly in Andhra Pradesh, and failed to achieve lasting impact. Not until India's economy was pried open in 1991 did the Naxals again emerge on the national stage.

This renewed campaign is focused on preventing the sale of India's significant mineral resources. Over the past twenty years, India has signed thousands of contracts that parcel out its reserves of bauxite, thorium, and coal, respectively 10 percent, 12 percent, and 7 percent of the world's reserves. India stands to do deals worth more than $80 billion, should the Naxals allow it.[3] Unfortunately, 80 percent of these natural resources are found in four Naxal-afflicted states that lack governance and opportunity. Furthermore, despite aggregate foreign direct investment of $145 billion in this sector since 1991, the Reserve Bank of India estimates these four states receive less than five percent of this cash flow.[4] As a result, these states constitute only 12 percent of the country's gross domestic product, and none of their per capita income levels surpasses $900 per year. A recent study found that, compared to states not affected by the Naxals, these resource-rich but prosperity-poor states lost on average 12 percent of economic productivity year on year.[5]

Sensing opportunity in globalization's uneven distribution of capital, energy, and people, the modern Naxals have pioneered a strategy that enables the organization to wield these very flows against the state.

A New Strategy

We are ready with a blueprint to prevent entry into the region.

—Rakeshji, Naxal Spokesman, Orissa

Modern Naxals have corrected the flaws in their revolutionary predecessors' model. Instead of relying on ideology to amass huge numbers with shared purpose, this generation is emphasizes execution: building tactical training capacity, capturing popular support, and stockpiling equipment. Instead of the bows and arrows, the new generation is armed with state-of-the-art weaponry. The goal remains the same—rendering the Indian state incapable of governing—but the means are notably different.

Overruns

On April 6, 2010, a convoy of 120 federal and state police forces returning to headquarters after operations deep in the forests of Dantewada was ambushed. Two land mines were detonated, and then three hundred Naxals swarmed the already fatigued troops. Reinforcements rushed to the scene, only to discover seventy-five dead policemen and the burning wreckage of a convoy that had been pillaged for firearms and equipment. This was the deadliest attack the insurgency had ever conducted.

Adopting a tactic from the Maoist model, Naxals regularly overrun targets—that is, concentrate overwhelming numbers and firepower on a single location. In contrast to a strategy designed to maintain control of an area, as in Naxalbari, this guerrilla approach prevents state troops from engaging the group and minimizes the exposure of the insurgency to harm. In particular, Naxals target police forces and more specialized paramilitary soldiers patrolling the forests. After executing a successful ambush, the insurgents retrieve what equipment was not destroyed and disappear into the night. Any loot is amassed at later time in a secure location. In a two-year period beginning in 2008, the Naxals conducted six thousand such attacks. In addition to ambushes, the insurgency has conducted other operations:

- They have used improvised explosive devices. Every year, dozens of police units inadvertently set off landmines placed in their path. To mitigate this, they began to use metal detectors able to find landmines just under the surface. But in response, Naxals adapted their approach. Now, the insurgency embeds explosives in roads while they are under construction. Naxals can simply connect their detonators to explosives already in place and lay in wait.[6]
- They have assassinated officials. In a stunning attack in May 2013, Naxals assaulted a convoy of leading Indian National Congress officials, then stabbed select politicians and their sons. In all, twelve senior politicians and eight policemen were murdered. In an effort to silence former chief minister of Jharkhand Babulal Marandi, the insurgency stormed a sporting event attended by his brother. In the hail of gunfire, they killed his son instead. Only months earlier, the Naxals had publicly shot a member of Parliament, Sunit Mahato, seven times and set his jeep ablaze.[7]
- They have destroyed police infrastructure. Naxals regularly overrun remote forest-ranger outposts as well as more urban police stations. The insurgency specializes in night raids that begin with grenades and are followed by indiscriminate automatic-weapons fire. In 2005, Naxals overwhelmed a jail in Bihar, setting free almost four hundred of their own. These prison breaks can even come from inside. A Naxal-led riot inside a Chhattisgarh prison overcame sixteen jailers.

In all, 253 prisoners escaped, fifty of them members of the insurgency.[8]

India is clearly under assault, and the situation is likely to worsen. Recognizing the disruptive value of thousands of overruns in rapid succession, Naxals have shifted their strategy to exploit this vulnerability.

Disruptions

The state-owned Coal India is the largest single holder of coal reserves in the world, at 64 billion tons. The company produces over 430 million tons of coal per year and held an initial public offering of its stock in 2010 that earned $53 billion. However, a deeper look at its portfolio reveals some troubling facts. A full 92 percent of the company's coal production is from eleven fields that sit squarely in Naxal territory.[9] As a direct result of the insurgency's violence, the state of Jharkhand has seen coal production losses double from 60,000 in 2007 to 110,000 in 2011.[10] Naxals attack not just the nodes but also the networks themselves.

Railways, roads, and telecommunications infrastructures are prone to disruption by the insurgency as well. There were nine hundred such attacks over the last four years—and the pace is quickening. In 2008, there were a reported thirty Naxal-related security incidents on the railways. This figure almost doubled—to fifty-eight—in 2009. These attacks include bombing freight trains; destroying tracks in order to derail trains; holding passengers hostage; and conducting hijackings in which only the train's engineer is left, but hundreds of paying passengers are removed and replaced with sympathizers.[11] These tactics require remarkably few resources to execute, yet generate out-sized returns. The case of the Jnaneswari Express—a fast passenger train—in 2010 illustrates the destructive potential of even the simplest of attacks. In the hours before the Jnaneswari was to pass by, Naxal-affiliated organizations pulled the spikes tethering fifty feet of the railroad tracks to the ground using only a shovel and a pick. The group also removed a one-foot section of the track itself. When the train approached, the tracks shook and destabilized the engine, and the train derailed. A freight train headed in the opposite direction was unable to stop and slammed into the thirteen carriages littered across the track. In minutes, 141 were dead and 180 were injured.

Even in instances when no one is hurt by a Naxal attack on the railway, the insurgency can cause major delays to cascade through the system, such as in 2010, when Naxals destroyed three feet of track and halted twenty-four trains.[12] Because of this threat, all night trains through insurgency-affected areas have been halted. Companies have resorted to transporting goods by road—incurring costly delays in the process. In 2009 alone, the Indian Railways lost $110 million—a 40 percent loss from the previous year.[13] There are long-term consequences as well. In Jharkhand, a $259 million increase in costs caused by frequent Naxal attacks has halted six major railway-development projects.[14]

The Mineral Development Corporation (NMDC), distressed by the inability of the railways to keep pace with the NMDC's production schedule, constructed a pipeline system, failing to note that this sort of infrastructure is particularly vulnerable to the same kind of attack. Sure enough, in June 2009, the Naxals blew up a critical pipeline and caused a loss of $200 million.[15] To prevent this from happening again, the NMDC is building a $200 million pipeline system along existing roads.[16] Unfortunately, the road network is easily disrupted as well. Naxals frequently attack contractors building roads and set vehicles and machinery on fire to delay construction.[17] These attacks are troubling, given that the NMDC relies on a single district in Chhattisgarh for 71 percent of its output, and that district is hard-hit by Naxals.[18]

In contrast to railways, pipelines, and roads, all of which have been in place for some time, telecommunications infrastructure is still in its infancy, having taken off only in 2004. Disrupting this system enables the Naxals to isolate rural areas from the flow of information. Informers and police forces are prevented from passing on intelligence or calling for reinforcements when mobile networks are down.

Since 2006, Naxals have destroyed more than three hundred cell-phone towers in six states. It is interesting to note that more than 60 percent of these attacks took place after 2008, in what is likely a response to the surge in the number of towers being built. In Jharkhand, there are already close to nine hundred towers, and Chhattisgarh has five hundred of its own. The government is intent on building an addition 550 throughout the Naxal-affected areas.[19] But this will be a turbulent process, should it happen at all. In 2009, the state-owned Bharat Sanchar Nigam Limited planned to build fourteen towers in south Orissa. After Naxals attacked three, causing $700,000 in damage, the company temporarily abandoned its plans to expand in the area. Despite this, plans proceed to install three thousand new towers throughout the affected areas.[20]

To mitigate this threat, in a tactic not unlike the NMDC's plan for locating pipelines along roads, the communications providers have taken to placing cell-phone towers within the walls of the network of police camps that litter the forests. The state views this as a way of controlling the battle space. Raids conducted by the Naxals, however have shown that this is not a deterrent, and in fact, it could present an incentive, as it provides the opportunity to attack two valuable targets at once. This begs the question: if the Naxals possess overwhelming force, the element of surprise, and the ability to successfully execute hundreds of these attacks per year, why aren't they concentrating on the highest-yielding attacks on critical infrastructure?

The Deviant Economic Engine

The Naxals see industry as a source of earning and won't ruin its work.

—Vishwa Ranjan, director general of police, Chhattisgarh

The answer is to be found in what is the clearest demarcation between Naxalbari's revolutionaries and the insurgency of today. This generation has embraced the very activity the Maoist ideology so vehemently opposes: profit. India's illicit economy is estimated to be between 40 and

71 percent of the size of the legitimate economy—somewhere between $500 billion and $1 trillion.[21] The Naxals underpin a huge segment of this growing market. Weaponizing capitalism has sparked a deviant economic engine that steadily burns through the poorest parts of India with minimal effort.

The Revolutionary Tax

In 2000, India began an ambitious project to connect at-risk villages with populations greater than one thousand to major road arteries by 2003. By 2007, it planned to connect all villages with more than five hundred people. It is a powerful initiative, and thus far India has built 175,000 miles of roads, though much of the remaining 1.6 million miles of rural road system remains barely passable. This project was reinforced in late 2010 by a $1.5 billion loan from the World Bank to build another fifteen thousand miles of road to the benefit of six million people.[22] The government and the people were not the only ones to cheer this initiative on. This investment represents a huge windfall for the Naxals as well. Former director of the Intelligence Bureau Ajit Doval estimates that between 30 and 40 percent of development funds have been captured by the Naxals.[23]

Having proven their ability to destroy critical nodes and crash networks, Naxals are now able to exact ransoms with the mere threat of violence. The insurgency extorts hundreds of millions of dollars from businesses and others, including small shops, paper and rice mills, doctors, and property owners. The insurgency calls this a "revolutionary tax." This strategy yields massive return. In Chhattisgarh alone, Naxals extorted $60 million from mining firms, the transportation sector, and government contractors in 2009.[24] That state's director general of police, Vishwa Ranjan, estimated the national revenue of the Naxals at $400 million per year.[25] Perhaps due to the outcry around these large figures, the following year's estimates were remarkably lower, at $30 million and $280 million, respectively.[26]

How much the Naxals are able to extort depends on to how much the government spends, and because of this, there is no sign that this source of revenue will diminish. The government has allocated $3 billion over the next decade for construction designed to dampen the Naxal threat, including affordable housing, roads, highways, hostels, hospitals, drinking water projects, and electricity networks.[27]

A Revolutionary Tax Economy

Whereas the state can levy tax only on legitimate enterprises, the Naxals have expanded their tax pool to include illicit actors as well, such as extortionists, smuggling rings, and drug producers. Rather than assume the costs of running these operations using their own human capital and assets, the insurgency incentivizes and enables others in the extortion ecosystem.

Each Naxal foot soldier is paid $60 per month, with a performance bonus based on how much revenue he or she brings in. The market sets pricing, though one captured leader revealed going rates for extortion (on a monthly basis): $2 for daycares, $4 for elementary-school teachers, $10 for high-school teachers, $4 for bank employees, $14 for bank managers, $100 for businessmen, and $.20 and a kilogram of rice for villagers.[28] This corporate model enables individual and organizational profit to grow together. This system steadily generates revenue for all parties involved, but given that individual cells and leaders manage their own budgets, their relationship with one another can be contentious. There have been several noted heists and conflicts between factions jockeying for larger shares.[29]

The Naxals are not only market makers but regulators as well. In Chhattisgarh, gangs of unemployed young men used to shake down businesses and government officers using letters that imitated those written by real Naxals. Only when victims complained that they were being asked to pay twice per month did the Naxals respond to this dilution of their brand. In 2009, they began to enforce a simple edict: gangs were allowed to extort so long as they did not cut into existing Naxal revenue. As a result, the criminals are now giving a portion of their revenue, estimated at more than $4 million, to the insurgency while seeking out new victims.

This deviant economic engine is being fueled not only by extortion. The model is leveraging a variety of illicit activity across the country:

- **Mining.** Government records show 182,000 instances of illegal mining across seventeen states, with 30 percent of those being found in the Naxal-affected area. There are an estimated sixty thousand illegal mines operating today, with five hundred million untrained laborers working in entirely unregulated conditions.[30] These mines are operated by criminal organizations that also pay into the Naxal revenue pool. Prasoon S. Majumdar, editor of economic affairs at *The Sunday Indian*, estimates that Naxals receive between 20 and 30 percent for each truckload of coal, with another 15 percent reserved for corrupt local bureaucrats and policemen.[31] To continue their work unhindered, illegal miners bribe individual police inspectors at the cost of $7,000 per year.
- **Narcotics.** India is the world's largest legitimate producer of opium for use by the pharmaceutical industry. Every year, it issues thousands of permits to farmers to match licit demand. Motivated by the potential for massive returns, some farmers operate outside this system, risking the wrath of security forces for a crop worth $80 per pound. The U.S. State Department estimates that as much as 30 percent of India's opium production is diverted to the black market.[32] Two districts in Jharkhand alone generate $200 million per growing season.[33] Naxals, noting this opportunity, step in and provide protection in exchange for a share of the proceeds. Though government forces destroyed more than $270 million worth of illegal crops in 2007 alone, farmers are still motivated to participate in this alternate economy.
- **Informal tolls.** Naxals and their affiliates are notorious for establishing roadblocks on major road arteries. While this is not a high-yield enterprise, it does amount to forcibly

transforming critical state infrastructure into an illicit profit center. These blockades are not complex affairs. Often, a few individuals knock down a tree, or a band of young men lock arms and form a human chain across the road. They then demand a two- to six-dollar payment from passing vehicles under the implicit threat of violence.

What money remains after covering operational expenses is used to expand and to arm. In 2007, the Naxals bought uniforms, AK-47s, vehicles, and medicine worth $35 million, a far cry from the days of bows and arrows. The Naxals are building an arsenal for the threat they see on the horizon.

A Strategic Half-Life

It's a fact that they have been robbed of their livelihood.
Therefore, they look to the Naxals for justice.

—Arvind Inamdar, director general of police, Maharashtra

While the illicit economy provides revenue, generates trained and hardened troops, and seeds rot in the heart of the state, the expansion of opportunity into their territory presents an existential threat to the Naxals. For now, the benefits of co-opted globalization sustain and enable the insurgency to surpass the wildest expectations of those who fought in Naxalbari, but a time draws near when Naxals will not be content with melting into the forest, partial systems disruptions will not cause enough damage, and the revolutionary tax across all sectors of the formal and informal economies will be outweighed by the impact of foreign investment on the lives of India's most removed citizens.

India's strategy of development-as-counterinsurgency is fundamentally sound. If capital finds its way to the edges of India, and if the government overcomes corruption, disruption, and overruns, rural citizens will advance. They will become better educated, find new work, or perhaps migrate to the cities. This is an unacceptable outcome to the insurgency, which is predicated on the suffering of this peasant base.

And so the Naxals prepare. In the densest of jungles, they silently shape the way the world invests in India, facilitate widespread corruption, and arm themselves for what they see as the fight for the future.

9 Mexico's Criminal Organizations

Weakness in Their Complexity,
Strength in Their Evolution

Samuel Logan and James Bosworth

Transnational organized crime exists as a networked system that creates a high degree of resiliency. Government systems laden by a pyramid-shaped bureaucracy and sovereignty have had little effect when attacking networks of organized crime in Latin America. This uneven playing field is easily observed at the strategic level, where non-state threats appear to run circles around slower-moving governments. The criminal system rapidly adapts, strengthens, and increases in violence, independent of whether different groups are fighting each other, government forces, or civilian vigilante groups. A warlord entrepreneur is inherently resilient, displacing from one territory to another and across international boundaries as market conditions or threats to organizational structures present themselves.

When looking at this system from the standpoint of any individual criminal or leadership group, however, one quickly sees that life is nasty, brutish, and short—a life in which most leaders find themselves in prison or dead within a few short years. The average life span for a budding warlord entrepreneur in Mexico or Central America shortens dramatically once he registers on the radar of the government or rival warlords. Organizations that seem strong at one point can quickly disintegrate once the military, police, and intelligence operations—or rival groups—target the top of their structure. Each individual organization is unlikely to have a long time horizon in which building sustainable services serves as a benefit. Any individual leader's ability to function as a warlord entrepreneur, providing government-like services to a population after his organization has displaced the government, is therefore quite limited. And the fallout—normally violence as a new leader seeks purchase—is never a benefit for the host community.

Why is this the case? A close review of criminal structures at the operational level reveals that many organizations are structured very much as governments are, albeit with different rules. They have a vertical bureaucratic structure, often with one strongman at the top supported by a tightly knit group of trusted operators, specific lines of command, and harsh penalties for stepping out of line.

While criminality—and the visibility and strength of the criminal system overall—has increased in Mexico in recent years, individual groups have actually proven to be relatively unstable and weak due to their structures. Evolving through the phases of growth and decline, most criminal organizations have found themselves in a cycle of violence that ultimately leads to failure.

As a result, the life cycle of many criminal organizations follows a similar, four-phased pattern:

- **Start-up:** Market entry and early-stage competition
- **Competition:** Intense fighting with rivals to establish market dominance
- **Dominance:** Consolidation of dominance and expansion into neighboring markets or product segments
- **Transition:** Succession challenges brought about (usually) by the death or capture of key leadership

Each phase overlaps the previous phase, and any given organization may find itself shifting from one phase to the next. There are no clean breaks.

The first phase is Start-up, during which an organization seeks to establish a foothold for itself in the black market by clearing and holding an existing market niche or by creating a new one (for example, bringing existing drugs to a new market or new drugs to an existing one). For each of Mexico's top-tier organizations—the Arellano-Félix, the Carrillo Fuentes, the Sinaloa Federation, the Gulf Cartel, La Familia Michoacana, and Los Zetas—this phase is already complete.

The second phase is Competition, during which a group must compete against its rivals in this space to establish market dominance. As in business, this phase appears to be endless for some groups, such as Los Zetas, who are continually at war with rival factions in an ever-shifting balance of power and influence. Some geographic areas of Mexico have calmed down when a criminal organization completes this phase and achieves dominance, such as Sinaloa and Sonora, where the Sinaloa Federation holds sway, while other areas are prone to flare up as smaller organizations form to fight the stronger criminal force.

The third phase, Dominance, largely involves market expansion, diversification, and brand protection. The organization focuses on expansion into neighboring areas (thereby beginning the cycle again at phase 1) or adjacent product segments. The third phase is also marked by efforts to clean out smaller groups that unofficially use an established group's criminal brand to further its own endeavor, such as Los Zetas, which are still struggling to establish themselves as an organization strong enough to exist at the highest order of criminal nobility, yet nimble enough to enforce its rule of law in every corner where it purports to operate.

In the final phase, Transition, the organization must deal with succession, normally caused by the death or arrest of a leader. This is often the most turbulent and violent phase of a criminal organization's life cycle. It also the phase in which criminal organizations operating under a vertical, government-like structure are most prone to fail. Groups often cannot sustain the scale to which they have grown at this phase, and they crumble under the loss of their leadership, fragmenting into smaller, competing organizations. We can see, for example, how the Arellano-Félix, Carrillo Fuentes, and Beltran Leyva (BLO) criminal syndicates have all dealt with the successive loss of their leaders (with varying degrees of stability)—with the BLO in 2008, 2009, and 2010 providing the best example of how a criminal organization passing through this phase often spins off smaller groups, which, in turn, begin their own cycles of violence.

Another example is the methamphetamine-producing subsidiary of the Sinaloa Federation, run by the late Ignacio "Nacho" Coronel Villarreal, which atomized after his death in July 2010. There are now several groups fighting for control of Guadalajara, when, less than a year ago, one organization controlled the territory. The Gulf Cartel also weathered this phase with a hostile spin-off—Los Zetas—that, as an independent group, began its own cycle of violence as it established itself as an independent organization in Mexico's criminal landscape and beyond.

The ultimate disintegration and weakness of individual criminal groups leads to several questions:

- How do governments exploit these weaknesses in individual terrorist and criminal groups to hasten their decline or disintegration?
- Can fear of a brief and awful life convince enough prospective warlord entrepreneurs to avoid the criminal routes.
- Do government operations to destroy individual groups actually make the problem worse by allowing the system to adapt more quickly?
- Do governments speed up the evolutionary adaptation process of the criminal system by undermining the individual groups within it?

It is that last question that is tangentially raised by critics of the Calderón administration's policy in Mexico. By going after the cartels with military force, Calderón appears to have accelerated the speed at which the criminal organizations go through stages of growth and decline, thereby creating more resilient organizations and increasing violence in their communities.

This strategy suggests that while going after the criminal leadership is necessary to defeat warlord entrepreneurs, it may also lead to more violence if it is not combined with stronger police and judicial institutions. Herein lies a paradox—conflict is necessary to defeat warlord entrepreneurs, but their very defeat catalyzes more violence and the rise of new warlords. In addition, states such as Mexico, Guatemala, Honduras, Colombia, and Brazil suffer from pockets of economic malaise, which (combined with ineffective sovereignty) provides a social perch upon which warlord entrepreneurs find purchase to establish a new presence in the black market. In effect, the very existence of such a vast and undulating criminal network is a symptom of deeper issues that observers have long identified as social—not security—problems. Yet the readily presented solutions attack the symptom, not the disease.

Unfortunately, Latin America relies on a strategy for public security that depends heavily on the military. This does not bring enough institution-building capacity to counter the criminal organizations in the one area of state building where they should be weak. As long as institutional reforms lag, every "win" for security forces creates a more atomized and violent set of drug-trafficking organizations. This is the pattern that explains why 2010 was so violent, in spite of numerous successes by security forces in Mexico, Guatemala, Honduras, and El Salvador. Moving forward, as this pattern repeats itself, leaders in Latin America may find themselves at the precipice of a new phase of the evolution of the criminal system, where successful warlords, such as Joaquín "El Chapo" Guzmán, the former leader of the Sinaloa Federation, seek to find sustainable power beyond the criminal realm—in the political world—where the transition from criminal king to political kingmaker is relatively swift to complete and nearly impossible to reverse.

Part 3

THE BRIGHT SIDE

10 The Politics of a Post-Climate-Change World

Pyongyang, Puntland, or Portland?

William Barnes and Nils Gilman

Beyond Political Decay

Editor's note: Modern industrialized states face a stark challenge when dealing with systemic risk. Such states are often large and locked into political pathways of growth predicated on increasing consumption and enhanced complexity. The authors of this chapter suggest that these pathways work strongly against the possibility of change and that under these conditions, existing institutions are likely to fail to adapt. This is particularly true against large, existential threats such as climate change, which the authors suggest is the largest and most important risk faced by society.

Despite these many difficulties, the authors propose a positive vision of political organization that they believe may be the only functional alternative to warlord entrepreneurship in post-crisis conditions. This vision, which they call "Green Social Democracy," focuses on localized productive capacity and strong civic values that, they hope, will provide both the economic self-sufficiency and political meaning necessary to combat the worst elements of warlordism. This sense of vision in the face of pessimism is our first example of a "bright side" example of post-collapse conditions.

A Thousand-Year Perfect Story

As the present volume documents, the early twenty-first century is a sea of icebergs, full of hazards, threats, and crises-in-the-making, whose obscured bulk we are just beginning to appreciate and map. Atmospheric carbon, accumulating out of sight for two hundred years, is a mega-berg, one with the potential to sink modern civilization by itself. Climate destabilization, now inescapable, promises to exacerbate other crises, turning this mix into a thousand-year "perfect storm." The long-term futures of societies all over the planet will be shaped in large part by their experiences of and responses to the destructive ramifications of climate change, especially as those ramifications interact with other crises. It is already too late to avoid a cascade of local and regional "natural" disasters in the medium term (i.e., by midcentury), and heroic near-term action will be required to drastically reduce greenhouse gas (GHG) emissions if a long-term civilizational catastrophe of historic proportions is to be avoided. This, in combination with the panoply of other system-threats and crises covered in this volume, is humanity's playing field going forward—like it or not.

The message of this volume is that on this playing field, those of us who see green social democracy as the only winning game plan are at a distinct disadvantage. Of course, we already knew that, but this volume adds a new dimension to the problem. Our adversaries and competitors are not just those wedded to the status quo—its official agents, champions, and beneficiaries—but also the protagonists of the deviant underside of that status quo: those amoral warlords, smuggler cartels, mafias, and narrowly self-interested profiteers, whose lack of scruples makes them better positioned to take short-term advantage of the weaknesses and breakdowns of established systems, and who have no interest in seeing those systems replaced by any more beneficial alternative.

One must begin these sorts of discussions by emphasizing that major breakdowns of the existing world system, and some kind of long-term transition to a more decentralized world, are now inevitable. As it becomes more and more difficult to remain blind to the handwriting on the wall, the sorts of adversaries and competitors discussed in this volume will nonetheless continue to pursue their narrow self-interests, no matter what the larger human costs. The key political question will be, what kinds of local and regional actors will predominate in the new ecology of the climate-changed world that is coming, and will any of them organize any larger positive hegemony—such as what we refer to here as Green Social Democracy—to partially replace the current "official" world system. Will the advocates of such Green Social Democracy (with whom the present authors identify) gain the ability to accomplish enough politically, programmatically, and institutionally that we can not only co-opt or neutralize most of the "liberal" and "conservative" defenders of the current status quo (as it declines and collapses), but also hold off the warlord entrepreneurs? Or will quasi-fascist larger-system-builders (perhaps warlords writ large) have outdone us in those regards and be the only serious adversaries of the run-of-the-mill warlords? Or perhaps we are destined for a mix: a world "governed" by alliances, truces, and modus vivendis between and among local warlords, criminal gangs and cartels, regional quasi-fascist regimes, and lucky and plucky city-states—with the latter perhaps joined in regional "Hanseatic Leagues," defending, and preserving for future use, something like Green Social Democracy.[1]

The Nature of the Looming Catastrophe

Indefinite business-as-usual GHG emissions are now virtually certain to increase planetary temperatures by at least several full degrees centigrade by the latter part of this century (perhaps sooner), and likely a good deal more thereafter.[2] But it is misleading to focus on increase in global average temperature per se. The essential point is that such warming will manifest in the form of regional extremes in temperature increase (multiples of the global average, including in the arctic and regions already prone to hot summers). These changes will be accompanied by the virtually complete disappearance of precipitation in some places, and frequent extreme rain and wind phenomena in other places. Such will produce extensive flooding in some areas and permanent drought in others, dramatically alter hydrologies on every continent, destroy the agricultural productivity of many of the world's bread baskets—and also allow the permanent spread of tropical disease-carrying insects and pathogenic microbes into regions where they formerly could not survive the nighttime low temperatures most of the year. In the longer term, these developments will raise sea levels, destroying coastal and river-delta cities that are home to several billion people and the majority of today's industrial and long-distance-transportation infrastructure. All of this will lead to massive refugee flows, as large areas and mega-cities become incapable of supporting more than sparse human population. Nor will these effects arrive smoothly or incrementally, allowing societies clear projections and ample time to adapt; rather they will unfold as cascading acute crises, producing social and political breakdowns in weaker nation-states, if not everywhere. Scarcity-fueled interstate conflicts will be likely, with conflict over control of fresh water sources and flows particularly threatening. All of these developments have already begun in some parts of the world, and the latest data show the above-referenced (midcentury) global-warming calendar accelerating.[3]

And it gets worse—because accelerating climate change is intruding into a world fraught with other profound ecological and human problems. Quite apart from any direct impact of climate change, inequality within and between societies has been increasing over recent decades (despite the rise of hundreds of millions from poverty into the lower middle classes in China, India, and other large "developing" countries), as has material and existential insecurity among the billions of poor—particularly in the Global South—in the form of rising crime, social violence, and governmental weakness and dysfunction. Additionally, the world is running short of clean, fresh water and easily accessed and processed stocks of many resources key to modern life, especially petroleum (the current moment of great fracking success not withstanding)—at the same time as population growth continues.[4] Moreover, no matter what we do going forward, increasing numbers of disasters related to extreme weather—especially in coastal Asia, Central Africa, and the Caribbean—are already baked into the future, the result of GHG emitted over the last two hundred years (because much GHG remains in the atmosphere long-term).

For the foreseeable future, barring major war or worldwide pandemic disease, the epicenter of social impact will be the megacities of the Global South. Dramatic warnings come from diverse perspectives. In 2010, Left urban theorist Mike Davis wrote, "For thirty years, cities in the developing world have grown at breakneck speed without counterpart public investments in infrastructure, housing or public health.... Sheer demographic momentum ... will increase the world's urban population by 3 billion people over the next forty years, 90 per cent of whom will be in poor cities. No one ... has a clue how a planet of slums with growing food and energy crises will accommodate their biological survival, much less their aspirations to basic happiness and dignity."[5] And counterinsurgency expert David Kilcullen writes in his 2013 book *Out of the Mountains: The Coming Age of the Urban Guerrilla.*

> Four megatrends are driving most aspects of future life on the planet.... These are rapid population growth, accelerating urbanization, littoralization (the tendency for things to cluster on coastlines), and increasing connectedness. If we add the potential for climate-change effects such as coastal flooding, and note that almost all the world's population growth will happen in coastal cities in low-income, sometimes unstable countries, we can begin to grasp the complex challenges that lurk in this future environment.
>
> This unprecedented urbanization is concentrated in low-income areas of Asia, Latin America, and Africa. Cities are expected to absorb all the new population growth on the planet by 2050, while simultaneously drawing in millions of migrants from rural areas.
>
> The world's cities are about to be swamped by a human tide that will force them to absorb—in just one generation—the same population growth that occurred across the entire planet in all of recorded history up to 1960. And virtually all this urbanization will happen in the world's poorest areas—a recipe for conflict, for

crises in health, education, and governance, and for food, energy, and water scarcity.

Cities are in a state of dynamic disequilibrium ... there is no status quo, no "normal" to which to return, no stable environment to police. Think about Dhaka, exploding from 400,000 to 15 million, or Lagos, growing from 3 to 20 million, or Mumbai from 2.9 to 23 million, all in the same time frame. These aren't stable systems; even if you could somehow temporarily get every city function under control, the frantic pace of growth would rapidly overtake the temporary illusion of stability. In fact, that's exactly what has occurred in many cities, where planners have repeatedly devised solutions to problems as they exist at one particular moment, only to find these solutions overtaken by events before they can be implemented.... Rapid dynamic change has gotten inside planners' and political leaders' decision cycles: they repeatedly develop policies that *would have been* adequate for a set of circumstances that no longer exists.[6]

The foregoing gestalt constitutes a constellation of mutually exacerbating "super wicked problems"—impossible to get a firm grip on, much less to bring under control or resolve.[7] And this super-wickedness is increasingly compounded by the fact that accelerating climate destabilization means that "stationarity" is increasingly dead. "Stationarity—the notion that natural phenomena fluctuate within a fixed envelope of uncertainty—is a bedrock principle of risk assessment. Stationarity makes the insurance industry work. It informs the engineering of our bridges, skyscrapers, and other critical infrastructure. It guides the planning and building codes in places prone to fires, flooding, hurricanes, and earth quakes."[8] In this super-wicked world, business as usual means that risk becomes increasingly incalculable; everything we do—including doing nothing—increasingly suffused with recklessness. Ultimately, if the alarms of those like James Lovelock are to be credited, the human carrying capacity of the planet will decline drastically.[9] Short of global thermonuclear war, modern civilization has never faced a more dire existential threat.

It is this world, not the world of the 1950s or 1960s, into which the effects of accelerating global warming are now intruding ever more powerfully.[10] If humanity fails to build up societal capacities for mitigation, adaptation, emergency response, and remediation in advance of this oncoming cascade of disasters, then, as such accumulate toward the middle of this century, all of our attention and resources will be sucked up by disaster management and short-term remediation and adaptation efforts—with nothing left to address longer-term solutions. At that point, the abstract technological feasibility of far-reaching "solutions" would become irrelevant.

To moderate the foregoing will require a profound remaking of contemporary industrial modernity. The vast majority of all industrial, agricultural, mining, transportation, and mechanical processes that rely on hydrocarbons for fuel (or that produce substantial greenhouse gases as byproducts) will have to be either converted to clean/green technology or drastically curtailed—on a planet-wide basis. Unfortunately, barring a technological deus ex machina, it is highly unlikely that effective clean/green technological substitutes will be developed and deployed to replace current industrial processes within the time frame required to avoid catastrophe.[11] Absent such new technologies—or even *with* the development of some such technologies—the only choice will be to cut back on our aggregate industrial output (including factory farming). This, in turn, will necessitate far-reaching changes in energy-intensive, high-waste, high-pollution lifestyles—not just for a decade or two of "emergency," but, for all practical purposes, permanently. In other words, irrevocably downshifting our production and consumption patterns is the only route open to us if we want to hold open a long-term future for other prized aspects of our existing civilization.

Much has been written about what might and should be done economically and technologically to mitigate and cope with climate-change issues. What gets less attention, however, is the magnitude of the *political* requirements for seriously addressing climate change.[12] In recent years, a steady accumulation of scientific evidence and opinion has generated a

broad consensus among policymakers and informed publics that anthro-
pogenic global warming is both real and a very serious long-term threat
to human well-being. This is good news. And yet that consensus has not
led to political action; attempts to create GHG abatement policies and
protocols have stalled, and the political will to make necessary changes
remains nonexistent—especially where it matters most, in the United
States, China, and India. Absent a radical revision to the very conception
of modern political legitimacy, such political will is unlikely to emerge.
That's not just bad; that's a potential civilization-killer.

Thus a realistic review of the challenge of climate change, representing
the leading edge of a whole series of systemic disruptions and crises, yields
the following syllogism: a drastic reduction (80 percent or more) in global
GHG emissions by the 2050s is required in order to avoid civilization-
killing climate change in the long term (and that reduction needs to be
front-loaded, or it will need to get close to 100 percent before 2050).[13] Such
a reduction can only be accomplished either by wholesale conversion of
the energy system to renewables or by a massive reduction in total energy
consumption (really a combination of a whole lot of one and a great deal
of the other).[14] Wholesale conversion to renewables within the specified
time frame is, even if technically possible in the abstract, an unimaginably
monumental—and politically impossible—undertaking. The only feasible alternative is a gross reduction in total energy consumption, combined
with as much conversion as we can get. And this, in turn, must mean a radical reduction in aggregate production and consumption of most classes
of material goods. It means not just smaller and fewer motorized vehicles,
but less travel, less heating in winter, less cooling in summer, less light
at night, less opulent housing, less electronic gadgetry and entertainment
extravaganza, much less meat ... the list goes on. In sum, with regard to
all forms of material production and consumption, serious emissions reduction boils down to just one word: LESS.

The conditions and inputs necessary to the maintenance of modernity's
"normal" levels of system functioning are, in a word, history. This chapter
attempts to move away from the wishful thinking that so often infuses and

clouds climate-change debates and instead proposes conceptually coherent and imaginable moves toward a realistic (albeit terrifically challenging) alternative. Rather than join the unrealism of the political hopes and technological utopianism of most environmentalists, we instead find promise in a different direction—one based on the possibility of retrieving, reformulating, and reinstating a once-prominent alternative form of "capitalist" political economy— early industrial "producerist republicanism"—as a constituent element of a forward-looking Green Social Democracy.

Why a Technological Fix Is Not in the Cards: Ecological Modernization Theory—Too Little, Too Late

Typically, when arguments such as we make here are introduced, liberals and green pragmatists step forward and say, "But wait, if we can just get the prices right on carbon, this will put in place the incentives that will inevitably push entrepreneurs, scientists, and inventors to perfect and deploy the technology necessary to radically reduce GHG emissions while still generating all the energy we need to maintain and spread our modern way of life." The hope that many pragmatists place in a technological fix is an expression of high-modernist faith in the unlimited power of science and technology as profound—and as rational—as Augustine's faith in Christ. The assumption here, often voiced explicitly without much hard evidence to back it up, is that "all the necessary GHG abatement technology already exists"[15] and only political gridlock, incompetence, or venality is preventing its deployment.[16]

Green technocrats, recognizing that most people don't want to give up their carbon-intensive habits or aspirations, assert that we must—and therefore we can—somehow find a way to reconcile decarbonization of the global economy with people's consumerist desires. Such self-described "ecological modernization theorists" insist that it is possible to give the modern global political economy an eco-friendly makeover. They promote the idea of making economic growth and affluence "sustainable," while remediating the environmental damage caused by earlier dirty growth and development.[17] The scholars and policy intellectuals in this tradition, it should be said, are not without their own politically audacious proposals, demanding massive public and private investments in the development and deployment of clean/green technology, as well as substantial institutional reform of capitalist political economy (typically in the vein of the "Third Way"[18]). What this literature shies away from, however, is the need for any fundamental change in culture or politics beyond that held to be already triumphant in the form of the "post-materialist" culture and politics of the "knowledge workers," the "creative classes," and the modern middle classes generally.[19]

Exemplary of this school of technological utopianism are Ted Nordhaus and Michael Shellenberger, authors of the acclaimed 2007 manifesto *Break Through: Why We Can't Leave Saving the Planet to Environmentalists* and founders and directors of the Breakthrough Institute (whose journal and blog serve as a leading platform for technocratic utopianism).[20] For them, prosperity, like consumption, is an entirely unproblematic concept. They see nothing excessive or unworthy in the hegemonic version of the American dream. This posture is related to the assumption, central to all earlier modernization theory, that modernization and modernity naturally and necessarily come as a coherent package—and that the materialistic affluence of upper and upper-middle classes is part of the package. The aspiration to share in that affluence, the "psychic mobility" that makes it possible to see one's own future in those terms, is an essential part of what it means to be modern.[21]

The "American way of life" is a gloss on that package, dressed up for popular consumption by the twentieth-century advertising industry. This is not to argue that all of the American dream's satisfactions are inauthentic—far from it. But, contrary to the thrust of both modernization theory and the advertising industry, there is no reason to believe that the integrity of those satisfactions depends on "having it all" or that toned-down, modest versions of such are not as good or better than versions-on-steroids. Work such as that of Nordhaus and Shellenberger begs the question of what constitutes adequate satisfaction of material needs and what constitutes the kind of overindulgence that actually stands in the way of recognizing and cultivating "higher" needs and values.[22] In any case, the climate change we now face means that the content of the high-modernist dream must be disaggregated and some heretofore preeminent parts of the package given up entirely—the legitimation of material luxury, the glorification of wealth, the prospect of possession without limit—we must end the orienting and preemptive power of such over the development of human aspiration and human capital throughout the world's population.[23] But for Nordhaus and Shellenberger and their ilk, this is anathema.

The foregoing reveals the pivot of our disagreement with Nordhaus and Shellenberger and with ecological modernization theory more generally. Ecological modernization theory remains wedded to the assumption that the post-WWII form of modernization was not a wrong turn, but rather a positive development that generated some unanticipated externalities. By contrast, we assert that we now know enough about the nature and consequences of those externalities—and of planetary sensitivities and limits—to realize that they put the nail in the coffin of modernization theory and its glorification of industrial productivity and high-tech mass consumerism. We must face up to the reality that the last thirty-five years of "turbo capitalism" has been the culmination of a grand, historical wrong turn that began in the last third of the nineteenth century and reached hegemony in the twenty years after World War II.[24]

Of course, Nordhaus and Shellenberger are well aware that their vision of modernization spreading from today's materialistically privileged minority to a much larger segment of the population through the application of current (fossil fuel) technology will have the unfortunate consequence of boiling the planet. Knowing this, Nordhaus and Shellenberger fall back on the classic high-modernist magic of the "technological fix." They assert, without any real basis, that clean/green technology will allow us to have our high mass-consumption cake on a global scale and yet eat it in a low carbon-footprint manner. To be sure, Nordhaus and Shellenberger recognize the magnitude of the technological investment and innovation that they are calling for and relying upon. But at the end of the day, their way out of the GHG emissions quandary is to assert that technological breakthroughs can and will lead the way through the coming travails to a new postmodernity that is simultaneously affluent, green, and global. Indeed, they seem to believe that the new technology will not only limit the damage from the climate change (which they acknowledge to be already baked-in) but also make it possible to restart and complete the spread of near-affluence throughout the world population without further exacerbating global warming. They can cite no persuasive evidence for either of these positions. Their program is as much a matter of quasi-religious faith as is new age environmentalism for its acolytes.

To realize the futility of hoping that a technological fix can solve our GHG problem without requiring a massive reduction in energy consumption, one must understand the dimensions of the global energy system. The current global economy requires the regular availability of about sixteen terawatts of electrical power generating capacity. Reducing GHG emissions by 80 percent over the next twenty-five years or so (and that target is an artifact of now outdated science—as of early 2014, it is clear that we need even greater reduction in that time frame[25]), can logically mean only one of two things: either we need to massively cut energy consumption (which necessarily will entail drastic cuts in aggregate economic output) or else we need to generate approximately thirteen terawatts of electric power from renewable sources.[26]

How feasible is the latter? An answer has been sketched by Saul Griffith, inventor, polymath, and recent MacArthur Fellowship winner: "Imagine someone said you need 2 terawatts of wind, 2 terawatts of photovoltaic solar, 2 terawatts of thermal solar, 2 terawatts of geothermal, 2 terawatts of biofuels, and 3 terawatts of nuclear to give you 13 new clean terawatts. You add the existing 1.5 terawatts of biofuels and nuclear that we already use. You can also get 3 terawatts from coal and oil. That would give humanity around 17.5 terawatts"—enough to allow "only" a 10 to 20 percent decline in energy consumption per capita over the coming generation.[27] "What would it take to do all that in 25 years?" he asks.

Two terawatts of photovoltaic would require installing 100 square meters of 15-percent-efficient solar cells [the best currently available commercially] every second, second after second, for the next 25 years. (That's about 1,200 square miles of solar cells a year, times 25 equals 30,000 square miles of photovoltaic cells.) Two terawatts of solar thermal? If it's 30 percent efficient all told [again, the best that is currently commercially available], we'll need 50 square meters of highly reflective mirrors every second. (Some 600 square miles a year, times 25.) Two terawatts of biofuels? Something like 4 Olympic swimming pools of genetically engineered algae, installed every second. (About 61,000 square miles a year, times 25.) Two terawatts of wind? That's a 300-foot-diameter wind turbine every 5 minutes. (Install 105,000 turbines a year in good wind locations, times 25.) Two terawatts of geothermal? Build three 100-megawatt steam turbines every day—1,095 a year, times 25. Three terawatts of new nuclear? That's a 3-reactor, 3-gigawatt plant every week—52 a year, times 25.[28]

Griffith argues that, were it built, this new global energy infrastructure would require a space approximately equal to the size of the United States, not counting the space needed for transmission lines, energy storage, materials, or support infrastructure—not to mention the costs of decommissioning coal plants, oil refineries, and all the rest of the infrastructure and detritus of two centuries of hydrocarbon indulgence. This, then, is the brutal physics and engineering of what it will take to make a wholesale conversion of the current global system from hydrocarbons to renewables, without reducing total energy usage.[29]

Griffith's calculations (and our use of them), particularly as to the magnitude of the space requirements of the new energy system, have been challenged by various techno-optimists. For the sake of argument, let us stipulate that the green techno-optimists are correct about the near-term technical feasibility of 100 percent conversion of the world to clean/

green energy—the readiness of solar and wind for deployment at scale; the manageable magnitude of the necessary physical plant, transmission infrastructure, and land footprint; and the relatively unproblematic efficiency of operation and maintenance of such massive structures and machinery, once in place. In fact, Griffith has said that he agrees as to technical feasibility in the abstract.[30] But as Griffith's description indicates, the manufacture of the components, the construction of the generation facilities and the storage and transmission infrastructure, and the retrofitting of major urban cores and industrial complexes to mesh with the new system will amount to the most monumental and complex engineering and construction undertaking in human history. Looking just at the societies with very large industrial, urban, and transportation sectors (roughly fifteen to twenty countries), such a project would dwarf the Manhattan Project, the Marshall Plan, or the U.S. national highway system—or, indeed, all of those combined. A more realistic comparison would be with the transformation of the U.S. industrial and energy systems over the entire half century from World War I through the first fifteen years of the post-WWII boom—with the added burden of dismantling and disposing of the system built over the subsequent half-century (and writing off sunk costs). But as we stand right now, we don't have half a century to work with.

Plus, the manufacture and rollout of the machinery and massive structures of this new energy system will themselves be highly energy-intensive, and, at least during the first phase, almost all that energy will have to come from burning hydrocarbons—without much, if any carbon capture and storage (CCS). And that may be true beyond the first phase, because there are real questions as to whether massive CCS will ever be viable.[31] So the creation of the new energy system will necessarily be carbon-intensive, meaning we will necessarily make our problems considerably worse—in a long-lasting way—before we start to become effective on the solution end.[32] There is simply no way out of this trap, absent something miraculous.

How much progress in building such systems and getting them up and running is conceivable, under the most optimistic assumptions, over the next ten, twenty, or thirty years? In the United States, major progress over the next ten years appears utterly impossible, even if the Koch brothers drop dead tomorrow. It is hard to believe that there will be much net progress over those years (i.e., increased burning of hydrocarbons—without CCS—will likely match or exceed increased clean power generation).[33] But let's suppose the improbable, that the United States and others attempt to enter upon a huge crash program early in the next decade. Is appreciable success in fulfilling the global conversion project (or even such a project for fifteen to twenty countries) conceivable under anything like existing institutional and decision-making structures?

The techno-optimists find all this perfectly feasible, because they imagine the availability, assemblage, and on-going management of huge expanses of land and massive material and technological resources, entirely abstracted from the political, legal, governmental, and organizational processes and transactions—and the human capital requirements—that would be integral to actually carrying out such a project in the real world. The problem is not just political feasibility narrowly conceived (winning elections, getting legislation passed, and prevailing in litigation, all in the face of deep-pocket opposition). Accomplishing systems-reconstruction of this magnitude within a time frame of several decades is radically beyond the system-capacities of the actually-existing governing entities of the world. Some vague recognition of this problem has very recently begun to appear among some techno-optimists, but as yet to no great result.[34]

Let us give the last word on this issue to Vaclav Smil, the world's leading expert on the historical development of modern energy systems.

> Installing in 10 years wind—and solar—generating capacity more than twice as large as that of fossil-fueled stations operating today while concurrently incurring write-off and building costs on the order of $4-5 trillion and reducing regulatory approval of generation and transmission megaprojects from many years to mere months would be neither achievable nor affordable at the best of times: At a time when the nation has been adding to its massive

national debt at a rate approaching $2 trillion a year, it is nothing but a grand delusion (to say nothing of the fact that solar generation is far from ready to be deployed on a GW scale).

And as with all technical innovations, a definite judgment regarding long-term capability and reliability of wind-driven or PV generation is still many years ahead. Decades of cumulative experience are needed to assess properly all of the risks and benefits entailed in large-scale operation of these new systems and to quantify satisfactorily their probabilities of catastrophic failures and their true lifetime costs. This means that we will be able to offer it only after very large numbers of large-capacity units will have accumulated at least two decades of operating experience in a wide variety of conditions. This ultimate test of long-term dependence and productivity will be particularly critical for massive offshore wind farms or for extensive PV fields in harsh desert environment.[35]

And Smil concludes a later article with this.

Turning around the world's fossil-fuel-based energy system is a truly gargantuan task. That system now has an annual throughput of more than 7 billion metric tons of hard coal and lignite, about 4 billion metric tons of crude oil, and more than 3 trillion cubic meters of natural gas. This adds up to 14 trillion watts of power. And its infrastructure—coal mines, oil and gas fields, refineries, pipelines, trains, trucks, tankers, filling stations, power plants, transformers, transmission and distribution lines, and hundreds of millions of gasoline, kerosene, diesel, and fuel oil engines—constitutes the costliest and most extensive set of installations, networks, and machines that the world has ever built, one that has taken generations and tens of trillions of dollars to put in place.

It is impossible to displace this supersystem in a decade or two—or five, for that matter. Replacing it with an equally extensive and reliable alternative based on renewable energy flows is a task that will require decades of expensive commitment. It is the work of generations of engineers.[36]

The Political Problem of "Less": Why an Economics of Decline Is So Hard to Imagine

We hasten to emphasize that our position in this chapter is not to be confused or conflated with the comprehensive rejection of ecological modernization theory cum Third-Way-capitalist/high-modernism characteristic of new age radical environmentalism.[37] Like us, such new age radicals recognize the inevitability of the decline and breakdown of existing systems—and the disappearance of high-modern abundance—under the stresses and strains of multiple crises in the context of permanent climate destabilization. And, like us, new age radical environmentalists accept the imperative of the human race as a whole (particularly the upper/upper-middle classes) making do with dramatically lower levels of materialism. But the new age hope of enacting that imperative depends upon the availability and effectiveness of a fix even more demanding than that relied upon by mainstream liberal environmentalists: a virtual spiritual revolution leading to an enlightened humanity voluntarily giving up modern materialism (not just luxury) as a practice or an aspiration. Such green radicals see this spiritual revolution as opposed primarily simply by the ignorant and the terminally greedy and selfish of the world—with the latter's hold over the thinking of the former (presumed to be the majority) seen as contingent and ultimately tenuous. In our view, this perspective greatly underestimates the character and scale of the opposition to the proposed new age "revolution" and the difficulty of the educational and political tasks at hand.[38] Moreover, left out of the picture entirely is the fact that, as things stand, warlord entrepreneurs and their ilk are much better positioned and prepared to benefit from system crisis and breakdown than are new age environmentalists.[39]

The optimism of the new age environmentalists is based on the conviction that the shift to a radically less materialistic, less narcissistic culture is, in the end, wholly for the good, because of the humanistic value of the expected spiritual outcome over the present materialistic lifeworld. The spiritual revolution is a winner because more and more people will come to appreciate this human truth. But this is optimistic in the extreme. The reality is that, even were it successful on its own terms (a major unknown), such a transition away from materialism would certainly come as a painful shock to the vast majority of today's non-poor, most of whom have focused their adult lives on securing and maintaining a modern middle-class standard of living. For many, the result would be, paradoxically, existential crisis and spiritually impoverished, if not corrupted, lives (as is common among the downwardly mobile in the United States today). For those whose level of materialism is well below real affluence, radically scaling back material consumption as part of a program to save the planet would be akin to getting a gangrenous leg amputated—there's nothing inspiring or ennobling about it, even if it is better than the alternative.

Continuing the metaphor, our problem is that, most of the time, this materialist gangrene actually feels good—and a variety of powerful forces assure us that the infection is not dangerous and urge us to enjoy it (here "legitimate" economic actors and deviant entrepreneurs are in full partnership). So how can people be convinced to accept amputation before it's too late? It would be one thing if entire populations could leap from where they are straight into a fully formed world of universal rights, reliable public goods, and rich social capital. That would be the equivalent of immediately being fitted with a state-of-the-art prosthetic. But, of course, the world does not work that way—not least because of the shared vested interests of "legitimate" economic actors and deviant entrepreneurs in precluding it from doing so.[40]

Realistically, the difficulty of making "less" work politically can hardly be overstated. "Less" is something that present-day political classes literally do not know how to think about, much less how to sell to a mass public raised on "more." Just look what happened to Jimmy Carter when he made a modest gesture in that direction—his sensible cardigans are still a political laughingstock, and not just on the Right. What would it take for politicians to champion—and publics to accept—levels of consumption well below those they have either become accustomed to or been taught to long for? Not "less" in the form of a one-time cut to material goods and energy consumption, but a steadily diminishing less, as the necessary changes are phased in over the course of a generation—less, then less, then even less, until, if we are lucky, we reach some kind of a safe plateau, as clean/green technology matures and population growth ceases planetwide.

For rich democracies, the prospect of such systemic change is politically intransigent. What elected politician can hope to sell diminishment to a population that for generations has been taught to consider a rising standard of living a birthright and has internalized the myth that "each generation does better than its parents" (where "better" means more material consumption)? From the eighteenth century on, Western visions of progress and national development have treated ever-increasing material abundance as table stakes in any definition of political or societal success. Modern and modernizing governments (of whatever ideological stripe, from Teddy Roosevelt and Lenin, through Thatcher and Gorbachev, down to the present American and Chinese leaderships) have staked their claims to legitimacy on the premise and promise of delivering MORE.[41] With a few frightening exceptions, such as Kim's North Korea or Pol Pot's Cambodia, all governments of the postwar period have promised a rising standard of living to most if not all of their people. Social compromises and political hegemonies have been brokered on the assumption that continually increasing economic productivity would neutralize distributional conflict.

To get a sense for how profoundly politics will have to change in order to fit an age of diminishment, consider how effectively the U.S. Republican Party was able to use the word "rationing" as political kryptonite in the 2009–2010 debate over health-care reform. Here was a case in which private insurers are *already* imposing rationing, and the government was *not* planning to impose any additional rationing, and *still* the charge was politically poisonous.[42] Now imagine the government trying to *actually* impose rationing—and rationing of a stringent sort—across every aspect of material production and consumption, in exchange for an uncertain outcome—amounting, at best, only to a reduction of secular trends from catastrophic to difficult. American conservatives are, in this respect, relatively clear-eyed about the political-economic implications of serious climate-change mitigation efforts. That they respond by mendaciously denying the climate science itself—and depicting environmentalism as nothing but a Trojan Horse for authoritarian statism—should not distract us from the fundamental political truth they are putting their finger on, namely, that any serious effort to restrain greenhouse gases must necessarily mean a full-scale assault on what they (and many others) mean by "the American way of life"; in other words, a dismantling of a way of life defined, to quote modernization theorist Walt Rostow's famous phrase, in terms of "the age of high mass consumption."[43]

As difficult as it may be to imagine American or European or Japanese publics accepting "less" rather than "more" as their national mantra, it is even harder to imagine the emergent middle classes of the Global South willingly leaving the promised land of consumerism just at the moment when they have finally arrived. Even in authoritarian systems such as China and Russia, elites seek to employ their populations in carbon-intensive modernizing projects for the nation, and coercion by itself does not work to keep those populations dutifully on-task; some degree of social contract, some substantial payoff, must be offered and at least partially honored. A decline in China's astounding growth rate is often cited as the single factor most likely to destabilize the political system of the world's most populous country.[44]

Ultimately, it is impossible to predict what confluence of environmental and political events could sufficiently galvanize political elites and wider publics to break this intellectual and political deadlock. The environmental changes associated with GHG emissions (as typical of major system shocks in general) are likely to be nonlinear, and the political reactions to any climate-related disasters are equally unpredictable, thus piling one radical uncertainty on top of another. Two things, however, are clear: the first is that decisive political leadership, rooted in a fundamentally different conception of the economy, is absolutely required in order to take the necessary steps; and the second is that denying the magnitude of the necessary economic and cultural change—as most of our elites and policy intellectuals continue to do—makes the emergence of such political leadership all but impossible. In this latter respect, it must be pointed out that even the most politically hardheaded portions of the contemporary environmental movement are still not admitting the magnitude of the required industrial changes and the consequent political challenges.[45]

As argued in the last section, above, the problem is not just political feasibility narrowly conceived (winning elections, getting legislation passed, and prevailing in litigation, all in the face of deep-pocket opposition). The required level of societal and cultural reconstruction is radically beyond the system capacities (particularly political/governmental, but also epistemological) of the world's governing entities as they actually exist. Given the existing political economies and cultures of the world—and their organizational instantiation—the broad, effective, lasting mobilization of the political and organizational will, creativity, leadership, discipline necessary to carry through a project of this magnitude, complexity, and inherent difficulty is simply unimaginable, even absent the determined opposition of well-endowed obstructionists. This is a super wicked problem that existing authorities are not going to solve.[46]

An Alternative Modernity?

The climate-changed and multiple-crisis-ridden world that is coming spells the breakdown of modernity as we have known it. What will follow? Other contributors to this book have noted the power that "deviant actors" can rapidly amass during and after crises. But the kinds of deviant actors they are referring to have two great advantages over the kind of progressive "deviant" political agents that we are hoping to see rally. First, warlord entrepreneurs and their ilk are on the path of least resistance—they go with the grain of the dominant materialism rather than against it. They encourage and profit from greedy, shortsighted consumerism. In a perverse paraphrase of the old song by the Police, in a world that's running down, they make the best (for themselves) of what's still around.

Second, these entrepreneurs seek to take advantage of systemic failures in order to further narrow agendas. They have no interest in contributing to repair, regeneration, and improvement of larger systems, at least not beyond the trade and finance networks they utilize. They prefer that larger systems remain weak, incapable of effectively monitoring or confronting the entrepreneurs' operations, and amenable to covert manipulation through bribery and intimidation. Thus, in crisis environments, warlord entrepreneurs have distinct operational advantages over actors with broader agendas and ambitions, both existing authorities committed to stabilization of existing systems, and radicals and humanitarians who seek system transformation in the name of a just and viable future for their grandchildren and humanity at large. Warlord entrepreneurs can focus their attention, their muscle, their human capital, and their resources much more narrowly and be more forceful and persistent in their targeted involvements. Unlike humanitarians of all stripes, warlords do not need to inspire idealistic commitment from far-flung cadres and mass bases in order to leverage limited material resources in the mounting of broad campaigns that neither return any direct pecuniary profit to the central leadership nor motivate the cadre with the prospect of quick enrichment via capture of spoils. Of course, in the climate-changed world that is coming, ultimately, only those truly ready to live by the principle "après moi, le déluge" will be able to maintain such advantageous freedom of maneuver.

It is true, as the editor of this volume has said, that particularly successful warlord entrepreneurs may "become large and invested enough to seek to stabilize their position and consolidate their gains. In this condition, they shift from entrepreneur/exploitation mode to service provider/maintenance mode, in which they become subject to implicit and explicit agreements with their customers/subjects/constituents for continued support. Thus over time, they begin to assume the role of the state itself."[47] This is still happening—and will continue to happen—on a localized level, but comprehensive extension over larger territories will become increasingly rare. In the climate-changed and multiple-crisis-ridden world that is coming, larger projects will become difficult or impossible without idealistically inspired, committed cadres and mass bases. It will be increasingly difficult to make the shift from local dominance to larger system-consolidation (requiring, among other accomplishments, the integration/subordination of all the other warlord entrepreneurs in the territory), except by committing to and sacrificing more immediate interests to some new social democratic vision—or some quasi-fascist vision. In short, transcending Puntland without becoming Pyongyang will require becoming a lot more like Portland (at its "best"), and a lot less like Houston.

Avoiding both the Puntland and Pyongyang scenarios requires developing an alternative political economy that can survive and cope in the face of the new world that is coming.[48] While large-scale governmental institutions will be important on certain crucial dimensions in any Green Social Democratic version of the climate-changed world of our future, in most ways, that world—whatever version eventuates—will necessarily be much more decentralized than the current world. What would such a political economy look like, and how might we get there from where we are now? What resources exist that might make possible the building of Green Social Democracy under such difficult conditions? While it *is not true* that we already have—even in the lab—everything we need in the way of clean/green technology, and all that is lacking is the will to fund full development and deployment, it *is true* that around the planet there are many people, groups, and communities that know and practice (at least in bits and pieces) something like the techniques, methodologies, and policies needed to step back from high-carbon materialism.[49] The state of Kerala in India, with a population of over thirty million, has been (in some respects) a striking large-scale example.[50] There are also many lessons, models, and toolkits to be picked up from communities and organizations around the world.[51] And cross-fertilization between all this and advanced clean/green technology has taken off. What we do not have is an example of a national society adopting such practices anywhere near comprehensively—or even trying to move decisively in that direction.

This is particularly true of the largest societies. As things stand, the voracious, high-ecological-footprint urban and industrial sectors of the largest societies will drag the rest of the world down into oblivion with them, no matter how green the rest of the world becomes.[52]

For national societies to move decisively toward institutionalizing appropriate practices and technologies, existing institutions must be reconfigured so as to enable, coordinate, and manage appropriate investments, and both institutional personnel and the population at large must buy into the program with some dedication.[53] This will require a profound switching of gears, an intellectual and political reorientation that, in turn, demands a retooling of the entire stock of human capital of the social sciences, the professions, organizational management, and public administration.[54]

So is there some way to gather the lessons, technological innovations, stores of knowledge, toolkits, and green practices that are accumulating around the world and to synthesize them into a set of models that majorities everywhere might be persuaded to choose among, adopt, and enact? Note that the result must include the legitimation and administration of lawful coercion—up to and including the use of paramilitary force, if necessary—against ostrich-like status-quo dead-enders and self-serving deviant actors. As we have laid out above, existing environmental movements aren't going to get that job done, given their reluctance to face up to the magnitude of the challenge—and given the power of elite opposition, the recalcitrance of majorities in thrall to materialistic modernity, and the tactical advantages of warlord entrepreneurs. What is needed then is a larger narrative with the potential to legitimize radical departure from the status quo to wider audiences, including renunciation of aspirations to affluence and the moral ostracism of those who insist on indulgence in material luxury. Neither radical environmentalism nor centrist ecological-modernization policy discourse is providing the larger narrative we need to challenge and replace the orthodoxy of neoliberal modernization theory and "the American way of life."

The twentieth century's leading sources of broad, transformative vision, the Marxist and socialist traditions, are largely unhelpful in this regard, given that they expected to build on the material abundance and technological wizardry of advanced capitalism. In most mainstream versions of socialism, capitalist consumerism was cast not as ecologically unsustainable, but rather as the penultimate form of economic modernity, one revolution short of the end game. In the finalized form, the entire population was to enjoy a version of the affluence formerly limited to the wealthy, as well as "higher" values. Even those who saw the early years of the "transition to socialism" as occurring in the context of Spartan Third World revolution assumed that the revolution would eventually fulfill itself in a socialism of mass abundance.[55] That a life of higher values might be constructed in the permanent—not temporary—absence of mass affluence was not contemplated in these traditions, at least not in their twentieth-century versions.

We propose looking to a different historical tradition, namely, the petty bourgeois political culture of capitalism's early and middle industrial eras in North America and Europe. This tradition did not call for the overthrow of capitalism but rather argued for a more modest and cautious (in a sense, more "conservative"), more egalitarian and democratic, more decentralized "producerist" capitalism.[56] A twenty-first-century producerist capitalism would recast this politically democratic tradition, but in the context of vigorously and comprehensively Green economics. This kind of robust, community-centric self-empowerment could perhaps be a viable alternative to going down with the ship of high-modernist capitalism as it breaks up or to taking to the lifeboats captained by warlord entrepreneurs.

Many countries can look back to their own early-modern experiences for something analogous to producerist republicanism. In Russia, they might look back to Bukharin and the New Economic Program years; in China, it would be the World War II cooperatives and the "Yenan Way" born out of that experience; for India, it would involve looking to how the Kerala of the last fifty years has built on Gandhi's movement.[57] But the history of conflicts within the development of capitalism in the United States is particularly instructive in this regard.

From the American revolution through the 1930s, the United States has a rich history of democratic radicalism and enlightened populism among skilled craftsmen, artisans, family farmers, business people, professionals, and intellectuals, centered on the lower middle class, but reaching up into the higher middle classes and down into the rural and urban working classes. These traditions have often been denigrated by both Marxists and liberals as entirely unenlightened—anti-industrial and antimodernist, prone to anti-Semitism, racism, and anti-intellectualism. But such judgments, while by no means entirely wrong, crudely homogenize a highly variegated history and set of movements.[58]

What these movements and traditions, at their best, had in common was along the following lines: the demand that self-managed, self-enhancing work and political citizenship be valorized and protected from the depredations of federalist aristocracy, the slave power, the robber barons, the trusts, Wall Street, and corporate capitalism. Most of the leaders and cadres of most of these movements and organizations, including many of the agrarian Populists, were neither wholly modernist nor wholly antimodernist. They were not enemies of commerce and industry per se. Many were professionals and teachers, tinkering "mechanics," agricultural and sociopolitical innovators, interested in science; they participated vigorously and rationally in the public spheres and civil societies of their days—indeed, they were among the most important authors of the greatly expanded public spheres of their days. By the later nineteenth century, a substantial proportion of the leaders and cadres of these movements were women, pioneers of female civic activism, who went on to be key leaders and cadres of the elaborate, Progressive civil society of the early twentieth century.

The social protection these movements sought included public construction and ownership of major infrastructure and government regulation of the corporate capital, finance, and the factory system. They promoted widespread small production, linked together in a "cooperative commonwealth" through large-scale producer co-ops and vigorous political organization. Social and political identities were understood to be rooted in such cooperative arrangements of production and community self-management, rather than in privatized, individualistic practices of consumption.

This political tradition provides an Archimedean point from which to critique the pop-modernization-theory view of economic viability and societal success that has become hegemonic over the past seventy-five years. Recapturing the energies and hopes of this lost political assemblage allows us to see more clearly the assumptions and limitations of the orthodox, growth-centered vision of modernity that has led us to the brink of global ecological catastrophe. From the Civil War to World War II, neither economic theory nor popular political folklore insisted that modernity necessarily came as an integrated package, a package whose central components include the unlimited pursuit of industrial revolution, incarnated in gigantic, ravenous factories; the transformation of the population into "personnel" within complex, hierarchical organizations; and the elaboration and institutionalization of a culture of material consumerism and high-tech entertainment. The hegemonic culture that sees these developments as central to modernity is not the product of the natural progress of efficiency, science, and rationality; a particular pattern of contingent political victories and defeats has played a major role. This pattern need not be accepted as irreversible; path dependency need not be enshrined as unbreakable.[59]

We now need to revive aspects of the popular political culture of petty bourgeois civic republicanism that valued community, solidarity, moral economy, meaningful work, self-management, and democratic citizenship over economistic individualism, material affluence, and private consumerism. Note that we are not saying that any of the earlier incarnations of producer republicanism could have been fully victorious in its time, nor are we saying that any could be or should be reincarnated whole now. Recovery must include critically-minded updating and reformulation in the light of the lessons of the past seventy-five years. In particular, we need to spike that heritage with a major dose of cosmopolitanism regarding race, gender, and sexuality,[60] and we must give up the vision of an eventual metamorphosis into a socialism of abundance. Such a project is surely not without intellectual rewards, and, as a leading historian of American Progressivism and petty bourgeois radicalism has said:

> Nor are such utopias unattainable.... Charles Sabel, Michael Piore, and Jonathan Zeitlin have created something of a school of political economy that has demonstrated the economic viability of small-scale production within flourishing, democratic economic networks. Historically, Sabel and Zeitlin reconstruct and rehabilitate a craft-based alternative to mass production, an alternative that had impressively strong roots in various cities and regions throughout the nineteenth-century transatlantic world. Flexibility and constant innovation in specialized production formed the foundation for a labor process that revolved around skilled workers ... with owners and workers often attaining a solidarity difficult for us to imagine as part of business relations. And despite the many defeats this small-scale alternative met at the hands of both capitalist and social democratic advocates of a mass-production economy, it did not disappear but merely went underground, showing a remarkable resurgence since the 1970s. Especially strong in western Europe, "flexible specialization," or "small firm networks," provide a contemporary living model of what Michael Albert has aptly characterized as "Capitalism against Capitalism."[61]

The ray of hope that we hold out is that our imagined Green Social Democracy, underpinned and legitimized by producerist republicanism, will ground itself in an acceptance of the limits imposed by the fecundity of local environments and networks, rather than a Promethean ethos of constant overcoming of those limits. As such, it would encourage localized sourcing, localized production, and localized consumption. It would focus on the conversion of public infrastructure to low-carbon, clean energy as quickly as possible. It would provide universal access to such infrastructure, while making private use of centrally generated power and water quite expensive above a very modest minimum allotment. Tax and regulatory policies would focus on environmental impact and resource management. Governments, educational systems, and civil society would prioritize training, equipping, and enabling the population to be low-carbon "producers" of useful goods and services (especially the "human services"), and informed, environmentally conscious, responsible citizens within local communities, organizations, and enterprises. In other words, it would be something like the comprehensive elaboration of an intensely green version of the "social economy" model that has worked on the local level in Quebec and other places, and the "transition town" model that has taken off in England.[62]

Given the scale of necessary systemic retrofits—and the onslaught of disasters that must be prepared for, engaged, and recovered from—there will be a huge amount of work in energy and manufacturing conversion, infrastructure adaptation, ecological reclamation, emergency response, human services, and community development, and so on. This will be a full-employment economy, for the most part locally focused. Moreover, such a political economy—one emphasizing high levels of environmentally conscious human and social capital, largely situated in small production units (owned privately or through co-ops or local government) and community-based human services, supported and coordinated (but not centrally planned or directed) by larger, environmentally informed public institutions—would enable cutting GHG emissions and render societies more resilient and adaptive in the face of climate change. It is plausible that people whose lives are rich in social capital, educational opportunity, interesting work, and citizenship rights and responsibilities will be more amenable to being weaned off materialistic addictions—or they wouldn't develop strong addictions in the first place—particularly if a supportive political culture has been brought into being in advance and is rising toward hegemony.

Why It Just Might Work

This brings us back to the question of whether there is any realistic prospect of overcoming the political obstacles that are so formidable as to render the programs of both radical and mainstream environmentalists unrealistic. Why should our suggested political project fare any better? Why should mixing environmentalism and producer republicanism produce a viable, powerful hybrid, much less a magic bullet? Why should a new Green Social Democracy, struggling to establish itself under the most difficult circumstances imaginable, do better in remaking failing systems than warlord entrepreneurs do in exploiting system breakdown? Is it at all realistic to think we might create a path whereby we eventually find ourselves with modest Portlands outnumbering Puntlands and Pyongyangs?

Hope arises from two fundamental and connected facts. First, none of the political economies and political cultures of the modern world is monolithic or completely controlled by those wedded to the status quo. They are shot through with tensions, ambiguities, and contradictions, even societies (such as the United States) where dominant groups have been quite successful in legitimating themselves and institutionalizing their hegemony. Middle classes and "publics" are highly variegated, both within and across societies, and full of ambivalence. This represents an opening for those who would save the system from itself. As system failures and breakdowns accumulate in the climate-changed and crisis-ridden world that is coming, along with ever more credible warnings of worse to come, the existing high-modernist narrative will become less and less convincing and its hegemony harder and harder to sustain. More people will be increasingly open to a new "education." Second, some of the necessary political culture is still there, deep in the American grain, substantially co-opted, but never eliminated by the hegemonic, hyper-materialistic version of the "American way of life." Elements of producerist republican political culture are, in fact, being asserted in current public debate, including in right-wing constituencies, whose knee-jerk opposition to environmentalism may be weakened by a green producerist republicanism that invokes new versions of familiar old values.[63]

Again, we note that the result must include lawful coercion—including the use of paramilitary force, if necessary—against ostrich-like status-quo dead-enders, their quasi-fascist successors, and self-serving warlords of all kinds. But it should also be noted that the producerist republican tradition is full of episodes of armed citizen militias—even rising to the level of armies—defending their way of life and their communities against enemies of various kinds. Historically, this may have been reprehensible as often as it was admirable—and we see quasi-fascistic manifestations of it all over the world today. But we can also find many episodes that contain positive examples and lessons that might be modernized and incorporated in the larger project we are proposing. The great French social democratic leader and theorist Jean Jaures proposed exactly such a project.[64] It is not unreasonable to dream of Portlands—joined in regional Hanseatic-type leagues—successfully defending themselves against warlords and perhaps even against fascist regimes (given that no one is going to be able to afford much in the way of air forces or missiles). (Of course, a lot will depend on whether the world still contains deliverable nuclear, chemical, or biological weapons.)

The most we can do now is prepare a suite of building blocks that might allow such a project to get off the ground once current political economies and governments are in profound, undeniable crisis due to the socioeconomic consequences of climate destabilization. Such preparation must include maximizing the development of clean-energy and decarbonization technologies and the elaboration of disaster mitigation, management, and adaptation programs. But above and beyond such efforts, we require the construction of a politics and a cultural narrative that prioritizes shared public goods and responsible citizenship, creating a higher capacity for authoritative, collective decision making. That new politics and cultural narrative must persuasively explain the need for everyone in the world to give up material affluence as either a practice or an aspiration (constructing what we might think of as an enlightened "lower-middle-class" model of material sufficiency and sharing—drawing on "producer republicanism"—as a universal moral imperative). Turning the social sciences, the professions, public intellectuals, academia, and the modern middle classes in general decisively in this direction—and away from technocratic utopianism—is the most urgent imperative, particularly in the United States. And none of this can be accomplished absent the decisive political defeat of those who are determined to maintain their wealth and privilege no matter the cost.

We recognize that realization of our hopes on any grand (i.e., sufficient) scale is unlikely, but the foregoing is the best strategy we can think of and, in any case, as Mike Davis says, "either we fight for 'impossible' solutions ... or become ourselves complicit in a de facto triage of humanity"—which Davis counts (quoting a UN report) as "a moral failure on a scale unparalleled in history."[65] Unlike much radical green thinking, our analysis is not predicated on semireligious or New Age hopes for a spiritual revolution; it is firmly rooted in class and social analysis. Clearly, in order to succeed at any grand scale, a broad, cross-class coalition must be developed, based on the conviction that continuing commitment to high-modernist affluence makes one complicit in a civilizational and human catastrophe of unfathomable proportions. Is it possible for the middle and lower-middle classes in the most advanced societies (and the largest societies, in particular) to become part of the solution instead of part of the problem? The human potential is there, but can it be widely realized within the current conjuncture and available time frame?[66] It may well be that we cannot retool (technologically, institutionally, culturally, psychologically) fast enough, given the inertia of the old ways and the power of those who blindly insist on carrying those old ways forward. We cannot know, but what we can say is that it looks like the next couple decades will be our last chance to build the political and human-capital base that might make the conversion possible.[67]

11 Bringing the End of War to the Global Badlands

Hardin Tibbs

Weapons production is a major global business. The Stockholm International Peace Research Insititurre estimates that by 2013 the total sales of the world's largest arms-producing companies had reached about $402 billion a year, a more than 20 percent increase since 2006.[1]

The international trade in small arms and light weapons is a booming part of the overall arms business. According to an estimate by the Project on Light Weapons at the American Academy of Sciences, in 2000 the legal trade was running at $7 to $10 billion annually, with perhaps $2 to $3 billion circulating through black-market channels.[2] In the 1990s, following the end of the cold war, more than one hundred ethnic and sectarian conflicts broke out, killing over five million people and creating tens of millions of refugees. Most of this devastation was caused not by heavy weapons but by handguns, machine guns, and grenades. These are the weapons of choice in internal conflicts, because they are so readily available, cheap, portable, easy to use, and deadly. And they are being mass-produced in ever-increasing numbers for a global market.[2]

Mass production of military equipment actually makes little military sense for nation-states, because overseas arms sales constantly erode national advantage (even if offset by technological back doors) and offer very narrow economic advantage in terms of jobs. But they do, of course,

131

continually throw up new opportunities for private profit. From a commercial perspective, the loss of national advantage through overseas sales, even in peacetime, becomes a justification for new products that offer further advantage, however transient. For example, if the United States loses its original advantage in night-vision technology because of the technology's widespread availability, commercial producers can persuade the government, say, to subsidize research and development to extend the performance of night-vision equipment in smoke by using new wavelengths.

This pattern is not new, but the growth drive of business and sheer scale of production, combined with an active black market, translates into out-of-control global overkill. It pushes national defense budgets deeper into unsustainability, and rather than addressing genuine threats, it is making them worse. Nation-states are being taken for a ride.

The status of weapons as just another globalized product category effectively means that weapons production is now suffering from *strategic reversal*. When a strategy is overused, it turns into its own opposite—a paradox that is well known to military theorists. The term is usually applied to the strategy of a combatant, as with the repeated use of maximum surprise by the Israeli army. Over time, Israel's adversaries came to anticipate surprise as the usual Israeli mode of operation, and the element of surprise became its own opposite.

We have now reached the point where strategic reversal even applies to war itself: or at least to the industrial-era idea of war—the notion of "total war" first described by the renowned military theorist Carl von Clausewitz. Total war turns out to be self-defeating when waged in a world in which postindustrial societies are steadily converging to form a single, global social and economic entity.

Consider the context in which industrial nation-on-nation war traditionally took place. In the nineteenth century, when Clausewitz was writing, the dominant international actors were clearly identifiable nation-states with small, culturally homogenous populations. Geographic distance was a significant form of deterrence, and advanced military technology was relatively slowly changing, predictably distributed, and affordable.

Everyday life for most people in most places was relatively circumscribed, with most social and business transactions simple and occurring locally. National decision making was largely independent of other nations, was not overly complex, and had implications that did not extend very far into the future. Indeed, it was mainly the present rather than the future that was considered, since events unfolded at a manageable pace.

These conditions still existed as recently as the mid-twentieth century. Today, literally none of them remains true. Nation-states are only one class of powerful global player, and geography is only partly a deterrent factor. Populations are large, highly mobile, and ethnically mixed, and social and business interactions are complex and global. Advanced technology is fast-changing, increasingly powerful, and highly disruptive. Advanced weapons are sold in a global marketplace, yet they may be unaffordable even to the countries that produce them, while the impacts of war on the natural environment threaten everyone. Events unfold rapidly in front of a global media audience, and national decision making is complex, risky, contested, globally interlinked, and to a great extent, focused on an uncertain future.

The loss of the effectiveness of conventional war has not gone unnoticed. In 1995, Israel's President Shimon Peres wrote, "True, there are still generals who don the uniforms of the past, but they are hard pressed to find fronts where their armies can be used."[3]

Strategic reversal applies to nuclear weapons too—the ultimate instruments of total war. Toward the end of his life, Robert McNamara, former U.S. Secretary of Defense and architect of the Vietnam War, proposed that nuclear weapons should be abolished, because they threaten "the destruction of nations"—the very thing they are supposed to protect. Similarly, Paul Nitze, who in 1950 drafted National Security Council Memorandum 68, the effective charter of American Cold War policy, said he could "think of no circumstances under which it would be wise for the United States to use nuclear weapons" and recommended that America should "unilaterally get rid" of them. These are explicit recognitions of strategic reversal.[4]

Though the strategic drawbacks of nuclear weapons have been appreciated for some time, the implications of the globalization of war have begun to sink in only more recently. Conventional war depends on the nation as the unit of war, but the industrial production of armaments for a global market makes no sense under the logic of nation-on-nation war and, perversely, only feeds asymmetric risk by arming non-state actors.

Perhaps instinctively appreciating these strategic reversals, hyperlinked affluent societies no longer feel as they once did about war. During most of the modern era, the cost and horror of nation-on-nation war was an acceptable trade-off, because war was acknowledged as a vital means of social protection.

Today, war is increasingly seen as pathological, even sociopathic. This is partly because it has been getting more lethal for civilians. The ratio of civilian-to-combatant casualties has been rising steadily since the eighteenth century. The civilian casualty rate was 40 percent in the First World War, over 60 percent in the Second World War, 85 percent in the Israeli-Lebanon war of 1982, and it has risen to as much as 90 percent for U.S. drone strikes in Pakistan, according to a 2009 estimate published by the Brookings Institute. The environmental consequences of war can also be a serious threat to health and well-being long after a conflict ends—and can become a significant liability for aggressors.[5] The high rate of birth defects in Iraq attributed to the use of depleted uranium in munitions is a case in point.

In addition, the cultural acceptance of war is changing. Over the last two decades, the level of psychological literacy in well-educated societies has been rising, and there is now very little tolerance for violence of any kind. At the same time, the horizon of ethical concern has been widening to encompass the planet as a whole, and this is one aspect of a deep shift in cultural values occurring around the world. Digital communications tend to make all actions transparent, and they highlight failures of ethics, principles, and accountability. In this context, any display of warlike behavior comes under increasing scrutiny, and any political leader initiating a war is likely to be seen as, at best, psychologically unsophisticated and, at worst, sociopathic. This helps explain worldwide consternation at the United States' circumvention of the Geneva Protocol and use of torture during the first decade of the twenty-first century.

The perception of sociopathy is reinforced when continuing military research leads to dehumanizing and ultimately delegitimizing innovations, such as pharmaceuticals to suppress guilt, robotic weapons, and drones operated from half a world away.

The shift in the cultural status of conventional war from social protection to social pathology is yet another example of strategic reversal. Taken together, all these instances of strategic reversal mean that the logic of full globalization transcends the logic of conventional war. This effect—and the future it points to—could be termed "the end of war." Yet, so far, it does not mean that security threats have disappeared.

The active threats now are not between nations in the pre-globalization sense, but in the ungoverned spaces created by incomplete globalization. All nations face this common challenge. Globalization without global governance is spawning a global badlands that is unstable, prone to state failure and economic breakdown, awash with illicit firepower, and a major source of asymmetric attacks.

Non-state warlords, whether politically motivated actors or the bosses of organized crime, exploit the veins of weakness that snake between and through nations, leveraging social asymmetries and disaffections, even as post–financial crisis spending cuts bite and weaken the influence of the state. The warlords are the unintended beneficiaries of the existing obsolete game of maximum global sales of weapons for total war. They are the ultimate unprincipled players with itchy trigger fingers, and they inherit the capability for overkill. This is *Mad Max*, armed courtesy of nation-states fatally attracted to nostalgic notions of punching above their weight.

If clinging to conventional preparations for war actually strengthens these asymmetric threats, what can be done? Global society wishes for an end to violence—something that can hardly be repudiated. Yet if violence still exists and threatens the progress that has already been achieved, it needs to be countered in some way.

The best way to think about this may be to view things in a much longer time window. We live in an interregnum between the national and the global. The world has already reached a stage of global development from which, thanks to digital communications and air travel, it seems unlikely to turn back. But this development falls short of its full potential. In an optimistic future, the end point of our current path of global development is global social and political integration, in which there is genuinely global governance able to address potential conflict of all types at all geographic scales.

The progression toward the end of war is clearly visible in the number of major conflicts. Reports from institutions in the Swiss-based International Relations and Security Network show that the number of major wars (conflicts with at least one thousand combatant deaths per year) fell from twenty-four in 1990 to only four in 2007.[6]

Similarly, Harvard professor Steven Pinker has assembled persuasive evidence that violence in human society is actually in decline.[7] According to the UCDP/PRIO Armed Conflict Database, worldwide battle deaths in the first decade of the twenty-first century were 0.5 per 100,000 a year, which is lower than the homicide rate in the world's least violent countries. In absolute numbers, annual battle deaths have fallen by 90 percent, from half a million per year in the late 1940s to thirty thousand per year in the early 2000s. During this period, interstate war shrank to vanishing point, and the greatest source of deaths was civil war. Even civil wars have become less lethal. In 1950 the average armed conflict of any kind killed thirty-three thousand people; by 2007 it killed less than one thousand.

Over the same period, the number of democratic nations has been growing and, according to Spencer Weart, former director of the Center for History of Physics at the American Institute of Physics, well-established liberal democracies have never made war on one another.[8] In 1989 the NGO Freedom House reported that only 41 percent of the world's nations were democracies, while in 2010 they reported a total of 60 percent. The predominance of industrialized democracies also suggests that even looming resource shortages are unlikely to lead to a resurgence of nation-on-nation war. The function of the resources is to allow production for the global market, while war tends to disrupt the global market, making it a counterproductive means of securing access. Technological developments that reduce the need for raw materials represent a more plausible line of response.

Nevertheless, we are still at an incomplete stage of global jurisdiction, with many lawless and law-deficient zones and some national jurisdictions, such as tax havens, that do not meet emerging global norms. From a global perspective, the existing situation is not systemically coherent, and the incoherencies become weaknesses that are easy to exploit asymmetrically.

These weaknesses—which include such things as social injustice, inequity, and corruption—will not be addressed by reverting to the modes of an earlier stage but rather by more fully adopting the modes that are emerging. Warlords will not be countered by increasing firepower or arming all sides or even by waging war, because these things have become self-defeating for everyone—including the warlords themselves. In the long run, this is the message of the end of war.

The warlords who hold sway in the global badlands are one aspect of incomplete global integration and represent a kind of litmus test for what needs to be done. The end of war means that a fully integrated world cannot be brought about by war among nations or even by a zero-sum competition of interests among nations (the old mode of diplomacy). Instead, if nation-states are to remain effective, they will find that their only viable forward role is as leading actors in enabling global integration.

Warlords can develop asymmetric power either where conventional modes of operating by nations are failing under new conditions, a situation which might be called *functional asymmetry,* or where the conventional modes are not delivering on their implicit promises about outcomes, which might be called *moral asymmetry.* The end of war creates functional asymmetries if nations continue to pursue conventional activities such as global marketing of light weapons. And the implicit promise in industrial societies of steadily improving economic well-being and social justice means that exploitable moral asymmetries will be created if, say, income polarization in national economies continues to grow.

To remove these asymmetries—and defuse the power of warlords—nation-states will have to act in a way that recognizes and delivers the promise of full global integration. They will have to be explicit about the social promise of a global society—and live up to it. This will mean developing a new "non-zero" meta-narrative about the benefits of cooperation to replace the existing "zero-sum" or winner-takes-all national rivalry. Nations need not lose their identity or their (already declining) autonomy, but they will certainly need to de-emphasize their self-defeating preparations for war and redirect their attention and resources to delivering on the values that give them social legitimacy.

Full global integration can only be achieved by following a new narrative of mutual predicament and shared interest. It will be too complex to hold together based on coercion and exploitation. It must be about the whole, and it must work for everyone. It must be centered on the principles of personal freedom and systemic coherence, and it must reflect democratic principles and processes.

Positive counterinsurgency in the global badlands must be tied to this new narrative. The security narrative of nation-states can no longer be about maintaining order elsewhere, as there is no "elsewhere" in a global society. To bring order to the badlands, global society must be brought into being. This too is essentially the message of the blowback from the War on Terror—that the clash of civilizations must be disarmed before the end of history can arrive.

This will be a hard, counterintuitive lesson for nations: as the world moves toward global integration, the actors who will withstand the tide of history are going to be those who abandon war. If nations can do this, it will immediately give them an advantage over the warlords, draining the swamp by removing moral and functional asymmetries. Conversely, if nations attempt to justify continued war preparations—particularly if they resort to amoral measures such as false-flag operations—they will place themselves on the wrong side of history and will ultimately lose, not least by creating moral asymmetries for new "white hat" actors to employ.

There is, in fact, no shortage of white hats. Civil society is busy pioneering the development of many of the positive, globally directed initiatives that nations could promote if they were to redirect existing defense budgets. From social enterprises to sophisticated skills in conflict resolution, the ideas and the means for transcending conflict are already available.

It is said that without a vision, the people perish, and this will be true of both nations and people who cannot follow the new story of global integration. Perhaps the ultimate security message conveyed by this vision is that as long as there is war in the human heart, there will be war in human society. A change for the better is ultimately possible only if we have reached the point where each one of us is willing to allow compassion for our extended human family to take the place of all the hatreds, large and small, we harbor within us.

12 The White Hats

A Multitude of Citizens

Paul Hilder

An open society can be only as virtuous as the people living in it.
—George Soros, 2008

In environments of chaos and disruption, where law and order fall away, only one thing counts: power. Raw force is the most obvious currency. Violence, money, or fear seem to hold sway.

Yet power in its essence is not first and foremost about what you can do *to* someone else. At its most fundamental level, power is not a warlord's gun or a superior's command. It is an invisible web of social relationships and expectations, a force field of trust, identity, and belief.

What Is Social Power?

Power is social before it is political, military, or economic. We all have social power, even if we don't realize it. This power is constantly being reshaped, both collectively and individually, and social power can be used not just for ill but also for good. Ideas of networked social power underlie disciplines as diverse as social marketing, counterinsurgency, financial trading, nonviolent conflict, or governance.

141

Everything begins with us: with people and our relationships. "Civil society" is perhaps most visible in peaceful revolutions. But social power and civil society are not absent in uncivil societies, nor are they dormant in mature, institutional democracies. They simply operate differently.

Often you will not see social power unless you know where to look. But when you know what to look for, you'll see it everywhere: in a bustling market square, in opinion polls about support for military forces or government policies, in a revelatory article and the way it spreads through social media, even in the way our children are educated—and in the things they say when they come home from school.

In chaotic, tipping-point situations, the leverage of individual social actors and groups can be extraordinary. This power is too seldom recognized or understood today by most mainstream analysts of conflict, complex emergencies, and fragile governance, just as it is often ignored by market regulators and government officials.

This gap of understanding is dangerous. It impoverishes our collective understanding of the threats to public good, and it leaves most people, including most politicians and policymakers, ignorant of the genuine wealth of resources available for positive social change. It also leaves some particularly fascinating social actors and networks operating in the shadows, without the transparency and accountability we need to ensure that they live up to their full potential as public servants. But most importantly, when citizens themselves do not understand their potential power, they cannot use it well.

Social power is the most influential, least understood, and most potentially transformative force in the world today. Only if it can be better mobilized will humankind be able to drive the progress and develop the resilience we urgently need to navigate the coming decades.

I believe it is time to shine the full light of day on citizens as transformational agents for change, to help many more people discover this possibility in themselves, and to help the democratic potential of social power be fully realized.

White Hats Versus Warlord Entrepreneurs

As a small contribution to that wider project, this essay seeks to sketch the outlines of a group which, to use an old Western cowboy metaphor, we might call the "white hats"—the private diplomats, social and political entrepreneurs, and the growing multitude of citizens and organizations of global civil society. Sometimes they stand as the last bulwark against a tide of chaos. Sometimes they may just offer one of the best hopes we have for building a better tomorrow. I believe warlord entrepreneurs play a huge part in our world today, and a growing one. But I also see growing numbers of white hats riding out to surround them.

Heroic storytelling is a powerful art. Most serious official analysis tends to focus on the placid valleys of official governance or on the transactional dimension of formal institutions. As the natural complement to this civilized scholarship, almost fetishistic amounts of media attention are paid to the "black hats"—uncivil actors such as al-Qaeda or the Movement for the Emancipation of the Niger Delta (MEND). Meanwhile, a slew of arguments—such as Robert Kaplan's *The Coming Anarchy*—have been written to describe the frontier-lands between our civilization and the barbarians. If these are frontier-lands, the logic follows, conflict must be inevitable.

History has not ended after all, we are told. Today, the twenty-first century and the stone age coexist—divided by thousands of miles, but connected by a globalized web of shipments of people and goods, information and ideas, and increasingly advanced technologies, which dissolves boundaries.

This story has, at its heart, an idea of polarized and radically different social worlds: order necessarily finds itself opposed to chaos, and our heroes are the champions of a just order, fighting that chaos out on the frontier. Combined with the reality of extraordinary interdependence and potential vulnerability, it is a storyline that powerfully reinforces the defensive reactions of our market states, our national dreams, and our fortress identities—from Texas to Kandahar.

This narrative is persuasive, and it is powerful. But it is also a dangerous and divisive lie. Two variants are "the clash of civilizations" or "the global war on terror"—tales that have been told from different angles not only by American foreign policy and military analysts like Robert Kaplan but also by frontier strategists like al-Qaeda's Ayman al-Zawahiri.

But the notion of the warlord entrepreneur has considerably broader explanatory power than may be obvious at first glimpse, including in market democracies. The people brokering and capturing flows of power in the undergoverned spaces of the world are not only figures like Palestinian liberation leader Yasser Arafat; Pakistani nuclear scientist A. Q. Khan; Jomo Gbomo, the shamanic spokesman of the MEND militants in Nigeria;[1] or Osama bin Laden.

The rather more interesting truth is that today there are countless warlord entrepreneurs living in the heart of Western democracies. They are taking pragmatic advantage of the undergoverned spaces in our most "sophisticated" and well-developed countries, as well as in some of the world's poorest countries. They are taking freewheeling advantage of the undergoverned spaces of global power and markets. And they keep their eyes peeled for all kinds of opportunities.

We have financial warlords like Lloyd Blankfein of Goldman Sachs, whose activities both in the lead-up to the 2008 crash and through the ensuing years of financial turbulence have appropriately come under increasing scrutiny. We have commodity warlords like the secretive trading companies who control a large proportion of the flows of the world's food and raw materials. We have entertainment warlords like Rupert Murdoch or like Sepp Blatter, who now stands almost unopposed at the helm of a multi-billion-dollar advertising and licensing empire, FIFA, having captured huge rents from the love of soccer felt by billions of people worldwide. And we have countless governmental, military, and security warlords scattered across a spectrum between public accountability and brutal self-interest.

When the ideal of democracy seems like a distant dream, it may not always be easy to hold fast to. But it remains essential. Civil society and democracy are fundamental pillars of human growth and sustained flourishing. They can ground and harness the turmoil of self-interested energies, channeling entrepreneurial energy for the common good. But civil society, democracy, and the rule of law are far from fully realized, even in the heart of the West.

Anyone seeking to build a better future must understand these basic facts. We cannot allow ourselves to be diverted by either the turbulent dramas of the frontier or the cozy stories that media-saturated market democracies tell us about our own order and safety. Most of our world is constructed close to home, by the warlords at the core of our world—not by the warlords of the periphery.

The white hats, the agents of change that I will describe here, frequently pit themselves against the warlords who build their fortresses in market democracies and offshore havens. They seek to change the warlords' behavior or to hold them accountable for their misdeeds. White hats sometimes operate on the geographic frontier, against those warlords of the periphery, but their role is equally important in the undergoverned spaces of so-called civilization.

In this essay, I introduce a handful of white hat actors, focusing on two extremes of the white hat spectrum, of which I have some personal experience: private diplomacy and mass organizing. There is, of course, a rich landscape that connects these two extremes: social innovators and entrepreneurs, community organizers and bridge builders, democrats, writers, revolutionaries, consultants in business and market transformation, and architects of new governance.

I have no space here to properly describe the fascinating activities of the white hat warlords (and yes, some warlords wear white hats), be they philanthropists like George Soros and Jeff Skoll, spymasters-turned-politicians like Israel's Ami Ayalon, or social business magnates like Bangladesh's Muhammad Yunus, who created the Grameen Bank—which prospered in microfinance thanks to its rootedness in social power and social benefit—and who has won enemies for his pains. There is a wealth of fascinating stories to be told about them. Soros alone is an extraordinary and ambiguous character: the speculator who crashed the pound out of the European Exchange Rate Mechanism and the donor who helped mid-wife peaceful revolutions in Eastern Europe. He has a deep understanding of social power, which is the golden thread connecting his financial-investment doctrine to his philanthropy, writing, and political views. And his worldwide network includes countless other figures—for example, Rob Johnson, a talented musician who helped organize the savings-and-loan restructure as a U.S. Senate staffer before working in the Quantum Fund, then helped organize the U.S. Democracy Alliance of progressive funders, and, most recently, set up the influential Institute for New Economic Thinking (with Soros backing) to help rebuild the disciplines of economics and global financial governance.

What follows is unavoidably biographical—and autobiographical. Some of these white hats I have worked with; others' stories I heard of at second or third hand. I will also suggest a few lessons learned. Take it with a pinch of salt. Every concept needs practical illustration, and every illustration is slanted. Nobody's hat is entirely white.

Lone Rangers and Badgeless Sheriffs

In *The Shield of Achilles,* the American constitutional and military scholar Philip Bobbitt tells the story of a novel published in 1912, entitled *Philip Dru: Administrator.* The novel is dedicated to "the unhappy many who have lived and died lacking opportunity because, in the starting, the world-wide social structure was wrongly begun." For those familiar with the libertarian legacy of Ayn Rand's *Atlas Shrugged, Philip Dru* may be something of an antidote. (Since this essay was first written, interestingly enough, the U.S. Tea Party talk radio warlord Glenn Beck discovered *Philip Dru* and decided to place it at the heart of his fantastical demonology of liberal conspiracies.)

The story runs as follows: Philip Dru is a young, idealistic graduate of West Point. He becomes a syndicated writer, drawing public awareness to social injustices and proposing solutions. Meanwhile, a political Machiavelli, Senator Selwyn, has conspired with robber-baron financier

John Thor (a stand-in for J. P. Morgan) to control the government through a huge political slush fund, which they manipulate to corrupt senators and an apparently progressive president.

When this scandal is leaked to the press, the president's recall is demanded, and a civil war breaks out. Philip Dru becomes a revolutionary general, takes over Washington, and decrees a series of democratic and progressive reforms. He reimposes control over corporate elites; creates rights to union membership, pensions, and unemployment insurance; and negotiates a world federation of peaceful democratic states. Finally, Dru refuses to stand in the elections he has organized, and he sails off into the sunset with the love of his life. *Philip Dru* is a utopian white hat fantasy of a citizen taking action to transform his own society, then stepping modestly back into private life.

Why, in a world-historical tome of constitutional realpolitik that begins with Thucydides and the rise of the Westphalian era before chronicling the rise and fall of the dreams of multilateralism, international law, and world peace, does Philip Bobbitt spend any time on this fiction? Because, as it turns out, *Philip Dru: Administrator* was almost certainly authored by Colonel Edward Mandell House, President Wilson's informal advisor and closest ally, and a man who has a strong claim to be one of the principal architects of the modern ideals of collective security, international law, and global civil society.

House played many roles, but he was a serial refuser of public offices. He was a member of the Texas elite, a ruthless political-campaign manager, an idealistic novelist, a private envoy for Wilson to the councils of war-torn Europe, and an informal architect of progressive policies and narratives (including many of those that appear in *Philip Dru*). Finally, House was Wilson's man at the Paris Peace Conference in 1919, where he championed the establishment of the League of Nations and other principles, and struggled—too often in vain—against some of the petty but fatal idiocies of the Allied Powers, such as the exclusion of the German delegation from full participation in the conference and the territorial humiliation of Italy.

Despite his close links to government, for me, House was undoubtedly a white hat. Although he harnessed the power of politics and the state, he never became consumed by them. He seems to have remained first and foremost a modest citizen of his country and of the world. We will return later to House's story and to that of Philip Dru, because they are paradoxical and illuminating in equal measure. They also provide a good preamble to the first type of white hats I want to chronicle: the private diplomats, practitioners of "Track II" informal negotiation channels, and envoys of global civil society.

All around the world, wherever there is conflict, there are also people seeking to resolve it. They trace root causes, they seek to understand the positions and cleavages of the parties and what might affect their decision making, and they advise the players and propose policies. Sometimes they even organize private negotiations and channels of dialogue or become the midwives of peace, reconciliation, and coexistence.

Governments are often involved in official efforts at conflict management or transformation. These efforts can be carried out by diplomats, spies, or politicians. But these people often find it hard to gain the trust of the parties, because they are perceived to come with their own agendas. So in a surprising number of cases, it is independent citizens—academics, religious activists, social organizers, or journalists—who have become the crucial catalysts of reconciliation. And even where governmental actors take the lead, they must usually adopt an independent white hat mentality to be successful.

Case studies and profiles form a significant part of this essay, because a mental picture is often worth a thousand words. There are dozens of fascinating and idiosyncratic stories to tell about these envoys of hope and civility. The Community of Sant'Egidio is one of the more well known examples. A Catholic lay movement of tens of thousands of people founded in 1968, the community began in Italy with students coming together to read the Bible, making contact with poor immigrants, and helping the immigrants' children learn to read and write.

The community developed social and humanitarian programs for the poor: first at home, then overseas. But increasingly, it realized that conflict was a major cause of the poverty and suffering it was trying to alleviate. So members of the community began to explore informal dialogues in conflict zones—most notably in Mozambique in the early 1990s, where the community was eventually accepted by both the ruling party and the rebels as a formal mediator, and it helped shepherd through a peace agreement, which was signed at its headquarters in Rome. It has engaged in similar activities in Lebanon, Algeria, the Democratic Republic of the Congo, and elsewhere.

These are fragile processes, depending deeply on trust and on the ethics of the mediator. The community's practice and values have been crucial to their impact. They have eschewed bombastic claims. Their founder, Andrea Riccardi, ascribes their contribution to their commitment to the security of the multitude of poor people affected by conflict: "Our moral power during the negotiations was being the mouthpiece of the suffering poor populace, sometimes the only one."

Another region that has been riven with conflict is the oil-rich Niger Delta of Nigeria, full of warlords, oil barons, and desperate but resourceful communities. Judith Burdin Asuni, an American married to a Nigerian, who has lived in the region for decades, is one individual who has played a fascinating white hat role in this region. Burdin Asuni is named in the prison chronicle of Mujahid Asari-Dokubu—the leader of MEND, the Movement for the Emancipation of the Niger Delta—along with Jomo Gbomo, the shamanic spokesman of the MEND militants,[2] and she was briefly arrested and accused of espionage by the Nigerian government for her contacts with the militias. But from her small organization, called Academic Associates PeaceWorks, she has worked on police reform and community development, and she has published important analyses and recommendations for the re-governance of the Niger Delta and how the basic grievances of its people could be addressed.[3] (There is a larger story here, to which we will return.)

A third example of a white hat worth mentioning here is Michael Semple. If we were casting a white hat Western, Semple might make a good lone ranger. An Irish national, he began working in Afghanistan in the 1980s. He ran the Oxfam's humanitarian and development operations there and later worked for the prominent Ismaili leader the Aga Khan.

In a remarkable talk to the Carr Center on Human Rights at Harvard University, Semple described his early civil-society experience in Afghanistan: "If you wrap enough bands of hand grenades around you, shoulder your Kalashnikov, and look fierce, the Pakistani border guards will salute you. It worked. But I wouldn't advise it.... You're much better off without them."[4]

Semple has moved on from his white hat civil-society origins. Today, his self-conceived identity appears to be close to that of the autonomous "political officer" of the British colonial frontier—for example, the Kashmiri operator Mohan Lal, a public entrepreneur on the chessboard of the Great Game in Afghanistan. But as he took on governmental roles, Semple appears to have only deepened his white hat commitment to and understanding of the social power and human security of the local population at large, something which many diplomats and other frontier officials today lack. He appears now almost as a hill tribesman.

Semple was serving as the deputy representative of the European Union in Afghanistan when, at the end of 2007, he was thrown out by the government for talking to the Taliban. He had, however, been working closely with the Afghan National Security Council on these questions. According to him, his expulsion can be traced not to any particular misdeed, but to the interests of a tribal leader and power broker. His book about the period leading up to this, *Reconciliation in Afghanistan*, is required reading for anyone who wants to understand events in that country today. Semple's EU superior, Francesc Vendrell, claimed not really to know what the Irishman had been doing. Of these events, he merely said, "Michael was a person who had a tremendous amount of initiative."

Semple then moved to the United States, where he shared his experience and insights, and, it seems, where he ran a subtle campaign to shift the policy and elite debate toward support for dialogue and the civilianization of international support to Afghanistan.

Like most people who know that country deeply, Semple seems to be concerned about three things: the deepening effects of massive Western counterinsurgency on various aspects of Afghan society; the risks of precipitate withdrawal; and the likelihood that the West may repeat its mistake of the early 1990s, when it cut off support after the mujahedin's victory over the Soviet Union, failing to help properly with reconstruction and development.

Elsewhere, Professor Mary Kaldor of the Centre for Global Governance and Global Civil Society at the London School of Economics—a white hat social activist as well as a formidable academic—has been riding forth to promote the paradigm of human security for militaries and foreign services. She has worked closely on this with some of the world's leading experts in stabilization and counterinsurgency operations.[5]

Replumbing the state to serve the people better is a continuous challenge. Valuing dialogue and prioritizing the bottom-up perspective of affected citizens are two common threads in white hat conflict transformation, whoever is doing it. The Community of Sant'Egidio worked with local missionaries in Mozambique to collect letters and petitions for peace. Through this process, the leader of the rebel delegation received a letter from his father, whom he had not seen for a decade.

The community's Riccardi says, "I believe in the power of dialogue till the very last moment. It is not easy. Dialogue means a conversion towards the other person: you have to try understanding him, and at the same time help him to change his agenda." These ideas of understanding and change bring us to the curious case of Conflicts Forum, which I had some experience with during several years working on the Middle East, but whose work in that arena was probably of more provocative interest than my own.

In 2002 in Jerusalem, journalists and experts were whispering about a man called Alastair Crooke. Crooke was reportedly a British intelligence officer living in caves with the Palestinian factions—like some latter-day Lawrence of Arabia—and working on cease-fires.

I failed to track him down at that time but managed instead to meet in Gaza with Ismail Abu Shanab, a Hamas leader involved in these contacts, as well as with the political independent Ziad Abu Amr, who later became a minister in both Fatah- and Hamas-led governments. These conversations took place a couple of days after Israel had dropped a bomb on Saleh Shehadeh, a head of Hamas's military wing. An extraordinary, poetic declaration had just been issued, signed only by the Tanzim militia, which declared a unilateral cessation of attacks on civilians. When we met, Abu Shanab was in no mood for compromise. Within a year he would meet the same fate as Shehadeh.

Crooke was removed from his post as "EU security coordinator" to the Middle East not long after. I suspect that, by then, he was already some way down a path that, by all accounts, led to him separating from the British secret service and moving to Beirut. Over time, I believe Crooke came to consider himself what we are calling a "white hat" (others have compared him to a John Le Carre character). He also began working closely with another man with white hat credentials, an American named Mark Perry. Both men had been involved in ceasefire conversations and in mediation around the siege of the Church of the Holy Nativity in Bethlehem.

Mark Perry had previously been a U.S. truckers' union organizer, a senior official of the Vietnam Veterans of America and the Campaign to Ban Landmines, a political consultant and lobbyist, an unofficial adviser to Yasser Arafat, and a prizewinning journalist and author. He is one of the most interesting historians of U.S. military leadership working today, and he has strong informal networks with people in the U.S. military and security establishment.

Crooke and Perry set up Conflicts Forum in 2004, in the crucible of the post 9/11 terror wars. It was the year after the invasion of Iraq. U.S. policymakers were still dreaming of creative destruction and secular domino effects. The coalition in Iraq had already made a series of fatal and hubristic mistakes in failing to engage with—or even gain a basic understanding of—that country's social fabric.

The declared purpose of Conflicts Forum was "Understanding Islam, Recognizing Resistance." Put differently, its purpose was to persuade

Western governments to accept that dialogue with Islamic political movements with political legitimacy and a broad base of popular support in their communities was sensible, and that not every Muslim entity currently on a terrorist list should be classed with al-Qaeda.

Perry and Crooke organized formal and informal meetings between former U.S. and European officials and representatives of Hamas, Hezbollah, and other movements linked to the Islamic revival, the Muslim Brotherhood, and the Iranian revolution. These were meetings of deep listening, but also of mutual challenge.

It is hard now to remember just how radical a move this was to make out in the open at that time. The Conflicts Forum enterprise has been far from fully successful, but it and similar initiatives, such as Forward Thinking, have had a deep impact over the last few years in reshaping some of the underlying mental models of decision makers and opinion makers—not just in the West, but also in the Middle East.

Bilateral advice was an important part of Conflicts Forum's approach. There are differing views about the shade of gray of the hats worn by the leaders of these movements, but there can no longer be any doubt that they are primarily political rather than terrorist organizations. Meanwhile, some of their underlying narratives and models of organization are now more contested than before, based on knowledge rather than ignorance, most importantly in their own societies.

Needless to say, this is a moment of great promise and danger in the Middle East. As someone connected to these processes said recently about the Arab Awakening, "There is a growing demand, not just for open, democratic and accountable states, but also for open, democratic and accountable *movements*." Despite the ups and downs of recent history, we have barely glimpsed the full potential for transformation across the landscape of Middle Eastern political and social organization.

A wave of change was already well underway when I met Perry and Crooke in 2005. Hamas and Hezbollah had moved closer to a full commitment to parliamentary politics, and tumultuous debates were unfolding across Arab and global civil society. Perry, Crooke, and I were among a handful of observers of the Middle East who were starting to plan for the likely rise of Hamas, the reconfiguration of the Israeli political landscape, the regional fallout of events in Iraq and Afghanistan, and the challenges and opportunities of these transitions.

We were good at predicting events, but less good at the white hat mission of decisively changing their course. Palestinian elections went ahead. But promising conversations were cut short immediately afterward by the Quartet principles agreed to by the United Nations, the European Union, the United States, and Russia, which set strict preconditions for any formal engagement with Hamas, and this shifted the balance of power away from advocates of a political path.

Despite private acknowledgments of unease or inconsistency, many Western politicians and decision makers were drawn into sponsoring civil strife among the Palestinians. I was in the region in late 2006. On learning that I had contacts in the British government, one Fatah security official asked me unashamedly for more weapons and training to fight Hamas. At the same time, others from a different wing of his movement were working toward reconciliation between the factions.

This process came to a bloody climax in June 2007 in Gaza, just months after a Palestinian unity government had been brokered in Mecca. Contacts had been tracking news of agitation, weapons transfers, and training for months beforehand. The neoconservative David Wurmser, who resigned as Dick Cheney's chief Middle East adviser the following month, later said, "It looks to me that what happened wasn't so much a coup by Hamas but an attempted coup by Fatah that was pre-empted before it could happen," adding that his own administration had been "engaging in a dirty war in an attempt to provide a corrupt dictatorship with victory."[6]

Still, stepping back for a moment, the careful reader may already have noticed the missing characters in this story. The only white hats visible so far are a small network of somewhat egotistical lone rangers.

This is a mistake which policy entrepreneurs and private diplomats very often make. They design elite processes of dialogue and policy change that fail to connect sufficiently with the legitimacy, the agenda-setting power, and the transformative potential of broader public engagement. Often, they take the legitimacy of the actors they are convening too much for granted, or they fail to recognize the forces of inertia.

A broad yet schismatic community of people and organizations have attempted to initiate channels of dialogue in the Middle East over the years. This became a veritable industry in the early 1990s, when a process run by Israeli and Palestinian citizens and facilitated by Norwegians led to the signing of the Oslo Accords between Israel and the Palestinian Liberation Organization.

The Middle East peace-industry dialogues were sometimes valuable, but they also proved increasingly inadequate, because they tended to engage only the "peace camp" on both sides, and they became more transactional than transformational. The interlocutors often had more in common with each other than with the consensus in their own societies, and they did too little to reach out to their own publics. After the collapse of negotiations and the resumption of hostilities in 2000, very few of these private peace dialogues proved to be of much value.

The legitimacy deficit proved also to apply to some of the work done by Conflicts Forum and others. Despite a number of provocative conversations about deliberative polling, locally legitimate security orders, or supporting all-party popular committees at the neighborhood level, these approaches were never sufficiently operationalized or owned by *local* white hats.

It was in an effort to learn these lessons that I focused my final project in this field on securing support for two parallel projects which I played little or no part in. The first was a scenario-building process that brought together Israelis across social divides to contemplate their shared future, led by Adam Kahane, who had run a similar process for South African leaders. The second was the Palestinian Strategy Study Group, facilitated by a Palestinian and an Egyptian, which brought together Palestinians across divides to develop a more effective and democratic national strategy.[7]

The importance of democratic civilian power cannot be underestimated in these processes. My personal experience of providing advice to politicians and policy makers on the Middle East over this period had shown me that, usually, they would acknowledge the force of the arguments, then make unconvincing realpolitik excuses about why they needed to stick to their existing strategy until it had finally and decisively failed. Bad policies have been kept on life support for years in this way.

These experiences of policy and elite failure were some of the experiences which led me to start organizing with new, people-powered networks and movements over the last half-decade. These movements and other "white hat Multitudes" will be described further in the final part of this essay.

One last piece of the Conflicts Forum story deserves to be shared, because it is, in some ways, the most telling. It concerns the path-finding and world-defining role of norms, values, and political identity and community, all of which are crucial if we are to take white hat action to scale. I was surprised to find myself having a couple of remarkable and wide-ranging conversations with Alastair Crooke about social values and the failings of Western capitalist modernity—and particularly about postmodern philosophy and the counter-globalization "movement of movements"— things I had some familiarity with. I discovered that these were topics that both Crooke and the Islamist movements were intensely interested in.

These conversations were stimulating, but they were also deeply disturbing for me. In my view, Crooke and movements like Hezbollah were placing existential "resistance" at the heart of their political narrative. They were attracted by the overlap with the stories told both by the radical vanguard of the "No Global" movement and by European philosophers from the generation of 1968.[8] But it had already become clear to me from my experience with those communities that resistance, when elevated to this existential level, becomes an emotionally narcotic dead end. The harder and more worthwhile task is building a better society.

I agreed with Crooke that there were powerful positive social traditions in Islam. But we found ourselves disagreeing on other points, for example, his views of Iran seemed to me sometimes to risk slipping toward

idealization of that curious state and the political networks that have colo-
nized it—and in a way that appeared to me naïve for someone of his background (although I should emphasize that these perceptions, reflections,
and experiences are my own, presented here as illustration, rather than as
the final word).

Another white hat, T. E. Lawrence, travelled a long way to find his
tribe. Still, I believe that if you are a true white hat, all states and power
centers deserve challenge and scrutiny, without exception.

A full exploration of white hat ethics is a topic for another time. But
when you are up against a black hat adversary, it is all too easy to find
yourself mirroring his or her cynicism or practices. During this period,
Ron Suskind described a conversation he had with an (anonymous) prominent Bush administration figure, later reputed to be Karl Rove.

> The aide said that guys like me were "in what we call the reality-
> based community," which he defined as people who "believe that
> solutions emerge from your judicious study of discernible real-
> ity." I nodded and murmured something about enlightenment
> principles and empiricism. He cut me off. "That's not the way
> the world really works anymore." He continued, "We're an em-
> pire now, and when we act, we create our own reality. And while
> you're studying that reality—judiciously, as you will—we'll act
> again, creating other new realities, which you can study too, and
> that's how things will sort out. We're history's actors ... and you,
> all of you, will be left to just study what we do."[9]

Compare this neoconservative doctrine[10] to Crooke's own words
about the Lebanese Shi'ite political Islam movement, Hezbollah, with
whom he seems to have worked closely.

> Hezbullah is using techniques that stand outside of the usual
> repertoire of western politics in order to transform Muslims....
> Hezbullah is using myth, archetypal narrative and symbolism to

explode the Cartesian severance between subject and object, and between objective reality, on the one hand, and fantasy, make-believe and superstition on the other. Hezbullah uses these means to re-ignite creative imagination. The opening of this intermediary layer in Cartesian dualism allows people to begin imagining themselves in a new way; and by imagining themselves differently, to begin to act differently. As they begin to imagine themes differently and act differently, the way they see the world about them changes also.[11]

Both these descriptions are, in a strict sense, accurate. But I do not think that we could call them *right*. The actions of the U.S. administration or Hezbollah can dramatically alter social realities, as can the actions of the white hats described in this essay. Such change can be good or bad.

But what is most striking in both the quotes above, to my mind, is the way they seem to affirm a kind of manipulative approach and a denial or denigration of the underlying realities: human hopes, human suffering, human lives.

What would a genuine ethos of democratic white hat transformation look and feel like?

The White Hat Multitudes

On February 15, 2003, tens of millions of people marched in eight hundred cities around the world to protest the impending invasion of Iraq. It was the biggest international march ever, and the marches in individual cities broke national records in much of Europe.

The Iraq marches prompted many (including UN secretary-general Kofi Annan, and the *New York Times*) to call global public opinion a second superpower. The street demonstrations were backed up by Pew Center polling showing large majorities against the war in most—though not all—countries. This "second superpower" failed, almost inevitably, to influence the U.S. decision. Yet many now reflect that those who marched were right to question the rush to war and the failure to respect international legitimacy.

The march was not a spontaneous event. It was midwifed in part through transnational conversations in circles linked to the European Social Forum and similar meetings in Porto Alegre and Cairo. The organizers included a rainbow of representatives of their societies, but almost nowhere did the demonstrations also oppose Saddam Hussein's crimes against his innocent citizens or present any positive alternative agenda. Still, February 15, 2003 was a network-centric and locally rooted mobilization that, for one day, channeled and gave thunderous voice to the will of a global multitude.

In London, the *Observer* newspaper wrote, "[As well as the] usual suspects—CND, Socialist Workers Party, the anarchists.... There were nuns. Toddlers. Women barristers. The Eton George Orwell Society. Archaeologists Against War. Walthamstow Catholic Church, the Swaffham Women's Choir and Notts County Supporters Say Make Love Not War (And a Home Win against Bristol would be Nice)."

The white hat multitude was on the march.

At the end of the day, however, the multitude went home. What's more, a few days later, with the invasion of Iraq, the multitude watched its own defeat live on television. Many of those who marched felt disenchanted and demobilized. More hardened radicals filled the vacuum and captured the banner of the peace movement, often to its detriment. Countless others started channeling their energies in new directions. And a few people started doing lessons learned.

The growth of the white hat multitude is not just about marches or petitions. It's a process with many aspects, from neighborhoods to the global public square. Part of it is about attitudes, beliefs, and behaviors. Part of it is about social capital. And part of it is about social infrastructure and the networks that connect us.

A year after the February 15 marches, individuals and small groups scattered around the world started to think hard about organizing infrastructure and narratives. Over time, we began to think, talk, and write about an internet-enabled movement that could become a rapid-response arm for the second superpower and a civil counterforce to the clash of civilizations. I was one of those people, as were the founders of the Australian movement GetUp and Eli Pariser, who had raised a huge global petition for a law-based response to 9/11. We had all become increasingly convinced that a global movement for direct, mass citizen action was a crucial part of the answer to the global challenges we faced. So in 2007, we launched Avaaz, which means "voice," "noise," or "people's song" in many languages.

But the momentum for what became Avaaz was generated overwhelmingly by three extraordinary white hats who had come together in an organization called Res Publica: Tom Perriello, later a U.S. congressman for Virginia; Tom Pravda, who has had a stellar career in the British Diplomatic Service; and, most of all, Ricken Patel, who became Avaaz's main founder and executive director.

As this book was in production, the Avaaz network had close to forty million members, and it is still growing fast. These citizens are taking action together through the internet across a dizzying range of global and national issues. Avaaz has members in every country of the world. Two of its largest national constituencies are now burgeoning in Brazil and India, southern democracies where its members have recently run mass national anticorruption campaigns.

The Avaaz movement, like the wider white hat multitude, is still in its infancy. So I will share just a handful of episodes from its first few years, in the hope that they may illuminate the potential of civil society coming together and becoming a more decisive actor for resilience and transformation.

In late 2007, a motley cast of characters arrived at a house on a hilltop a few miles outside Granada in Spain. Some had never seen each other face-to-face. These were the organizers of Avaaz, and we had planned to be strategizing for the long-term development of our movement. But as it turned out, we had more important things to do. Thousands of monks and hundreds of thousands of citizens had taken to the streets of Burma in antigovernment protests, and a campaign was going viral across the internet. So we descended en masse on the nearest internet café and got to work.

That campaign received over eighty thousand signatures. It was delivered to UN Security Council members, and its message was spread via a full-page advertisement in the *Financial Times* and in private meetings with diplomats. It was followed up with thousands of messages sent by citizens of the European Union, Singapore, and India, pressing their own governments to act, and with a global day of action organized through Facebook and global trade union and NGO networks. Avaaz members also donated hundreds of thousands of dollars to help break the communications blackout in Burma, providing vital equipment and other support to hard-pressed civil-society movements there.

But the story didn't end there. Perhaps its most important chapter was still to come. The following May, Cyclone Nargis hit the huge Irrawaddy Delta in Burma, killing tens of thousands of people and devastating communities. The government was very slow to accept aid, and there were multiple problems over the following weeks getting official and NGO aid supplies and workers into the country.

By contrast, within twenty-four hours, Avaaz were in touch, via Burmese counterparts, with networks of monasteries and community-based organizations across the delta. We established that we could get funds into the country directly through the *hundi* money transfer system, which carries huge volumes and is used by the diaspora for remittances and by businessmen for payments, to defray payments for community-based relief and reconstruction that urgently needed to begin. Within days, Avaaz members had donated more than $2 million to these locally sourced and community-based efforts—a greater contribution than the government of France made, channeled in faster, with less obstruction, and to more reliable destinations.

Another interesting moment in the history of Avaaz came at the Bali conference on climate change in 2007, where Avaaz mobilized a full-spectrum campaign of petition signatures, phone calls, and *Titanic*-themed advertisements to personally target the leaders of the three most obstructive countries, Japan, Canada, and the United States, in the final seventy-two hours. Japan and Canada folded, leaving the United States isolated to be browbeaten into agreement by the delegate from Papua New Guinea.

In the heat of the moment, we were not sure just how much impact our members' pressure had in this process. But a couple weeks later, we received an email from one of our Japanese members with a scan of a full spread from the *Asahi Shimbun,* Japan's second biggest newspaper. The article told the tale of Japan's "Bali Shock." In a vivid scene, it described the environment minister putting a newspaper down on the cabinet table in front of the prime minister, telling him that this was how Japan was being seen in the world and that a change of policy was needed. The newspaper was the *Jakarta Post,* and on the back page was Avaaz's *Titanic* advertisement. That advertisement achieved iconic status in some circles in Japan and later made its way onto the wall of the headquarters of the Democratic Party of Japan.

It should by now be clear even to the skeptical reader that we are not talking about a banal and misleading stereotype of "clicktivism." Avaaz became one of the backbones of the global movement on climate change by 2009. It ran dozens of national and global campaigns on climate change in the run-up to the Copenhagen summit, including an election campaign in Germany that engaged the leaders of the main parties personally. Its members organized thousands of flash mobs and vigils globally, culminating in a vigil inside the Copenhagen summit addressed by Archbishop Desmond Tutu, a mass global telephone conference with British prime minister Gordon Brown, a plethora of rapid-response campaigns targeted at the main dramas of that summit, and the delivery of millions of petition signatures.

Copenhagen fell short of the "real deal" Avaaz and NGOs had been calling for, but as one member said in an email, "the elephant is moving." Avaaz's membership has exploded since then, and other social campaigns are gathering momentum all around the world.

It may be worth sharing one more sequence of stories from Avaaz's campaigning, as it connects to the other white hat stories discussed above. Early on, we created a short YouTube video called "Stop the Clash of Civilizations," designed to give voice and hope to everyone who felt unrepresented by the two sides in the terror wars or who resented how it had dominated headlines and imaginations for so long. "Stop the Clash" shows the misperceptions, manipulation, and ventriloquism at the heart of this false conflict. It asks whether Arab strongmen and the leaders of the G8 really speak for us as global citizens, and it outlines an alternative agenda of people power rising up to change flawed policies, change misperceptions, and transform our world for the better.

"Stop the Clash" was watched by millions of people around the world in several languages, including Arabic. It was voted "Best Political Video of 2007" by YouTube users, beating the much-touted "Obama Girl." For a time, it was the second most discussed video ever on YouTube, and it became the basis of conversations with policy makers and opinion makers in the United States and the Middle East. It is now used as a teaching material in many schools around the world.

Perhaps most importantly, "Stop the Clash" helped set an agenda for white hat movement building and campaigning over the following years. Avaaz's contributions to this process have included the deliberative promotion of a peace plan for Iraq based on negotiations, empowerment, legitimacy, and withdrawal; pressure for a comprehensive Gaza ceasefire; and an Indian social resilience viral after the Mumbai bombings, signed by a Muslim Bollywood actress, which carried the message "don't let them divide us."

Recently, with me long gone, Avaaz has campaigned intensively in support of the Arab Awakening. Its most significant practical intervention here is probably the tens of thousands of donations that have been channeled into support for Arab civil society within weeks, including smartphones, satellite communications, training, and connections to the global media.

Controversy was also sparked over Avaaz's involvement in the botched smuggling of British journalist Paul Conroy out of Syria. The operation was led by Free Syrian Army networks, and activists died in it. Ricken Patel's public version of this story can be found on the Avaaz website, although there may be aspects which cannot be openly discussed to this day for reasons of safety, as is often the case in conflict zones.[12]

Strikingly, for an organization with a history of questioning imperial adventurism, Avaaz also delivered almost a million messages of support to the UN Security Council for a no-fly zone over Libya, after polling its membership and receiving an overwhelming majority of support. Susan Rice, the American ambassador to the United Nations, publicly welcomed this campaign.

It is probably too early to tell, on balance, what the net consequences of this work have been, in a turbulent and complex time of transition. But Avaaz's Libya decision, made by a mass membership, was, in my view, a significant milestone in the evolution of the white hat multitude. Avaaz uses a continuous model of participatory-democratic accountability and steering to make sure it stays close to its members. Regardless of their views today on the Libyan intervention, they are certainly committed to the civilian-led transformation of the Middle East.

Avaaz is now an institution as well. Because of its openness to and complete dependence on its membership, its future success is more dependent than that of most institutions on trust and a growing practice of open accountability. The contrasts between Avaaz and a project such as Wikileaks should be clear. I will not venture to suggest what color Julian Assange's hat is, although I have met him. Many of his interventions seem to have contributed considerably to the public good. But it seems to me that his operating method at Wikileaks may have been closer to that of the warlord entrepreneur. Nor is Avaaz a vehicle for anarchic swarms like those of Anonymous. More Avaaz members are businesspeople and parents than hackers and students, and that is much of its strength.

In the Middle East today—and in many other regions—social norms and means of organization are being transformed. The ideas, identities, and social technologies that facilitate self-organization through networks are spreading. So are open-source strategies of popular struggle articulated by white hats like Gene Sharp (the supposed éminence grise of nonviolent conflict), the Serbian resistance movement OTPOR, and others—who have themselves become the subjects of sharp controversy.[13]

Charismatic individual leaders like former Google executive Wael Ghonim, who created the Facebook network that prepared the ground for the Egyptian revolution of 2011, are important in these processes, as is clear from his autobiography; but they are also fragile and perilous sources of legitimacy and hope.[14]

It is crucially important that the new organizers and participants in these movements do not romanticize the spontaneously self-organizing potential of networks like Facebook or Twitter. These platforms are not yet naturally designed to support the resilient new forms of social capital and democratic organization that will be necessary for the full flourishing of white hat transformation. Avaaz itself is far from perfect in channeling the energies of its members, and, like other such movements, it is only a beginning. We need to broaden the base much further and to build better channels for white hats of all kinds to step up.

Some of the new frontiers in white hat organizing are in undergoverned spaces like Pakistan or Nigeria. Other frontiers involve working more closely with the warp and weave of the popular imagination, our media and our daily lives, to evolve positive frames and values. The work of analysts like George Lakoff and Drew Westen hold promise in this arena, not least because both promote an ethic of transparent reframing that, instead of manipulating the emotions, lays out its arguments on the table for all to see.[15]

The restless work of the white hats is crucial, because our existing paradigms of global governance, economic prosperity, and social order often seem to be failing. The market states, the Hobbesian attitude to the global commons, and the bent toward global counterinsurgency outlined in the work of Philip Bobbitt, Robert Kaplan, and other scribes of the establishment may still be dominant, but these paradigms are also, I believe, inadequate to delivering order or prosperity in a fractured, turbulent, and unequal world.

Global laws can and should be further solidified, contrary to Bobbitt's dismissal of the dream of Edward Mandell House. Yet hopes of a better global society also rest fundamentally on networks of association and creativity, on the health and vibrancy of the global public sphere, and on the growing global conversation about norms and values.[16]

In *Philip Dru: Administrator*, in an argument with his prospective father-in-law, the hero states:

> The moral tone and thought of the world is changing. You take it for granted that man must have in sight some material reward in order to achieve the best there is within him. I believe that mankind is awakening to the fact that material compensation is far less to be desired than spiritual compensation. This feeling will grow, and when it comes to full fruition, the world will find but little difficulty in attaining a certain measure of altruism. I agree with you that this much-to-be desired state of society cannot be altogether reached by laws, however drastic.

As the awakening process of global civil society converges with the mega-trends of economic transformation and disruption, we must keep clear in our minds the impossibility of achieving human flourishing solely through control, counterinsurgency, or the rule of law. We must develop and preserve systems of public authority that extend beyond the state, deep into society and the market. And we must construct new identities and designs for living, as well as new frameworks of social regulation and action.

Fortunately, the white hat ethos is one of mutual generosity, based on a logic of abundance rather than scarcity. Reality-based, but questioning and endlessly creative, it is the essence of the human spirit and the good society. This is something we can all share.

⊹

This article is dedicated to a young, unemployed Palestinian man whom I met in a Hamas minister's office. His elder brother had been elected for Hamas to lead the Palestinian student unions but had been killed in office. The young man leaned in close to me as we took the elevator down to the ground floor. He had something very important to tell me. Was it a point of religious doctrine, a vow of martyrdom, or a claim to represent the Palestinian people?

The young man whispered passionately that he loved to dance the tango.

In hidden dancehalls all over the world, social power is brewing.

What will we change? The decision is ours.

13 Beyond Survival

Pioneering as a Response to Crisis

Graham Leicester

Hell is a most popular subject today because so many people are in it.
Hell is very stimulating and easy to understand. Paradise is very difficult
to understand, and also, there is in Paradise a rebuke. In that Paradise
there is a purity which reveals one's own sense of impurity.

—Cecil Collins, *Theatre of the Soul*

The Marvelous and the Murderous

The essays in this volume are compelling. They bring into the harsh light of rational examination and understanding some of the dark forces at work in the world. They lay bare the ways of power that inevitably find their opportunity when order collapses and scarcity reins. At such times, we might find it a struggle to articulate an alternative to "going down with the ship of high-modernist capitalism as it breaks up or taking to the lifeboats captained by warlord entrepreneurs" (as Barnes and Gilman put it).

Expressing a credible alternative is bound to be challenging. It is not just that "the devil always has the best tunes." It is also that, by contrast, the music of the spheres is more demanding of the listener. It is easier to dismiss alternatives as unrealistic and utopian rather than accept, as Cecil

Collins suggests in the epigram to this essay, that their very imagining represents a challenge to who we are, how we live, and what we are prepared to stand for today.

Yet lessons can be learned from the rich history of human action in periods of challenge and duress that offer us a sense of what's possible. Those who emerge from crisis with both their aspirations and their humanity intact appear to follow a journey in four phases. The first step is survival, the sine qua non. But what should we do beyond that? The next step must be to generate fresh insight into our new situation. The third step involves maintaining the will to act and to persevere—survival now with a purpose. The final factor is hope, without which we cannot even start the journey.

These phases are described in more detail below. But these are not lessons only for those of us unfortunate enough to find ourselves in the badlands of globalization's ungovernable spaces. We live in a world of such boundless complexity, radical interconnectedness, and rapid change that we are all already, as Harvard psychologist Robert Kegan pointed out back in the early 1990s, "in over our heads."

The core challenge in these circumstances is to learn how to draw upon strengths and inner resources we may not think we have and that our typical defensive responses to crisis deny us. These strengths are not technical or structural or theoretical; they are existential. It is our artists, our poets, our mythmakers who have constantly brought them to mind for us for generations.

One touchstone for me is Seamus Heaney's extraordinary acceptance speech for his 1995 Nobel Prize for Literature. In it he tells of his own experience of losing hope during the "harrowing of the heart" that he experienced during the years of conflict in his native Northern Ireland. He describes how, during those decades, he bent over his desk like a monk, going through the motions of writing, "blowing up sparks for meagre heat."

But then, "finally and happily," he "straightened up." He found his inner strength again. As he puts it, "I began ... to try to make space in my reckoning and imagining for the marvelous as well as for the murderous."

Heaney illustrates the point with a story about a group of workmates ambushed by the roadside in those times. The armed gunmen line the men up against a wall and ask that any Catholics among them step forward. The assumption is that these are Protestant paramilitaries, and that the Catholics will be shot dead.

The one Catholic among them, "caught between dread and witness," makes a motion to step forward. But at that moment, in the darkness, he feels the Protestant worker next to him take his hand and squeeze it, as if to say—don't worry, we will not betray you, stay in line. But it is too late. He has already made a motion. He expects to be shot, but instead is thrown aside as the rest of the men are gunned down. The gunmen themselves are Catholic, presumably members of the Provisional IRA.

The image haunts Heaney—as it must anyone who reads his speech. It is a reminder of the utter inseparability of the marvelous and the murderous, both ever present and always available in the same image. The squeeze of the hand is as real as the volley of gunfire, and as much a part of our human nature.

Yet, as Heaney puts it, "as writers and readers, as sinners and citizens, our realism and our aesthetic sense make us wary of crediting the positive note." It is the gift of poetry, in particular what he calls "the necessary poetry," to lend power to the positive, to hold both the murderous and the marvelous "in a single thought."

As we contemplate dark times ahead, we too must be open to the marvelous, ready to see and to respond to hope amid despair. Not false hope, not blithe optimism, not the fantasy of rescue, but the mature hope that brings with it its own burden, its own challenge. Heaney concludes his speech by pointing to the contradictory needs we experience at times of crisis: "the need on the one hand for a truth telling that will be hard and retributive, and on the other hand, the need not to harden the mind to a point where it denies its own yearnings for sweetness and trust." In light of the dark imaginings of much of this collection, the few words of practical hope that follow are offered in this spirit.

Lesson 1: Survival

I spend my professional life encouraging people to think and to reflect. Yet I have lost count of the number of senior figures who, at times of crisis, have told me they are not interested in new thinking and ideas just at the moment, thank you. Their first priority is survival.

Fair enough. They need to batten down the hatches, concentrate on the short term, look after the staff, cut costs, lie low for a while—keep themselves and their organizations viable while waiting for recovery.

They evidently don't know much about survivors. Studies of accidents, plane crashes, shipwrecks, and people who get lost in the wilderness show that those who decide to sit still and wait for things to get better are far more likely to perish. Rule one for survivors is "discard the hope of rescue."

That is a challenging stance—which is why we don't generally go there. But think about the costs of waiting for rescue. It leaves you as a victim in your own eyes. It relieves you of the need to make sense of the condition you find yourself in. It clothes you in false comfort. And ultimately, if things don't improve, it leads to growing anxiety, panic, and finally resignation, as it becomes clear that the moment for effective action has long gone, and rescue is not on the way. All a bit gloomy, I'm afraid. So if you are committed to survival in difficult times, don't go about it that way.

What's the alternative? Many survival schools (which are enjoying boomtown business, incidentally, since the prophets of planetary doom found their voices) use the acronym STOP: stop, think, observe, plan ... and then, crucially, act.

The first three are linked. They are about coming to terms with new circumstances. We automatically resist this. It has something to do with maintaining our emotional stability: we do not like to admit to being confused. People who wander off the trail and get lost almost never turn back. They press on, convincing themselves that they are still on track and that they will come across a landmark on the trail just around the next corner.

This is called "bending the map." Survivors don't make the mistake of imposing old patterns on new information.

Maintaining that level of awareness, however, is tricky. It requires a recognition that our emotions condition our thinking. We are more likely to believe what we feel than what we know. And when we are in danger or under pressure or anxious, our emotions tend to crowd out rational thought. That's why fighter pilots have such intensive training, so the right thing to do becomes instinctive when the body is suffused with fear. As one instructor says, "when you climb inside the cockpit, your IQ rolls back to that of an ape."

That's why it is important to slow down, to maintain the balance between emotions and reason. And observe. Really observe. Don't just see what you expect to see, what you hope to see. Make sense of your situation anew—in all its fearful complexity.

This is where new thinking comes in. Malcolm Gladwell writes pithily about the ability to perform under pressure: "Choking [in a sport] is a result of thinking too much. Panic is a result of thinking too little." So try to think just enough, and in a way that acknowledges the new landscape of the crisis and with an emotional quality that allows our understandable fear and anxiety to express itself in creative impulse rather than blinkered denial.

New thinking is a survival strategy. In fact, it is *the* survival strategy. Is anybody interested now?[1]

Lesson 2: Insight

I wrote in the previous lesson about the extensive research on the qualities of survivors—how they react to danger, how they think and respond in a crisis, what they do, and how they pull through. There are clues here for what constitutes intelligent behavior at a time of crisis.

The survival drama has three acts. Act 1 is the descent into chaos. Act 2 is confusion, commitment to survival, and the subsequent struggle. Act 3 brings us, at last, to reemergence into safety. The critical task at the entry to act 2 is to maintain the energy and adrenaline that fear generates, but not to descend into panic. Manage the anxiety; take a long, hard look at the situation; recognize that you are off the map; and generate the one thing that is going to help you survive: fresh insight.

Most of us are not in life and death situations today. But we are no strangers to feeling overwhelmed, anxious, or stressed—when things get out of hand at work, for example—and struggling, in those circumstances, to perform at our best, precisely when our best is most needed. On top of these normal pressures, today we are operating in a complex world running constantly in failure mode (as Charles Perrow puts it in his book *Normal Accidents*)—a world in which small errors in any part of the system can rapidly escalate, with critical and unforeseen consequences. The disruption of the financial system in 2007–2008 is just one example. We hope that small failures in systems of governance in the face of the growth of transnational crime described elsewhere in this volume do not escalate. But we cannot be sure. As pressures mount, the threat of at least a partial collapse of contemporary civilization is frighteningly plausible.

The important thing is how we respond. Most people go into denial: carry on, ignore inconvenient evidence, and hope for the best. Others commission extensive research to assess future risk: analyze trends and develop scenarios. But that too is of no value if it simply feeds complacency in the present: "It's okay, we did the scenarios exercise, and we're future-proofed."

No, you're not. Because what we need to be prepared for is unpredictable, disruptive change. That is what triggers a crisis. And at that point, it is your instincts that kick in—who you are, not what you know. If you have a habit of relying on plans and numbers you will cling on to them more tightly than ever. But if you are a survivor, you will adapt to the new circumstance. You will take careful stock of the new situation. What is this place? What opportunities does it offer? What sense can I make that will allow me to take the first step out of the crisis rather than just waiting for it to pass?

How can we do that? We can take a longer-term perspective—recognizing that our sense of the future inevitably colors our reading of the present. We can start to notice things we have previously missed through inattention, prejudice, or cultural habit. Psychiatrists notice subtleties of behavior that others miss. Naturalists notice entire ecologies on the underside of a leaf. Recognizing that we typically have a limited view and taking steps to identify our blind spots and to find alternative ways of perceiving expands the space in which fresh insight may emerge.

And insight is not inert. It is not 'blue skies' thinking. Insight demands action. And that in turn will bring something new into the world and provide the source for new scanning and fresh insight. Our first steps will kick start a learning cycle. We cannot plan but we will learn our way out of crisis.[2]

Lesson 3: Perseverance

Up to now I have treated "survival" broadly as a metaphor. But we also know that times of crisis are truly testing. We are stressed; some will become depressed; levels of suicide rise; violence increases. New thinking and fresh insight are crucial for future prosperity. But so too will be actions to look after ourselves, to maintain our energy to persevere, and to care for the wounded.

The warning signals have been mounting for decades. The World Health Organization suggests that by 2020 depression will be second only to heart disease as a source of illness and premature death in the world. Rising levels of divorce, family breakdown, burnout, stress, drinking and drug problems, domestic and other violence, accidents at work, absenteeism, diagnosed depression, mental illness, and suicide—all have been steadily rising to global epidemic proportions. We live in powerful times, and we are not coping well.

On top of this, some societies and nations are having to come to terms with the psychological impact of crushing natural disasters. The

Philippines has been struck by a category 5 typhoon—killing over ten thousand. Cities from New York to Tokyo continue their cleanup from natural disasters that cost billions in damages years earlier. And the rise in more conventional violence shows no let up. At the time of writing, nearly eighty thousand people have been killed in violence among drug cartels in Mexico between 2006 and 2014. Syria has experienced over one hundred thousand casualties in less than three years of its civil war. Countries from Sudan to Egypt continue their descent into darkness. How can we maintain composure in this sea of troubles?

At a human level, we effectively face a choice between awareness and growth or denial and decline. Denial and decline occur when we stop learning—when we respond to new challenges with the same old routines. When our certainties are threatened, we have a natural tendency to invest in them even more heavily. In organizations, this shows up as micromanaging systems of accountability in order to regain control: stricter discipline and closer oversight, more metrics, harder work. But in example after example, we see the results of this turning of the screw simply leading to increased pressure on organizations and individuals.

We must be able to rise above this instinctive, neurotic defense. Ian Mitroff's leading edge work on crisis management in organizations confirms that lesson: "You can and will survive—even prosper—but if, and only if, you are prepared emotionally, physically, intellectually, and spiritually." Mitroff's "seven essential lessons for surviving disaster" apply equally to individuals, corporations, maybe even societies. The first is "right heart"—emotional resilience. Another is "right soul"—"effective crisis management requires a special type of inner spiritual growth. Nothing devastates the soul as much as a crisis." These are lessons derived from over twenty-five years of experience. They point to the fact that even complex organizations can do "inner work" to build their capacity and resilience.

David Bolton established the Centre for Trauma and Transformation in Omagh, Northern Ireland, after a bomb devastated that community in 1998. The center worked for a decade in disaster zones around the world, from New York after 9/11 to earthquake relief in Nepal, and all points in between. The center always leads with the same simple, practical message to launch the rescue and recovery operation. It comes in two parts. The first is that, whatever the circumstances, we will recover: we all have the untold and usually untapped inner resource to manage this. The second is that the best way to find these resources in ourselves, to survive and recover from crisis, is to help somebody else do the same.[3]

Lesson 4: Hope

And finally comes the poet. So wrote Walter Brueggemann, the Old Testament scholar, about what he called "the prophetic imagination." His contribution to the survival debate is less about technical skills and more about inspiration and leadership. But without these, there is no point in surviving.

The role of the prophet is threefold. To warn about the dangers and iniquities of the existing system. To paint a desirable vision of the promised land. And to maintain energy and commitment in the people during the forty years in the wilderness it will take to make the transition.

This is the role of imagination, and of hope.

When business-as-usual systems and practices begin to fail, the task is to innovate. Managers must keep the present system running while the innovators get to work fashioning offerings better suited to the times. Clayton Christensen identifies the moment when the new offerings become more successful than the legacy product as a "disruption."

What Brueggemann adds to this model is a third horizon. The first horizon is failing. The second is innovating. But if there is no vision of a desirable third to which an innovation is heading, change is merely opportunistic.

The third horizon makes a distinction between "innovation" that props up the old system and innovation that paves the way to a new, sustainable system fit for changed times. Without a vision of a third horizon pulling us forward, there can be no such distinction, and all innovation will inevitably draw us backward toward an improved version of the past.

The philosopher Jonathan Lear, in his book *Radical Hope—Ethics in the Face of Cultural Devastation,* tells the story of Plenty Coups, chief of the Crow Indians at the end of the nineteenth century. His tribe was coming under pressure from white people to give up their way of life and enter the reservation. It was a moment of cultural crisis. The bottom had dropped out of the Crow Indian world.

Plenty Coups described the transition many years later: "when the buffalo went away the hearts of my people fell to the ground, and they could not lift them up again." As one Crow woman said, "I am trying to live a life I do not understand."

Some tribes gave in to despair and accepted white people's superiority—throwing in their lot with "business as usual." Resistance was futile. Some—like Sitting Bull and the Sioux—chose violence. They went down fighting—to the bitter end, as it turned out. Their vision of the third horizon was psychotic and destructive rather than aspirational. Neither was successful in negotiating a cultural transition.

But Plenty Coups had a dream that, although the buffalo would vanish, the Crow—provided they kept attuned to changing conditions—would come through to find a new way of living. Lear calls this "radical hope"—the hope for cultural rebirth, but without any predetermined vision of what that rebirth will look like. In the event, Crow youth learned the white people's law, negotiated favorable settlements, maintained far more of their land than any other tribe, and came to reinvent notions of honor and courage in a world without warriors.

Lear writes, "There may be various forms of ethical criticism that one might be tempted to level at this form of hopefulness: that it was too complacent; that it didn't face up to the evil that was being inflicted on the Crow tribe. But it is beyond question that the hope was a remarkable human accomplishment—in no small part because it avoided despair."

I regard this as a story for our times. As the skies turn dark and the "imminent collapse of civilization" literature grows, we too are in need of inspiration if we are to avoid the predictable future. How might we navigate our way through the present crisis "toward the hope of a better day"? Put simply, we need to find among us individuals and organizations willing to connect their actions today to a vision that is more than a patched-up version of the past. These will be the pioneers.

Where innovators and entrepreneurs are opportunistic, pioneers are visionary. They display all the characteristics I speak of in these pages. They are not waiting to be rescued. They are aware of the larger, shifting context for their actions. They are not afraid of big thoughts and wide ambition. They have strong values that feed their capacity to persevere through good times and bad. They provide inspiration to others. They are the individuals who turn radical hope into reality.

We all have this capacity within us. It is no more than the stuff of life. Václav Havel, in his inspirational essay *The Power of the Powerless* (1978), calls it "living in truth." He boldly predicted at the time of its writing—shortly before he himself was imprisoned—that the accumulation of actions in that spirit would eventually bring down the totalitarian regime in Czechoslovakia. He was proved right. But he was not calling for acts of great leadership or superhuman courage. "Living in truth covers a vast territory whose outer limits are vague and difficult to map," he wrote, "a territory full of modest expressions of human volition, the vast majority of which will remain anonymous." In the end, he asked of himself and others only something very simple: "Most of these expressions remain elementary revolts against manipulation: you simply straighten your backbone and live in greater dignity as an individual."

This may seem an embarrassingly simple response to the depth of challenge outlined elsewhere in this collection. But the fact is that if we are to fashion any viable alternative in dark times to "taking to the lifeboats captained by warlord entrepreneurs" then we must start—each of us, personally—from a strong sense of what it is we wish to save. Havel, like Heaney, encourages us not only to recognize but also to enact the marvelous, even in the presence of overwhelming oppression. They both speak from experience. If we cannot live in truth, they challenge us, even at the most modest of levels, are we really "living" at all? It was Havel's conviction that seeing this capacity in others would appeal to the same suppressed instinct in his oppressors—and that eventually a system that denied it would collapse. He was right.

It is vital then that we find this capacity in ourselves and support it in each other if we are to thrive amid the worst of what may yet lie ahead.[4] This is, and has always been, the true source of radical hope.

Epilogue

Into the Future

Daniel S. Gressang

The future is now. Technological innovation—not just in today's digital age, but since the harnessing of steam—has reshaped society and governance in subtle and profound ways. As technology has advanced, it has both rapidly expanded the reach of government and dramatically increased the rapidity of that transformation. The telecommunications and computer revolutions have had the greatest impact, it would seem, in increasing, yet again, the reach of both government and the people, allowing rapid interaction across vast distances.

The contributors to this volume paint a picture that is both disturbing and hopeful. On the one hand, the emergence of warlord entrepreneurs and their ability to enter, control, and in some instances, dominate segments of society casts serious doubt on the future of government and its ability to function effectively. The governance space is becoming more contentious, with myriad claimants to authority and legitimacy challenging the prerogative of the state. Organized criminal enterprises, narcotics traffickers, warlords, and other non-state actors lay claim to neighborhoods, slums, favelas, and largely ungoverned spaces seldom touched by state authority, creating a parallel structure for control and social interaction. Yet that is not a new phenomenon, as we sometimes like to think it is. The Westphalian state has always faced challenges to its authority in both urban and rural backwaters.

And on that front, the authors here also offer hope in suggesting concrete, actionable ways forward, charting a path by which state legitimacy and authority can be extended to those areas where it has yet to fully assert its rights or where it has abdicated its responsibilities. Changing attitudes and patterns of consumption—while simultaneously doing better at managing expectations—offers opportunities to reshape social interactions and the relationship between government and the governed in such a way as to bring the benefit of globalization to a greater percentage of the world's people. But, as the authors acknowledge, the choices that must be made and the behaviors that must be modified will present significant challenges far into the future.

One of the questions raised in this volume is one of the more fundamental issues we must address before any path forward can be identified: where are we? Does the Westphalian state represent the epitome of social and political development, such that the emergence and activities of warlord entrepreneurs represent a devolution of structure and process? If so, then the very existence of warlord entrepreneurs represents a serious threat to all nation-states, demanding determined effort to boost the actual and perceived legitimacy of government, to suppress the activities and curtail the spread of warlord entrepreneurs, and to strengthen and redefine the relationships within the governance space. Or, on the other hand, are we not at the pinnacle of social and political development? Is the Westphalian state instead a local maxima, a developmental mountaintop, to use a common complexity metaphor, with the "devolution" represented by the rise of warlord entrepreneurs perhaps little more than the necessary transition through a valley before we can climb to the next, higher mountaintop? If this accurately describes the evolutionary path we see, we may want to think more in terms of managing the transition process effectively and asking instead how we can leverage change to ultimately achieve greater good.

At the same time, the essays in this volume raise equally fundamental questions about our understanding of the Westphalian state. In considering the wisdom and insights offered in each chapter, we are left with a degree of uncertainty about the fundamental soundness of the state construct, particularly in terms of incomplete and uneven globalization. While many scholars have championed the Westphalian state model, it could also be argued that warlord entrepreneurs have found opportunities to emerge and, in some places, flourish, because they fill a need. If that need exists, it suggests the state is unwilling or unable to meet the needs of some segment of the population. Which should, in turn, prompt questions about whether the state construct is flawed or whether our efforts to apply that construct are flawed. Regardless of the answer, the question itself should point us to an area ripe for additional inquiry.

If the future is now, what does the farther future look like? We can envision at least three possible futures based on the essays here, each of which offers opportunities and dangers in the years to come. In the first, suggested by complexity literature, we appear to be in a transition period. The question we have yet to answer, however, is whether we are witnessing the transition to a Hobbesian future or a more equitable future, as suggested by visions of more complete and effective globalization. Are we, to use the terrain metaphor favored by some, heading down the mountain only to stay mired in the valley below, or will our trip through the valley be little more than the necessary path to greater heights on the next mountaintop? In the first, we could envision a future that is nasty, brutish, and short, with ineffective, incomplete, and uneven globalization creating and empowering more—and more assertive—warlord entrepreneurs who may, though their ruthless disregard for society's rules, challenge and perhaps even replace government? Such a future dominated by warlord entrepreneurs would be rife with uncertainty, leaving us to wonder if the exercise of authority where government fails would be more akin to feudalism or whether it would be some form of heretofore unimagined benevolent sharing between non-state and state actors. In the latter, the emergence and activities of warlord entrepreneurs, while unwanted, could be a temporary phenomenon, soon to fade into the mists of history as society and government create a new model that more fully embraces the benefits of globalization. In this future, our study of warlord entrepreneurs may well be an interesting, but ultimately fleeting, arena for study.

A second possible future sees the continuance of today, a form of stasis, where little ultimately changes from what we have seen for at least several centuries. Here, we would acknowledge the fallibility and limits of both government and globalization, recognizing that the construct will remain imperfect and that that opportunities for warlord entrepreneurs will remain. In this future, the identities, locations, and relative strengths of the warlord entrepreneurs may ebb and flow, but government's reach will not be pervasive or compelling enough to eliminate the ungoverned backwaters. Warlord entrepreneurs will remain, at the global level, irritants to society and government, to be dealt with on a case-by-case basis. Realistic challenges to government supremacy—and to the Westphalian state construct itself—will be rare, yet demanding of a not insignificant application of scarce resources.

A third possible future is a hybrid future, where the roles and responsibilities of the state are ceded to some degree to the warlord entrepreneur. Here, states come to recognize their own inability to meet expectations of one or more segments of the population, and they come to see the non-state actor as better suited and better positioned to provide specified, perhaps local and limited, goods and services, freeing government to focus on a separate and broader set of public goods. This future could offer a symbiotic relationship between warlord entrepreneurs and government designed to ease government's burden in light of dwindling resources and growing demands placed upon it. The application of a hybrid form may be limited spatially or by specified service, and the non-state entities filling the breach may transition from charity to association to criminal enterprise and back. That future is not so hard to imagine in light of the examples we see operating today.

At present, the likelihood of each of the three possible futures seems about equal, with none enjoying a compelling advantage over the others. The actions of governments, as well as of the people and the warlord entrepreneurs themselves, will shape the future in unforeseen ways. Given the uncertainty of both the near and distant futures, the challenges to the state, and the growing awareness of warlord entrepreneurs, we should ask additional questions about the direction in which globalization—with its uneven application—may be taking us. How is the future unfolding, and are there signposts we might discern that can tell us where we're heading? And if that direction is not to our liking, how might we affect desired change? We need additional research and critical thought to determine whether we can, indeed, understand the path we are on; what impact our decisions, both major and minor, will have on our developmental trajectory; and what might be the viability of our efforts to affect change.

Our perceptions of the present and expectations of the future color our analysis. A significant proportion of the literature on both globalization and warlord entrepreneurs seems to hold the Westphalian state as not simply the epitome of social and political development, but the ultimate desired end state. While there is nothing wrong with such a perspective, we must recognize that it defines the way in which we understand the state and warlord entrepreneurs, casting one automatically in a more favorable light than the other, to be protected and strengthened. It also defines for us, in a very real sense, the nature and scope of the problem. Warlord entrepreneurs are interlopers on government authority at best, devious and ruthless adversaries that must be eliminated at worst. The vision of warlord entrepreneurs, in turn, guides us to a predefined way of thinking about the problem itself and its possible solutions. Yet that thinking also predisposes us to see warlord entrepreneurs as a solvable problem, if only we can identify the appropriate countermeasures—whether it entails more effective globalization, extending the reach and boosting the legitimacy of government, transitioning to a more eco-friendly set of consumption behaviors, or any one of myriad other avenues for action. We may, however, serve ourselves and our efforts well by taking a step or two back and asking if, in light of growing expectations and demands for "more," we might be looking not at a solvable or tame problem, but at a wicked problem that will defy both effective definition and solution.

One can easily interpret warlord entrepreneurs as a wicked problem. The problem is difficult to define in clear, unambiguous terms. Would Hamas or Hezbollah, both of which are providers of essential government services to specific segments of their respective populations, be on par with Mexican narcotics distribution networks and Afghan warlords? The boundaries of the warlord entrepreneur problem are vague, at best, leading to multiple interpretations of the problem that prevent us from making a compelling case about who qualifies for consideration and who doesn't. Likewise, there are no definitive solutions to the problem of warlord entrepreneurs, as any solution brought to bear offers only a single attempt, unique in time and space, offering no opportunity to learn best practices by trial and error. What may work in Mexico is unlikely to be effective in Afghanistan or the Gaza Strip. Each warlord entrepreneur is as unique as the environment in which he works, suggesting that we cannot even enumerate all possible solutions. And were we to stumble upon an effective solution to the problem in one instance, that solution could be expected to disenfranchise, displace, disempower, or deflate expectations of others, giving rise to new opportunities for the emergence of new nonstate claimants to authority and control.

If the warlord entrepreneur problem is a wicked problem, do we simply accept it as a new norm and move on to other areas of inquiry? That would certainly be the easy way out of our dilemma, but hardly satisfying and definitely not worthy of us and our society. There are questions and avenues to explore, solutions to be sought, for if we have anything to offer, we are certain to touch lives and help improve the human condition. Maybe the state will be strengthened and warlord entrepreneurs significantly weakened as we move forward in exploring the problem. Maybe the warlord entrepreneurs will prove more adaptive and resilient than we might imagine. And maybe additional digging into the topic will lead to our uncovering more problems and more issues to confront in the near and far futures rather than leading us to useful insights, offering probative understanding, and allowing for the design of effective countermeasures and solutions. Maybe. But the potential remains for generating insights that can help society and political structures evolve in a beneficial way, allowing insights generated to be leveraged for the greater good. For this reason alone, the essays in this book offer a starting point for digging deeper into the dynamics of governance and warlord entrepreneurialism and for asking the questions that still need to be asked.

Notes

Foreword

1   Forrest D. Colburn, *Post-Revolutionary Nicaragua: State, Class, and the Dilemmas of Agrarian Policy* (Berkeley: University of California Press, 1987), 120.
2   William Gibson, *Burning Chrome* (New York: Ace Books, 1987), 116.
3   Charles Tilly, et al, "War Making and State Making as Organized Crime," *Bringing the State Back In*, edited by Peter B. Evans, Dietrich Rueschemeyer, and Theda Skocpol, 169–91 (Cambridge: Cambridge University Press, 1985).
4   Martin van Creveld, *The Transformation of War* (New York: Free Press, 1991), 197.

Introduction

1   "Cali Cartel Fronts International Network", Department of the Treasury Office of Foreign Assets Control, http://www.treasury.gov/press-center/press-releases /Documents/js9152.pdf, (2003).
2   Paul Kaihla, "The Technology Secrets of Cocaine Inc.," *Business 2.0*, (2002).
3   Elaine Shannon, "The Cali Cartel: New Kings of Coke," *Time*, (1991).
4   Adriaan Alsema, "Cali Crime Statistics," http://colombiareports.co/cali -crime-statistics/ (2013).

Chapter 2. Social and Economic Collapse

1   Joseph A. Tainter, *The Collapse of Complex Societies* (Cambridge: Cambridge University Press, 1988); Norman Yoffee and George Cowgill, eds., *The Collapse of Ancient States and Civilizations* (Tucson: U of Arizona, 1988).
2   Martin J. Rees, *Our Final Century: Will the Human Race Survive the Twenty-first Century?* (London: William Heinemann Ltd., 2003); James Martin, *The Meaning of the 21st Century: A Vital Blueprint for Ensuring Our Future* (New York: Riverhead Books, 2006); Vaclav Smil, *Global Catastrophes and Trends: The Next Fifty Years* (Cambridge, MA: MIT Press, 2008); Chris Patten, *What Next? Surviving the Twenty-First Century* (London: Allen Lane, 2008).
3   See, for example, Thomas Homer-Dixon, *The Upside of Down: Catastrophe, Creativity, and the Renewal of Civilization*, (Washington: Island Press, 2006).
4   This is not to propose, however, an abandonment of scholarly work focused on the negative impact of the absence of a monopoly over violence.

Chapter 3. Innovation, Deviation, and Development

1   For further reading on global guerillas, see John Robb, *Brave New War* (Hoboken, NJ: Wiley and Sons, 2008).

Chapter 4. Sovereignty, Criminal Insurgency, and Drug Cartels

1   According to Gary King and Langche Zeng, "Improving Forecasts of State Failure," *World Politics*, 53, (July 2001): 623-658.

2   Jack A. Goldstone, Goldstone, Robert H. Bates, David L. Epstein, Ted Robert Gurr, Michael B. Lustik, Monty G. Marshall, Jay Ulfelder, and Mark Woodward, "A Global Model for Forecasting Political Instability," *American Journal of Political Science*, Vol. 54, No. 1, (2010): 190–208.

3   United Nations Office on Drugs and Crime (UNODC), "Threat of Narco-Trafficking in the Americas," (October 2008).

4   United Nations Office on Drugs and Crime (UNODC), "The Globalization Of Crime: A Transnational Organized Crime Threat Assessment," June 2010.

5   UNDOC, (2008): 1.

6   Manuel Castells, *The Information Age: Economy, Society, and Culture: The Rise of the Network Society (Volume I)*, (West Sussex, UK: Wiley-Blackwell, 2010); *The Power of Identity (Vol. II)*, (Blackwell: Malden, MA, 2004); and *The End of Millennium (Vol. III)*, (Blackwell, Malden, MA, 2008).

7   John Arquila and David Ronfeldt, *Networks and Netwars: The Future of Terror, Crime, and Militancy*, (Santa Monica: RAND, 2001).

8   John P. Sullivan, "Criminal Netwarriors in Mexico's Drug Wars," GroupIntel, 22 (December 2008), at http://www.groupintel.com/2008/12/22/criminal-netwarriors-in-mexico's-drug-wars/.

9   Martin van Creveld, *The Rise and Decline of the State*, (Cambridge: Cambridge University Press, 2009).

10   Manuel Castells, *The Information Age: Economy, Society, and Culture: The Rise of the Network Society (Volume I)*, (West Sussex, UK: Wiley-Blackwell, 2010); *The Power of Identity (Vol. II)*, (Blackwell: Malden, MA, 2004); and *The End of Millennium (Vol. III)*, Blackwell, Malden, MA, 2008); Manuel Castells, *Communication Power*, (Oxford: Oxford University Press, 2009); and Martin Carnoy and Manuel Castells, "Globalization, the knowledge society, and the Network State: Poulantzas at the millennium," Global Networks, 1,1, (2001).

11   Philip Bobbitt, *The Shield of Achilles: War, Peace and the Course of History*, (New York: Knopf, 2002) and Philip Bobbitt, *Terror and Consent: The Wars for the Twenty-First Century*, (New York: Knopf, 2008).

12   Vanda Felbab-Brown, *Shooting Up: Counterinsurgency and the War on Drugs*, (Washington, DC: Brookings Institution Press, 2009) and Vanda Felbab-Brown, "Conceptualizing Crime as Competition in State-Making and Designing an Effective Response," (Speech at Conference on Illicit Trafficking Activities in the Western Hemisphere: Possible Strategies and Lessons Learned, Brookings Institution, 21 May 2010), http://

www.brookings.edu/speeches/2010/0521_illegal_economies_felbab
brown.aspx.

13   Saskia Sassen, *The Global City*, (Princeton: Princeton University Press, 2001); Saskia
      Sassen, *Territory, Authority, Rights: From Medieval to Global Assemblages*, (Princeton:
      Princeton University Press, 2006); and Saskia Sassen, "Neither Global nor National:
      Novel Assemblages of Territory, Authority and Rights," *Ethics & Global Politics*, Vol,
      1, No. 1–2, 2008, p. 61.

14   Robert J. Bunker, (Ed.), *Networks, Terrorism, and Global Insurgency*, (London & New
      York: Routledge, 2005) and Robert J. Bunker, (Ed.), *Criminal States and Criminal
      Soldiers*, (London & New York: Routledge, 2008).

15   Richard J. Norton, "Feral Cities—The New Strategic Environment," *Naval War
      College Review*, Vol. LVI, No. 4, (2003).

16   Ivan Briscoe, "Trouble on the Borders: Latin America's New Conflict Zones,"
      (Madrid: FRIDE, July 2008).

17   Max G. Manwaring, *A Contemporary Challenge to State Sovereignty: Gangs and Other
      Illicit Transnational Criminal Organizations (TCOs) in Central America*, (El Salvador,
      Mexico, Jamaica, and Brazil, Carlisle Barracks: Strategic Studies Institute, January
      2008) and Max G. Manwarning, *A "New" Dynamic in the Western Hemisphere Security
      Environment: The Mexican Zetas and Other Private Armies*, (Carlisle Barracks: Strategic
      Studies Institute, September 2009).

18   Eric Hobsbawn, *Bandits*, (New York: The New Press, 2000).

19   Phil Williams, *From the New Middle Ages to a New Dark Age: The Decline of the State and
      U.S. Strategy*, (Carlisle Barracks, Strategic Studies Institute, June 2008) and Gregory
      O'Hayon-Baudin, "Big Men, Godfathers and Zealots: Challenges to the States in the
      New Middle Ages," (Doctoral Dissertation, University of Pittsburgh, May 2003).

20   See John Agnew, *Globalization & Sovereignty*, (Lanham, MD: Rowman & Littlefield,
      2009) and Macur Olson, *Power and Prosperity: Outgrowing Communist and Capitalist
      Dictatorships*, (New York: Basic Books, 2000).

21   UNDOC, 2010.

22   John P. Sullivan, "Criminal Insurgencies in the Americas," *Small Wars Journal*, 13
      (February 2010).

23   UNDOC, 2010.

24   John P. Sullivan, "Cartel Info Ops: Power and Counter Power in Mexico's drug
      War," *MountainRunner*, (15 November 2010) at http://mountainrunner.us/2010/11
      /cartel_info_ops_power_and_counterpower_in_Mexico_drug_war.html.

25   John P. Sullivan and Keith Weston, "Afterward: Law Enforcement Responses
      for Criminal-states and Criminal-soldiers," *Global Crime*, Vol. 7, No. 3–4. (April-
      November 2006), 615-628.

26   John P. Sullivan and Carlos Rosales, "Ciudad Juárez and Mexico's 'narco-culture'
      Threat," *Mexidata*, (28 February 2011) at http://mexidata.info/id2952.html.

27   John P. Sullivan, "Terrorism, Crime, and Private Armies," *Low Intensity Conflict
      & Law Enforcement*, Vol. 11, No. 2/3, (Winter 2002), 259-253.

28   John P. Sullivan, "Post-Modern Social Banditry: Criminal Violence or Criminal

Insurgency?" (Paper presented to Drug Trafficking, Violence and Instability in Mexico, Colombia, and the Caribbean: Implications for US National Security, University of Pittsburgh and Strategic Studies Institute, US Army War College, Pittsburgh, PA, 29 October 2009) and John P. Sullivan and Adam Elkus, "Cartel v. Cartel: Mexico's Criminal Insurgency," *Small Wars Journal*, (February 2010).

29   World Bank, "Governance Matters 2009: Worldwide Governance Indicators, 1996–2008" at http://info.worldbank.org/governance/wgi/index.asp.

Chapter 5. From Patronage Politics to Predatory States

1   U.S. District Court of California, *United States v. One Michael Jackson Signed Thriller Jacket and Other Michael Jackson Memorabilia; Real Property Located on Sweetwater Mesa Road in Malibu, California; One 2011 Ferrari 599 GTO, Case No. CV 13-9169-GW-SS*, October 10, 2014, www.justice.gov/sites/default/files/press-releases/attachments/2014/10/10/obiang_settlement_agreement.pdf.

2   Maïa de la Baume, "A French Shift on Africa Strips a Dictator's Son of His Treasures," *New York Times*, August 23, 2012, www.nytimes.com/2012/08/24/world/europe/for-obiangs-son-high-life-in-paris-is-over.html.

3   UNDP Human Development Report 2014: Equatorial Guinea, http://hdr.undp.org/sites/all/themes/hdr_theme/country-notes/GNQ.pdf.

4   Stanislav Andreski, *The African Predicament: A Study in the Pathology of Modernisation*, (London: Michael Joseph, 1968).

5   De la Baume, "A French Shift on Africa Strips a Dictator's Son of His Treasures."

6   Axel Dreher, Andreas Fuchs, Roland Hodler, Bradley C. Parks, Paul A. Raschky, and Michael J. Tierney, "Aid on Demand: African Leaders and the Geography of China's Foreign Assistance," Working Paper 3, *AidData*, November 2014, http://aiddata.org/sites/default/files/wps3_aid_on_demand_african_leaders_and_the_geography_of_chinas_foreign_assistance.pdf.

7   Bruce J. Berman, "Ethnicity, Patronage and the African State: The Politics of Uncivil Nationalism," *African Affairs* 97, no. 388 (1998): 305–41.

8   Jeffrey Herbst, *States and Power in Africa: Comparative Lessons in Authority and Control Princeton*, (NJ: Princeton University Press, 2000).

9   M. Utas, "Introduction: Bigmanity and Network Governance in African Conflicts," introduction to *African Conflicts and Informal Power: Big Men and Networks*, ed. M. Utas (London: Zed Books, 2012), 1–31.

10   H. Vigh, "Critical States and Cocaine Connections," in *African Conflicts and Informal Power: Big Men and Networks*, ed. Mats Utas (London: Zed Books, 2012), 145.

11   K. Annan, "The Causes of Conflict and the Promotion of Durable Peace and Sustainable Development in Africa," United Nations General Assembly Security Council, April 13, 1988, S/1998/318, 4, www.securitycouncilreport.org/atf/cf/%7B65BFCF9B-6D27-4E9C-8CD3-CF6E4FF96FF9%7D/CPR%20A%2052%20871.pdf.

12   Leonardo R. Arriola, "Patronage and Political Stability in Africa," *Journal of Comparative Political Studies* 42, no. 10 (2009): 1339–62.

13   World Bank, "Vulnerability to Violence," in *World Development Report 2011: Conflict,*

Security and Development, 74–89. http://web.worldbank.org/archive/website01306 /web/fulltext.html.

14   International Crisis Group, *Mali: Avoiding Escalation*, Africa report no. 189, July 18, 2012, www.crisisgroup.org/~/media/Files/africa/west-africa/mali/189-mali -avoiding-escalation-english.pdf

15   International Crisis Group, *Mali: Reform or Relapse*, Africa report no. 210, January 10, 2014, 1, www.crisisgroup.org/~/media/Files/africa/west-africa/mali/210-mali -reform-or-relapse-english.pdf.

16   Bridges from Bamako, "IBK One Year On: A Voter's Remorse," September 5, 2014, http://bridgesfrombamako.com/2014/09/05/ibk-one-year-on-a-voters-remorse.

17   Diarra Soumali, "Mali Government Pressured to Make Arrests in Bribery Scandal," *Reuters*, November 7, 2014, http://allafrica.com/stories/201411071845.html.

18   IRIN News, "Nearly 25 Million Food Insecure in the Sahel," October 29, 2014, www.irinnews.org/report/100769/nearly-25-million-food-insecure-in-sahel.

19   Martin Meredith, *The State of Africa: A History of the Continent since Independence* (London: Simon and Schuster, 2011), 374–76.

20   Akpan Hepko, "Economic Development under Structural Adjustment: Evidence from Selected West African Countries," *Journal of Social Development in Africa* 7, no. 1 (1992), 25–43.

21   *Global Witness, Time for Transparency: Coming Clean on Mining, Oil and Gas Revenues*, March 2004 www.globalwitness.org/sites/default/files/pdfs/oil_061.04.04.pdf.

22   *Economist*, "China Investment Fund: The Queensway Syndicate and the African Trade," August 13, 2011, www.economist.com/node/21525847.

23   S. Ibi Ajayi and Leonce Ndikumana, *Capital Flight from Africa* (Oxford: Oxford University Press, 2015).

24   Africa Progress Panel, *Equity in Extractives: Stewarding Africa's Natural Resources for All*, Africa Progress Panel Report 2013, www.africaprogresspanel.org/publications /policy-papers/africa-progress-report-2013.

25   James S. Henry, *The Price of Offshore Revisited: New Estimates for Missing Global Private Wealth, Income, Inequality and Lost Taxes*, Tax Justice Network, July 2012, www.taxjustice.net/cms/upload/pdf/Price_of_Offshore_Revisited_120722.pdf.

26   Mark Shaw and Tuesday Reitano, "Cocaine Politics in Guinea Bissau: The Link be- tween Drug Trafficking and Political Fragility and Its Wider Implications," *Columbia Journal of International Affairs* (January 25, 2013), http://jia.sipa.columbia.edu /cocaine-politics-in-guinea-bissau.

27   "Mauritania Police Chief Jailed over Cocaine Ring," *BBC News*, February 12, 2010, http://news.bbc.co.uk/2/hi/africa/8512195.stm.

28   "Jackie Selebi: South Africa's 'Corrupt' Police Chief," *BBC News*, July 2, 2010, www.bbc.co.uk/news/10489457.

29   Rukmini Callimachi, R., "Paying Ransoms, Europe Bankrolls Qaeda Terror," *New York Times*, July 29, 2014, www.nytimes.com/2014/07/30/world/africa/ransoming -citizens-europe-becomes-al-qaedas-patron.html.

30   Mark Shaw and Fiona Mangan, *Illicit Trafficking and Libya's Transition: Profits and Losses* (Washington, DC: U.S. Institute of Peace, February 2014).

31   I. Briscoe, *Crime after Jihad: Armed Groups, the State and Illicit Business in Post-Conflict Mali* (The Hague, Netherlands: Clingendael Institute, May 2014), 29.

32   West Africa Commission on Drugs, *Not Just in Transit: Drugs, the State and Society in West Africa*, June 2014, 20–22.

33   Peter Gastrow, *Termites at Work: Transnational Organized Crime and State Erosion in Kenya* (New York: International Peace Institute, 2011), http://reliefweb.int/sites /reliefweb.int/files/resources/Full_Report_2562.pdf.

34   Moisés Naím, "Mafia States: Organized Crime Takes Office," *Foreign Affairs*, May/ June 2012, www.foreignaffairs.com/articles/137529/moises-naim/mafia-states.

35   Aimee-Noel Mbiyozo and Tuesday Reitano, *Unholy Alliances: Organized Crime in Southern Africa*, report of an expert seminar hosted by the Global Initiative against Transnational Organized Crime and the Rosa Luxemburg Foundation in Cape Town in April 2014, www.globalinitiative.net/unholy-alliances-organized-crime-in -southern-africa.

36   Jakkie Cilliers, "Africa, Root Causes and the 'War on Terror,' " *African Security Review* 15 no. 3 (2010): 57–71.

37   World Bank, "The Interlinked and Evolving Nature of Modern Organized Violence," in *World Development Report 2011: Conflict, Security and Development*, 67–68, http://web.worldbank.org/archive/website01306/web/fulltext.html.

38   United Nations Security Council, " 'Arc of Instability' across Africa, If Left Unchecked, Could Turn Continent into Launch Pad for Larger-Scale Terrorist Attacks, Security Council Told," May 13, 2013, www.un.org/News/Press/docs /2013/sc11004.doc.htm.

39   Abdelkader Abderrahmane, "The Sahel: A Crossroads between Criminality and Terrorism," *Institute Français de Relations Internationales*, October 10, 2012, www.ifri.org/fr/publications/editoriaux/actualite-mom/sahel-crossroads-between -criminality-and-terrorism.

40   Tuesday Reitano, "What Hope for Peace? Grief, Grievance and Protracted Conflict in Somalia," *Yale Journal for International Affairs*, April 2013, http://yalejournal.org /2013/04/02/what-hope-for-peace-greed-grievance-and-protracted-conflict-in -somalia.

41   C. S. Chivvis and A. Liepman, "North Africa's Menace: AQIM's Evolution and the U.S. Policy Response," *Rand Corporation*, 2013.

42   START (National Consortium for the Study of Terrorism and Responses to Terrorism), *Global Terrorism Database* (data file), www.start.umd.edu/gtd.

43   *Economist*, "Why America Refuses to Pay Ransoms," August 24, 2014, www.economist.com/blogs/economist-explains/2014/08/economist-explains-18.

44   World Bank, "Repeated Violence Threatens Development," in *World Development Report 2011: Conflict, Security and Development*, 52–66, http://web.worldbank.org /archive/website01306/web/fulltext.html.

Chapter 6. Warlord Governance

1 In terms of motivations, the explanations put forward take different forms, all of which—to a significant extent—are linked to the issue of legitimacy, both directly (raising social capital), as well as indirectly (deterring potential defections or "robbing the state of the legitimacy it derives through the social contract"). See Alexus G. Grynkewich, "Welfare as Warfare: How Violent Non-State Groups Use Social Services to Attack the State," *Studies in Conflict & Terrorism* 31, no. 4 (2008), 350–70.

2 Lindsay Heger and Danielle F. Jung, "Negotiating with Rebel Governments: The Effect of Service Provision on Conflict Negotiations," (paper presented at the Sié Research Seminar Series, Joseph Korbel School of International Studies, February 4, 2013).

3 This difference is clearest when we consider that warlords' longer-term status in the local community depends simultaneously on the extent of their military prowess and their social responsibility toward the community under their control—and less on hereditary prestige or strictly defined territory.

4 Both have currently enrolled in the 2014 race for presidential elections in Afghanistan—Ismail Khan for vice president on the ticket with the controversial Abdul Rasul Sayyaf, Dostum as a vice-presidential candidate on a ticket with Ashraf Ghani, the final winner of the elections. In what seems to shape as an electoral confrontation between (former?) warlords in 2014, other figures include Gul Agha Sherzai and Mohammad Mohaqiq. As the former UN special representative to Afghanistan between 2008 and 2010, Kai Eide explained, "the prominence of the old warlords on the candidates' list reflects the reality of Afghan society today." See Kai Eide, "Wooing the Warlords," *Foreign Policy*, (November 18, 2013), available online at http://afpak .foreignpolicy.com/posts/2013/11/18/wooing_the_warlords.

5 William Reno, *Warlord Politics and African States* (Boulder, CO: Lynne Rienner, 1998), 94.

6 Antonio Giustozzi, "Respectable Warlords? The Politics Of State-Building in Post-Taleban Afghanistan," Crisis State Research Center working paper 33, (London: LSE Crisis States Programme, 2003), 3.

7 Francisco Gutiérrez Sanín and Mauricio Barón, "Re-Stating the State: Paramilitary Territorial Control and Political Order in Colombia (1978–2004)," Crisis State Research Center working paper 66 (London: LSE Crisis State Programme, 2005), 9.

8 For more details, rarely discussed, see Garry Leech, *The FARC: The Longest Insurgency* (London: Zed Books, 2011), especially chap. 3, "The FARC's Social Project," 38–55.

9 Sanín and Barón, "Re-Stating the State," 27.

10 Sanín and Barón, "Re-Stating the State," 26.

11 Kirill Nourzhanov, "Saviours of the Nation or Robber Barons? Warlord Politics in Tajikistan," *Central Asian Survey* 24, no. 2 (2005): 110.

12 William Reno, "Political Networks in a Failing State: The Roots and Future of Violent Conflict in Sierra Leone," *International Politics and Society* 2, no. 2 (2003): 61.

13 Conrad Schetter, "The 'Bazaar Economy' of Afghanistan. A Comprehensive Approach," *Südasien-Informationen* 3 (2004): 6, pointing to the the case of Nouristan and Hazarajat.

14   Giustozzi, "Respectable Warlords?" 2. As this chapter intends to show, while the most compelling evidence of the development of the warlord domain as a form of "political complex" are the insights, old and new, from the Chinese case of the 1920s and 1930s, contemporary cases—among which Afghanistan figures prominently—also contain elements that justify his remarks.

15   Olivier Roy defines the "group of solidarity" in terms of the feeling of "belonging to a local primary group, to which one is attached through birth and which determines an informal network of loyalties and solidarity … which can be itself hierarchically organized." While kinship affiliation plays a significant role in the definition of the solidarity group referred to in Afghanistan as qwam, it is not the only form of its manifestation. To the clan or tribal affiliations of the qwam, one might add ethnic or linguistic affiliations. For more details, see Olivier Roy, *Afghanistan: La Difficile Reconstruction d'un Etat*, Chaillot Papers 73 (Paris, Institute for Security Studies, 2004), 22.

16   Barnett Rubin, *The Fragmentation of Afghanistan: State Formation and Collapse in International System* (New Haven, CT: Yale University Press, 2002), 220.

17   Rubin, *The Fragmentation of Afghanistan*, 234–35.

18   Gordon Peake, "From Warlords to Peacelords?" *Journal of International Affairs* 56, no. 2, (2003): 188.

19   Brian Glyn Williams, *The Last Warlord: The Life and Legend of Dostum, the Afghan Warrior Who Led US Special Forces to Topple the Taliban Regime* (Chicago: Chicago Review Press, 2013) 167.

20   M. George, "Profile: Ismail Khan". *BBC News Online*: 2 December 2002.

21   Gulshan Dietl, "War, Peace and Warlords: The Case of Ismail Khan of Herat in Afghanistan." *Alternatives: Turkish Journal of International Relations* 3, no. 2–3 (2004), 48.

22   Peter Marsden, "Afghanistan: The Reconstruction Process," *International Affairs* 79, no. 1 (2003).

23   Roy, *Afghanistan: La Difficile Reconstruction d'un Etat*, 39.

24   Mark Duffield, quoted in Jonathan Goodhand, "From War Economy to Peace Economy? Reconstruction and State Building in Afghanistan," *Journal of International Affairs* 58, no. 1 (2004): 159.

25   Amin Saikal, *Modern Afghanistan: A History of Struggle and Survival* (London, I. B. Tauris & Co, 2004): 208.

26   Roy, *Afghanistan: La Difficile Reconstruction d'un Etat*, 24.

27   Paul B. Rich, ed., *Warlords in International Politics* (Basingstoke and London, Macmillan Press, 1999), xv.

28   Alfred H. Y Lin, "Building and Funding a Warlord Regime: The Experience of Chen Jitang in Guangdong, 1929–1936," *Modern China* 28, no. 2 (2002): 183.

29   Robert I. Rotberg, ed., *State Failure and State Weakness in a Time of Terror* (Washington, DC: Brookings Institution Press, 2003), 15 (my emphasis).

30   Nourzhanov, "Saviours of the Nation or Robber Barons?" 110.

31   Sanín and Barón, "Re-Stating the State," 25.

32   Reno, *Warlords Politics and African States*.

33   Olivier Roy, "Afghanistan: Internal Politics and Socio-Economic Dynamics and

Groupings," *Working Paper* No 14. Geneva, UNHCR Emergency and Security Services, (2003): 2.

34   Andreas Mehler, "Oligopolies of Violence in Africa South of the Sahara," *Nord-Süd Aktuell* 18, no. 3 (2004): 540–41.

35   Mehler, "Oligopolies of Violence in Africa South of the Sahara," 541.

36   I am using here the terminology of Joel Migdal as presented in his influential *Strong Societies and Weak States: State-Society Relations and State Capabilities in the Third World* (Princeton, NJ: Princeton University Press, 1988).

37   William Reno, *Warlords Politics and African States*, 97.

38   Schetter, "The 'Bazaar Economy' of Afghanistan," 12.

39   Georg Elwert, "Intervention in Markets of Violence," in *Potentials of Disorder, Explaining Conflict and Stability in the Caucasus and the Former Yugoslavia*, edited by Jan Koehler and Christophe Zurcher (Manchester, U.K.: Manchester University Press, 2003), 219.

Chapter 7. 5GW

1   William S. Lind, Colonel Keith Nightengale, Captain John F. Schmitt, Colonel Joseph W. Sutton, and Lieutenant Colonel Gary I. Wilson, "The Changing Face of War: Into the Fourth Generation," *Marine Corps Gazette*, (1989).

2   See Chet Richards, *If We Can Keep It: A National Security Manifesto for the Next Administration*, (Washington: Center for Defense Information, 2008).

3   Ibid.

4   Robert C. Tucker, *Stalin in Power: The Revolution from Above, 1928–1941*, (New York: W. W. Norton & Co Inc, 1990).

5   Simon Sebag Montefiore, *Stalin: The Court of the Red Tsar*, (London: Weidenfeld & Nicholson, 2003).

6   Ben Kiernan, *The Pol Pot Regime: Race, Power, and Genocide in Cambodia under the Khmer Rouge, 1975-79, Third Edition*, (New Haven: Yale University Press, 2008).

7   Ibid., 294.

8   Ibid., 271.

9   Samantha Power, *A Problem From Hell: America and the Age of Genocide*, (New York: New Republic Books, 2002).

10   Chris McGreal, "French Politicians Accused of Assisting Rwandan Genocide," *Guardian*, August 5, 2008, www.theguardian.com/world/2008/aug/06/rwanda.france.

11   Interviews: Philip Gourevitch, 2008.

12   Thomas P. Odom, *Journey into Darkness: Genocide in Rwanda*, (College Station: Texas A&M University Press, 2005).

Chapter 8. Weaponizing Capitalism

1   Mahendra Kumawat, "Naxal Movement Has Shown Tremendous Grit," *Rediff News*, April 9, 2010.

2   Waquar Ahmed, Amitabh Kundu, and Richard Peet, *India's New Economic Policy: A*

Critical Analysis (New York: Routledge, 2011).

3   Bibhudatta Pradhan and Santosh Kumar, "Pillai to End Maoist Grip on $80 Billion Investments," *Bloomberg Businessweek*, September 17, 2010.

4   Government of India, "Fact Sheet On Foreign Direct Investment (FDI)," *Ministry of Commerce and Industry*, February 11, 2011, http://dipp.nic.in/fdi_statistics/india _FDI_February2011.pdf.

5   Rahul Nilakantan and Saurabh Singhal, "The Economic Costs Of Naxalite Violence and the Economic Benefits of a Unique Robust Security Response," 2010. www.aae .wisc.edu/mwiedc/papers/2011/Singhal_Saurabh.pdf.

6   "Chhattisgarh's Entire Forest Area A Minefield?" *Times of India*, May 10, 2010.

7   Manoj Prasad, "Former Jharkhand CM Marandi on Their Hitlist, Naxals Kill Son, 17 More," *Indian Express*, October 28, 2007.

8   Press Trust of India, "Maoists Storm Jehanabad Jail," *Rediff News*, November 14, 2005.

9   Sudheer Pal Singh, "Illegal Mining May Impede Divestment in Coal India," *Business Standard*, August 21, 2010.

10   Government of India, "Loss of Coal Production in Naxalite Areas," *Press Information Bureau*, August 4, 2010, http://pib.nic.in/newsite/erelease.aspx?relid=64116.

11   "Chronology of Naxal Attacks on Trains," *India Today*, May 28, 2010.

12   Law Kumar Mishra, "Maoists Blow Up Track on Gaya-Dhanbad Section, Rail Traffic Disrupted," *Times of India*, September 13, 2010.

13   "Naxal Attacks Doubled in 2009, Rlys Lost Rs 500cr: Mamata," *Times of India*, April 23, 2010.

14   Manoj Prasad, "Naxal Attacks, Escalated Cost Derail Jharkhand Railway Projects," *India Express*, April 12, 2010.

15   Ishita Ayan Dutt, "Naxal Hits to Pull NMDC Net Down by Rs 1,000 cr," *Business Standard*, April 20, 2010.

16   "NMDC to Lay 12 mt Pipeline on Highways to Avoid Naxal Attacks," *The Financial Express*, July 20, 2010.

17   "Naxals Obstruct Road Works," *The Hindu*, May 9, 2011.

18   Dutt, "Naxal Hits to Pull NMDC Net Down by Rs 1,000 cr."

19   Sandeep Joshi, "550 More Mobile Towers to Boost Fight Against Naxalites," *The Hindu*, June 30, 2010.

20   Baba Umar, "A Mobile War against the Naxals," *Tehelka*, June 15, 2013, www.tehelka .com/a-mobile-war-against-the-naxals.

21   Manu Joseph, "India's Underground Economy", *The New York Times*, June 25, 2014: Venu, M.K. "Opinion: For Black Money, Look in India, Not Switzerland—NDTV." Profit.com. July 7, 2014. Accessed July 20, 2014. http://profit.ndtv.com/news/opinions /article-opinion-for-black-money-look-in-india-not-switzerland-584565.

22   "World Bank Approves $1.5 Billion for India's Rural Roads Scheme," *Press Trust of India*, December 22, 2010.

23   Prassana Mohanty, "Maoists' Financing—The Blood Flows as Long as the Cash Flows," *Governance Now*, April 7, 2010.

24   Sujeet Kumar, "Maoists Extort Rs 300 Crore Annually in Chhattisgarh," *The Economic Times*, July 5, 2009.

25   Bharti Jain, "Rs 150 Crore: Maoists Extortion Amount From Chhattisgarh SSIs," *The Economic Times*, April 10, 2010.

26   Ajit Kumar Singh and Sachin Bansidhar Diwan, "Red Money," *Outlook India*, April 5, 2010.

27   Ministry of Home Affairs, *2010–2011 Annual Report* (Delhi: Government of India, 2011).

28   Mohanty, "Maoists' Financing—The Blood Flows as Long as the Cash Flows."

29   Bhupendra Pandey, "Naxal Ranks Split Over Share in Extortion Spoils, Say Cops," *Indian Express*, December 13, 2009.

30   Shaikh Azizur Rahman, "India's Illegal Coal Mines Turn Into Death Pits," *The Washington Times*, November 24, 2006.

31   Prasoon Majumdar, "Our Own Banana Republics!" *Indian Institute of Planning and Management*, August 26, 2010, http://prasoonmajumdar.blogspot.com/2010/08/our-own-banana-republics.html.

32   United Nations Office on Drugs and Crime, "India is a Major Drug Hub: US," September, 2007, http://www.unodc.org/india/en/rajiv_quoted_et.html.

33   "Maoists extort up to Rs 2,000 crore across India" Rediff News, April 28, 2010. http://news.rediff.com/slide-show/2010/apr/28/slide-show-1-drugs-extortion-violence-fund-maoists-movement.html.

Chapter 10. The Politics of a Post-Climate-Change World

1   It is possible that relatively compact, well-established, high-functioning nation-states, or regional/metropolitan subunits of such, that have secure access to fresh water, that are remote from major refugee flows and powerful aggressors, and whose territory is mostly at considerable altitude or at 40 degrees or more above or below the equator (and not subject to inundation by rising sea levels) will survive for a long time, perhaps even long enough to weather the thousand-year storm—perhaps linked to, and protective of, surviving city states beyond their boundaries, perhaps even organized into one or more international federations capable of environmental cooperation and collective self-defense. But would such be fortresses of privileged survivalists, waiting out (and forcefully insulating themselves from) hundreds of years of horrific mass suffering and death in the rest of the world? Or might they (or some of them) devote themselves to doing everything possible to support the survival of wider humanity and parts of the natural world? Sad to say, the former seems more likely. As the classic American "wise man," George Kennan, famously wrote in his February 1948 secret memo to his fellow wise men, Secretary of State George Marshall and Under Secretary Dean Acheson: "Furthermore, we have about 50% of the world's wealth but only 6.3 of its population.... Our real task in the coming period is to ... maintain this position of disparity.... To do so we will have to dispense with all sentimentality and daydreaming;... We need not deceive ourselves that we can afford today the luxury of altruism and world benefaction.... We should dispense with the aspiration to 'be liked' or to be regarded as the repository of a high-minded international altruism. We should stop putting ourselves in the position of being our brothers' keeper and refrain

520025

222002

from offering moral and ideological advice. We should cease to talk about vague ... unreal objectives such as human rights, the raising of living standards, and democratization.... The less we are hampered by idealistic slogans the better." Department of State, Policy Planning Staff Memorandum No. 23, February 1948 (declassified June 17, 1974); quoted in Ross Jackson, *Occupy World Street: A Global Roadmap for Radical Economic and Political Reform* (White River Junction, VY: Chelsea Green, 2012), 125. It should be noted that this quotation is taken from the section of Kennan's memo devoted to the "Far East," and amounts to a "realist" refutation of the McCarthyite accusation that China was the United States's to "save" and the State Department had "lost" it. Nonetheless, Kennan's views warrant rebuke.

As Christian Parenti writes, "There is a real risk that strong states with developed economies will succumb to a politics of xenophobia, racism, police repression, surveillance, and militarism and thus transform themselves into fortress societies while the rest of the world slips into collapse. By that course, developed economies would turn into neofascist islands of relative stability in a sea of chaos. But a world in climatological collapse—marked by hunger, disease, criminality, fanaticism, and violent social breakdown—will overwhelm the armed lifeboat. Eventually all will sink into the same morass." *Tropic of Chaos: Climate Change and the New Geography of Violence* (New York: Nation Books, 2011), 20.

2   New data and analysis over the last three years has led many climate scientists to conclude that we are on the brink of definitively blowing by any possibility of limiting global warming to two degrees centigrade (above preindustrial levels) over the next twenty to thirty years, and are on track for at least three to four degrees by early in the second half of this century, if not sooner—and if we continue with business as usual for very much longer, we may well entrain six to eight degrees of warming by the end of the century. Andrew Jordon, Tim Rayner, Heike Schroeder, Neil Adger, Kevin Anderson, Alice Bows, Corinne Le Quéré, et al. "Going Beyond Two Degrees? The Risks and Opportunities of Alternative Options," *Climate Policy* 13, no. 6. (2013), 751–69, http://dx.doi.org/10.1080/14693062.2013.835705 and Camilo Mora, Abby G. Frazier, Ryan J. Longman, Rachel S. Dacks, Maya M. Walton, Eric J. Tong, Joseph J. Sanchez, et al., "The Projected Timing of Climate Departure from Recent Variability," *Nature* 502 (October 10, 2013), 183–87. Also see the following three articles, all in *Four Degrees and Beyond: The Potential for a Global Temperature Increase of Four Degrees and Its Implications*, edited by Mark New, a special issue of *Philosophical Transactions of the Royal Society A* 369 (2011): Kevin Anderson and Alice Bows, "Beyond 'Dangerous' Climate Change: Emission Scenarios for a New World"; Richard Betts, Matthew Collins, Deborah L. Hemming, Chris D. Jones, Jason A. Lowe, and Michael G. Sanderson, "When Could Global Warming Reach 4°C?" and Mark New, Diana Liverman, Heike Schroder, and Kevin Anderson, "Introduction: Four Degrees and Beyond: The Potential for a Global Temperature Increase of Four Degrees and Its Implications."

For general summaries, see International Energy Agency, "Redrawing the Energy-Climate Map" and PricewaterhouseCoopers LLP, "Too Late for Two Degrees?": "The PwC Low Carbon Economy Index evaluates the rate of decarbonization of the global economy that is needed to limit warming to 2°C.... The global economy now needs to cut carbon intensity by 5.1% every year from now to 2050 to achieve this carbon budget. This required rate of decarbonization has not been seen in a single year since the mid-20th century when these records began. Keeping to the 2°C budget will require unprecedented and sustained reductions over four decades. Governments' ambitions to limit warming to 2°C appear highly unrealistic" (3).

For terrifying discussion of the unexpected 2012–13 rapid increase in the level of methane release from defrosting Arctic and Siberian tundra, see Dahr Jamail, "Are We Falling Off the Climate Precipice?" TomDispatch.com, December 17, 2012, www.tomdispatch.com.blog/175785. For an earlier warning on this, see K. M. Walter, et al., "Methane Bubbling from Siberian Thaw Lakes as a Positive Feedback to Climate Warming," *Nature* 443 (September 7, 2006). For the most recent, most advanced computer simulations of interactions among multiple mutually exacerbating feedbacks, see David Wasdell, "Sensitivity, Non-Linearity and Self-Amplification in the Global Climate System," (Presentation to the Club of Rome, Ottawa, Canada, September 20, 2013). In any scenario approaching the foregoing level of warming, "average temperatures over much of the inland United States would be a scorching 20°F hotter. Soil moisture would drop 50 percent or more over much of the country. Prolonged drought would ravage much of our cropland, turning breadbaskets into dust bowls. Sea-level rise of 80 feet or more would be inevitable. We would exceed global temperatures before the Antarctic ice sheet formed, when sea levels were 70 meters (230 feet) higher on our planet." Joseph Romm, *Hell and High Water: Global Warming—the Solution and the Politics—and What We Should Do about It* (New York: William Morrow, 2006), 94.

For a recent comprehensive review of environmental problems and threats to societal functioning, see Paul R. Ehrlich and Anne H. Ehrlich, "Can a Collapse of Global Civilization Be Avoided?" *Proceedings of the Royal Society B, Biological Sciences*, 280, no. 1754 (2013), http://rspb.royalsocietypublishing.org/content /280/1754/20122845, and their response to criticism from climate change–denier Michael J. Kelly (a professor of engineering) several months later, "Future Collapse: How Optimistic Should We Be?" *Proceedings of the Royal Society B, Biological Sciences*, 280, no. 1767 (2013), http://dx.doi.org/10.1098/rspb.2013.1373. See also World Bank Report, "Turn Down the Heat: Climate Extremes, Regional Impacts and the Case for Resilience," June 2013, www.worldbank.org/en/topic/climatechange /publication/turn-down-the-heat-climate-extremes-regional-impacts-resilience; and The Overseas Development Institute, "The Geography of Poverty, Disasters and Climate Extremes in 2030," October 2013, www.odi.org/poverty-disasters-2030.

3   Nils Gilman, Doug Randall, and Peter Schwartz, "Impacts of Climate Change: A System Vulnerability Approach," GBN white paper, www.gbn.com/consulting /article_details.php?id=61. Brahma Chellaney, *Water, Peace, and War: Confronting the Global Water Crisis* (Lanham, MD: Rowman & Littlefield, 2013; Jeffrey Mazo, *Climate Conflict: How Global Warming Threatens Security and What to Do about It* (London: Routledge, 2010); Nils Gilman, Doug Randall, and Peter Schwartz, "Climate Change and National Security: An Analytic Framework," in *The Oxford Handbook of Climate Change and Society*, edited by John Dryzek (Oxford: Oxford University Press, 2011).

4   Thomas Pogge, *Politics as Usual* (Cambridge: Polity Press, 2010); Thomas Pogge,

"Poverty, Human Rights and the Global Order: Framing the Post-2015 Agenda," www.crop.org; Branko Milanovic, *Worlds Apart: Measuring International and Global Inequality*, 2005 and Miklanovic, "Global Inequality Recalculated and Updated: The Effect of New PPP Estimates on Global Inequality and 2005 Estimates," *Journal of Economic Inequality* 10 (2012); see also Mike Davis, *Planet of Slums* (New York: Verso, 2006); UNDP, *Human Development Report 2007/08: Fighting Climate Change: Human Solidarity in a Divided World* (New York: Oxford University Press, 2007); Diane E. Davis, "Non-State Armed Actors, New Imagined Communities, and Shifting Patterns of Sovereignty and Insecurity in the Modern World," *Contemporary Security Policy* 30, no. 2 (2010), 221–45; Richard Heinberg, *The End of Growth: Adapting to Our New Economic Reality* (New Society, 2011); and Steven Solomon, *Water: The Epic Struggle for Wealth, Power, and Civilization* (New York: HarperCollins, 2010). Paul Ehrlich has also observed, "The 2.5 billion people projected to be added to the human population by midcentury will have a much greater destructive impact than the last 2.5 billion. People are smart and therefore naturally use the most concentrated, highest-grade resources first. So each additional person must be fed from more marginal land, equipped with objects made of metal won from poorer ores, supplied with water from more distant sources or expensively purified, and so on." Paul Ehrlich, "On Closing the Culture Gap," *SEED Magazine*, April 8, 2010, http://seedmagazine.com /content/article/on_closing_the_culture_gap.

5   Mike Davis, "Who Will Build the Ark?" *New Left Review* 61 (Jan/Feb 2010): 39–40.

6   David Kilcullen, *Out of the Mountains: The Coming Age of the Urban Guerrilla* (New York: Oxford University Press, 2013), 25, 29, 39,102, 241–42 (italics in original).

7   The term *wicked problem* was coined to reference social-policy planning issues and dilemmas that are so complex—with so many uncertainties and/or irregularly fluctuating moving parts and feedbacks—as to defy any firm conceptualization or analytic purchase, much less any reliable plan of organized attack or preconceived solution /end-state. H. W. J. Tittel and M. M. Webber, "Dilemmas in a General Theory of Planning," *Policy Sciences* 4, no. 2 (1973): 155–69. *Super wicked* appears to have been coined by K. Levin, B. Cashore, S. Bernstein, and G. Auld in "Playing It Forward: Path Dependency, Progressive Incrementalism, and the 'Super Wicked' Problem of Global Climate Change" (2007) later published as "Overcoming the Tragedy of Super Wicked Problems: Constraining Our Future Selves to Ameliorate Global Climate Change," *Policy Sciences* 45, no. 2 (June 2012): 123–52.

8   Laurence Smith, *The World in 2050* (New York: Dutton, 2010), 108–9, citing an article by prominent hydrologists, P. C. D. Milly, Julio Betancourt, Malin Falkenmark, Robert M. Hirsch, Zbigniew W. Kundzewicz, Dennis P. Lettenmaier, and Ronald J. Stouffer, "Stationarity Is Dead: Whither Water Management?" *Science* 319, no. 5863 (2008): 573–74.

9   James Lovelock, *The Vanishing Face of Gaia: A Final Warning* (London: Allen Lane, 2009). For somewhat less apocalyptic visions of collapse, see Dmitry Orloff, *The Five Stages of Collapse: Survivors' Toolkit* (Gabriola Island, BC: New Society, 2013); James Howard Kunstler, *Too Much Magic: Wishful Thinking, Technology, and the Fate of the Nation* (New York: Grove Press, 2012); and Ross Jackson, *Occupy World Street: A Global Roadmap for Radical Economic and Political Reform* (White River Junction, VT:

Chelsea Green, 2012).

10   From 1980 to 2015, total global carbon dioxide emissions from energy consumption will have doubled, from about 18 billion metric tons to about 36 billion metric tons.

11   Indeed, that time-frame has very likely already passed, at least in terms of avoiding increasingly frequent major natural disasters world-wide beginning in ten to twenty years and continuing throughout the balance of the century – absent miracles in the development of CCS.

12   Typical in this respect is Anthony Giddens, *The Politics of Climate Change* (London: Polity Press, 2009, 2nd ed. 2011), a book filled with sage advice about the governmental policies that ought to be implemented but with almost nothing to say about the political obstacles to achieving these policies, much less about how those obstacles might be overcome. The same might be said of Juliet Schor's useful handbook on alternative economics, *Plenitude* (New York: Penguin, 2010). Even those who stress the need for fundamental change in our civilization typically do not take on the question of the political requirements—or even highlight the centrality and magnitude of that issue, beyond one-sentence acknowledgments. See, for example, the otherwise admirable Nick Brooks, Natasha Grist, and Katrina Brown, "Development Futures in the Context of Climate Change: Challenging the Present and Learning from the Past," *Development Policy Review* 27, no. 6 (2009): 741–65. Thomas Homer-Dixon goes further than most in explaining that politics is a big part of the problem (without making this point central to his overall argument), see *The Upside of Down* (Washington, DC: Island Press, 2006), 214–19.

Discussion of the essential political problem has begun to appear since our earlier version of this paper. See John Barry, *The Politics of Actually Existing Unsustainability* (Oxford: Oxford University Press, 2012); Paul G. Harris, *What's Wrong with Climate Politics and How to Fix It* (London: Polity Press, 2013); John S. Dryzek, Richard B. Norgaard, and David Schlosberg, *Climate-Challenged Society* (Oxford: Oxford University Press, 2013); Dale Jamieson, *Reason in a Dark Time: Why the Struggle Against Climate Change Failed—and What It Means for Our Future* (Oxford: Oxford University Press, 2014); and Roger E. Kasperson and Bonnie J. Ram, "The Public Acceptance of New Energy Technologies," *Daedalus* (Winter 2013): 90–95.

13   The 2014 IPCC Report is being published as we complete this paper. It makes clear that the 2007 Report generally underestimated the rate of climate-change acceleration and the risks posed thereby. According to the IPCC 2007 Report, reaching a sustainable level of GHG emissions – one that will keep CO_2 to under 450 ppm – would require reducing emissions by 80 percent over the subsequent 25 years or so. That estimate is now overcome by the combination of growth in GHG emissions since 2007, the more rapid than predicted arctic snow and ice melt (and consequent albedo reduction and transfer of solar energy from the hard work of melting massive ice to the easier work of heating liquid water), and the elimination of any prospect of near-term front-loading of emissions reduction. Such front-loading is crucial because the great majority of the CO_2 added to the atmosphere remains in on-going circulation between the atmosphere and short-term "sinks" on the Earth's surface (or just below) for from hundreds to thousands of years. Only small amounts of atmospheric carbon per year are naturally sequestered in long-term (more or less permanent) "sinks."

Once emitted into the atmosphere, CO2 is a gift that keeps on giving, coming back
again and again after relatively brief vacations incorporated in living things and surface water (the short-term "sinks").

14 Techno-salvationists are constantly proliferating optimistic scenarios, most of which
are more or less in the realm of science fiction. For example, various people have
proposed that massive programs of carbon sequestration could help; they would
indeed, except that the technology doesn't yet exist and promises to be highly energy-
intensive. More recent discussions have centered on "geoengineering" options—for
example, putting shields in outer space to block incoming solar radiation or somehow
fixing carbon from the atmosphere on a massive scale. Even if these solutions became
technologically viable, the political obstacles to implementing them would remain
vast—a point that the engineers usually remark on only in passing. See Clive Hamilton, *Earthmasters: Playing God with the Climate*, (Allen & Unwin, 2013); David Biello,
"What Is Geoengineering and Why Is It Considered a Climate Change Solution?"
Scientific American (April 6, 2010) and David G. Victor, M. Granger Morgan, Jay Apt,
John Steinbruner, and Katharine Ricke, "The Geoengineering Option: A Last Resort
against Global Warming," *Foreign Affairs* (March/April 2009).

15 The claim that all the necessary technology already exists is put forth so often, and
with so little justification, that it seems unfair to pick on any particular advocates.
But here are a few high-profile ones: Sir John Houghton, "Overview of the Climate
Change Issue," Presentation to Forum 2002, St. Anne's College, Oxford (July 15,
2002), www.jri.org.uk/resource/climatechangeoverview.htm; Katie Fehrenbacher,
founding editor, Earth2Tech, www.economist.com/debate/days/view/208; and the
European Green Party, www.greens-efa.org/cms/default/dok/134/134192.climate
_change_facts@en.htm.

16 See the interviews of Mark Delucchi and Mark Jacobson (coauthors of the widely
noted "A Plan to Power 100 percent of the Planet with Renewables," *Scientific American*, November 2009) in John Wiseman, *Post Carbon Pathways: Conversations with
Leading Climate Change Researchers, Policy Makers and Activists* (Melbourne, Australia:
Centre for Policy Development, April 2013), http://cpd.org.au/wp-content/uploads
/2013/04/Post-Carbon-Pathways-2013-interview-transcripts.pdf, 32–37, 92–95.

17 The basic ideas of "ecological modernization" have become commonplace over recent
years, but the term itself is not well known outside the academic field of environmental sociology. Ecological modernization theory first appeared among German and
Dutch environmental sociologists and social theorists in the early 1980s, in response
to neo-Marxist theories of the irremediable ecological destructiveness of advanced
capitalism. By the mid 1990s, ecological modernization was a flourishing academic
field with a broad literature. See Arthur P.J. Mol, Gert Spaargaren and David A. Son-
nenfeld, eds., *The Ecological Modernization Reader* (New York: Routledge, 2009). The
school of thought had precursors among policy intellectuals in the mid-1970s, reacting
to the 1973 energy crisis and the growing first-world environmental movement of the
time, such as the work of Amory Lovins on "soft energy paths" and "natural capitalism." See Lovins, "Energy Strategy: The Road Not Taken," *Foreign Affairs* (October
1976); Paul Hawken, Amory Lovins, and Hunter Lovins, *Natural Capitalism: Creating*

the Next Industrial Revolution (New York: Little Brown, 1999).

18   See Anthony Giddens, *The Third Way: The Renewal of Social Democracy* (London: Polity Press, 1998).

19   Ecological modernization theory dovetails with (and at times explicitly relies upon) the neo-modernization theory of Ronald Inglehart and the "creative class" theory of Richard Florida. See Inglehart, *Modernization and Postmodernization* (Princeton, NJ: Princeton University Press, 1997); Inglehart and Christian Welzel, *Modernization, Cultural Change and Democracy: The Human Development Sequence* (Cambridge: Cambridge University Press, 2005); and Florida, *The Rise of the Creative Class: And How It's Transforming Work, Leisure, Community and Everyday Life* (New York: Basic Books, 2004). Inglehart posits that a turn away from high-carbon "more" toward post-materialist values is a natural and inevitable feature of a maturing modernity. The "creative class," as depicted by Florida, is made up of highly educated knowledge workers committed to social tolerance and diversity and an upscale, neo-bohemian lifestyle that includes positive appreciation of nature. Florida casts the creative class as a vanguard that will lead an eco-friendly technological revolution that will make economic growth endlessly sustainable.

20   Breakthrough Institute web address, and see, e.g. Earl Ellis.

21   The classic statement of this position is Daniel Lerner, *The Passing of Traditional Society* (Glencoe, IL: Free Press, 1958). This understanding of modernization and modernity, based in Talcott Parsons's and Edward Shils's translation of Durkheim and Weber into social systems theory, is still present at the heart of Ron Inglehart's influential revitalization of modernization theory over the last twenty years.

22   Not to mention the question of how such overindulgence has been historically constructed and reproduced—not out of purely natural, spontaneous human impulse, but by the exercise of power—and how what transition to higher needs has occurred has been due to bitter political struggles and partial historical victories by various movements that, in effect, demanded that "higher needs" (like civil rights) be put ahead of material affluence. Moreover, there is now an extensive literature in social psychology questioning the presumed contribution of material affluence to human happiness. Summarized in Juliet Schor, *Plenitude* (New York: Penguin, 2010), 176–180.

23   By this, we do not mean to reject the upscale neo-bohemian lifestyle of the "creative class" (satirized by David Brooks's *BoBos in Paradise* [New York: Simon & Schuster, 2000]) as without integrity. It is arguable that this lifestyle—at least in outline—is a version of the good life that stands up existentially and that would stand up normatively if it were universally available and could be pursued without violating norms of justice, but it's not and it can't—not on this planet after the history that's already happened. No technological fix is going to overcome these limits—that is, there is simply no reason to believe that there is a possible technology, waiting over the horizon, that would allow six or seven (much less eight or nine) billion people to all live like Bobos on this planet. Any such way of life will continue to be limited to a privileged minority; its pursuit—by anyone anywhere—will continue to violate norms of justice.

24   The political economy suggested by ecological modernization theory (and Third Way politics) might have been viable if its working out and implementation had begun

immediately after WWII—if the New Deal had continued in a green vein, leading to the greening of the Marshall Plan and Truman's Point Four program. This kind of program might still have had a chance of success if launched strongly in the 1960s or early 1970s and continued uninterrupted from there. But the scientific and techni- cal knowledge of the earlier period was insufficient, and Right, Left, and Center all had other priorities and other trajectories throughout those years. Instead, we got the glorification of suburban home-ownership, the automobile, electric appliances, and consumerism in general as central to the good life. In the late 1950s and early 1960s, a hopeful moment of critique of the affluent society and its culture and politics flowered, only to be overtaken by the conflicts over the Vietnam war, black power, and women's liberation. After some strong environmental beginnings in the 1970s, the subsequent rise of the New Right, carried forward by the Reagan/Thatcher revolution with its glorification of private wealth and denigration of public goods, and followed by post– Cold War neoliberal triumphalism, left both ecological modernization and the Third Way largely bottled up in "old" Europe and scattered local refugia (e.g., Portland, Oregon). Now it is simply too late for the half-measures of ecological modernization theory (even if there has been a substantial resurgence of innovating green livlihoods in the last several years, as Schor 2010 reports).

25 See note 3, above.

26 Of course the choice between production cutbacks, on one hand, and improvements in renewable-energy and materials sciences and technologies on the other hand, is not either/or and presumably will come in the form of some combinatory mix. But even if technology can make up half of what needs to be done, that still implies a 40% cut in production and consumption across the global economy – presumably most of which will need to be borne by wealthy economies. Such a drop in industrial output is far greater than any industrialized economy has ever experienced, even during the Great Depression.

27 How much per capita decline is required depends on global population growth. The "official future" calls for global population to max out (and then stabilize) around 9 billion around 2050. It's worth noting, however, not only that the accuracy of popula- tion projections over that time span have a notoriously poor track record, but also (and not coincidentally) that the theory of the demographic transition is entirely tied up with modernization theory; see Simon Szreter, "The Idea of Demographic Transi- tion and the Study of Fertility Change: A Critical Intellectual History," *Population and Development Review* 19, no. 4 (1993): 659–701. For a lower estimate on probable population growth, see Jorgen Randers, *2052: A Global Forecast for the Next Forty Years* (White River Junction, VT: Chelsea Green Publishing, 2012).

28 Griffith quoted in Stewart Brand, *Whole Earth Discipline: An Ecopragmatist Manifesto* (New York: Penguin, 2009), 14.

29 Griffith himself is convinced that, while a monumental undertaking, such a remak- ing of the world's energy infrastructure is technically perfectly feasible, were the political will and funding forthcoming (which we regard as so highly unlikely as to be utopian—and note that we have not included the additional task of transition- ing the world's vehicle fleet from hydrocarbons). In any case, political issues aside, there is significant debate about the theoretical and practical feasibility of current and

emerging green technologies as full replacements for existing conventional energy infrastructure. But what's striking is how hedged even the most optimistic arguments are. Consider the reasonable case made by Mark Z. Jacobson and Mark A Delucchi, "A Plan to Power 100 Percent of the Planet with Renewables," *Scientific American* (November, 2009). To make the numbers work, Jacobson and Delucchi make sanguine assumptions about efficiency gains during the conversion process. They also concede that dire new materials shortages are likely to arise (for uranium, as well as various rare minerals required to build batteries, gears, and photovoltaic cells), and they wring their hands about the political challenges associated with trying to replace the large majority of the world's energy generation, transmission and consumption infrastructure. For more, see Benjamin K. Sovacool and Charmaine Watts, "Going Completely Renewable: Is It Possible (Let Alone Desirable)?" *The Electricity Journal* 22, no. 4 (2009): 95–111. Vacliv Smil criticized the Jacobson and Delucchi 2009 Scientific American article in the below-quoted post. Jacobson and Delucchi maintained their 2009 posture without change in their (with coauthors) fifty-four-page May 2013 paper "Evaluating the Technical and Economic Feasibility of Repowering California for All Purposes with Wind, Water, and Sunlight" (subsequently published in *Energy Policy*), as did Jacobson in a presentation at UC-Berkeley on September 11, 2013, in the face of sharp challenges from the audience (including from Barnes). But see the Jacobson and Delucchi interviews in Wiseman et al., *Post Carbon Pathways.*

30   When we communicated to Griffith that his calculation of the necessary land-footprint was being sharply challenged by critics of our earlier paper, he stuck to his guns in that respect. We have not attempted to resolve this particular issue as we do not see it as a main point.

31   Clive Hamilton, *Requiem for a Species* (Earthscan, 2010), 159–67.

32   See N. P. Myhrvold and K. Caldeira, "Greenhouse Gases, Climate Change and the Transition from Coal to Low-Carbon Electricity," *Environmental Research Letters* 7 (2012), www.stacks.iop.org/ERL/7/014019. "The use of current infrastructure to build this new low-emission system necessitates additional emissions of greenhouse gases, and the coal-based infrastructure will continue to emit substantial amounts of greenhouse gases as it is phased out. Furthermore, ocean thermal inertia delays the climate benefits of emissions reductions.... We show that rapid deployment of low-emission energy systems can do little to diminish the climate impacts in the first half of this century" (from abstract).

33   Ibid.

34   See Wiseman, et al., *Post Carbon Pathways* interviews and discussion paper.

35   Vaclav Smil, *Energy Transitions: History, Requirements, Prospects* (Santa Barbara, CA: Praeger, 2010) 119, 134–35, 142, 146, 148.

36   "A Skeptic Looks at Alternative Energy," by Vaclav Smil, *IEEE Spectrum*, (July 2012). See also Robert W. Fri, "The Alternative Energy Future: The Scope of the Transition," *Daedalus* (Winter 2013): 5–7.

37   In fact, the world of environmentalism is broader, more diverse, and more complexly internally conflicted than we have explained in either version of this chapter. A crude summary maps three coalitions, overlapping at the margins: (1) radical Greens, romantic left antimodernists, radical antiglobalists, and anarchists; (2) centrist, high-modernist

science-and-technology enthusiasts, ecological modernization theorists, policy intellectuals, and green capitalists, who see themselves as the only pragmatists; and (3) an "in-between" grouping of critical modernist radical reformists, largely in academia and nongovernmental organizations—with which we identify.

38   See Dale Jamieson, *Reason in a Dark Time: Why the Struggle against Climate Change Failed—and What It Means for Our Future* (New York: Oxford University Press, 2014), chap. 3; Roger E. Kasperson and Bonnie J. Ram, "The Public Acceptance of New Energy Technologies," *Daedalus* (Winter 2013): 90–95.

39   New age radical environmentalists often envision a worldwide simple-living, back-to-the-farm-and-village movement that will naturally exfoliate across the landscape in the wake of the self-inflicted implosion and collapse of existing nation-states and political economies. We don't know of any version of this scenario that takes realistic account of the threats to such an idealistic lifeworld posed by the warlords and other deviant actors discussed in this volume.

40   This seems to us to also apply to the somewhat less radical hopes of a rapid transition to the "plenitude" model. Juliet Schor, *Plenitude* (New York: Penguin, 2010).

41   The ideology of endless growth is the common assumption across all modern political systems; it is the fundament of how modern societies and polities understand what they are all about; it is baked into the core of virtually all contemporary social contracts. See Bjorn Hettne, *Development Theory and the Three Worlds: Towards an International Political Economy of Development* (London: Longman, 1995). The ideology of endless growth has long been challenged by counterculture environmentalists, without, until recently, much impact on the mainstream social sciences. "Economic growth has become the secular religion of advancing industrial societies: the source of individual motivation, the basis of political solidarity, the ground for the mobilization of society for a common purpose.... If there is no commitment to economic growth, what can the Soviet Union—or Japan, or the United States–hold out as a social goal for its people?" (Daniel Bell, *The Cultural Contradictions of Capitalism*, 1976). "If one were to choose a single word to characterize [what it means to be an American in the twenty-first century], it would have to be *more*. For the majority of contemporary Americans, the essence of life, liberty, and the pursuit of happiness centers on a relentless personal quest to acquire, to consume, to indulge, and to shed whatever constraints might interfere with those endeavors." (Andrew Bacevich, *The Limits of Power*, 2008).

42   Kevin Drum, "The Rationing Canard," *Mother Jones* (August 28, 2009), http://motherjones.com/kevin-drum/2009/08/rationing-canaard.

43   Walt Whitman Rostow, *The Stages of Economic Growth: A Non-Communist Manifesto* (New York: Oxford University Press, 1961). See Naomi Klein, "Climate against Capitalism," *The Nation*, November 11, 2012.

44   Minxin Pei, "Communist China at 60," *Carnegie Endowment for International Peace*, September 30, 2009), www.carnegieendowment.org/publications/index.cfm?fa=view&id=23922.

45   Some are inching this way, see the interviews in "Post Carbon Pathways," especially the interviews of Mark Delucchi and Mark Jacobson, co-authors of the widely noted *Scientific American* article "A Plan to Power 100 percent of the Planet with

Renewables," in John Wiseman, et al, *Post Carbon Pathways: Conversations with Leading Climate Change Researchers, Policy Makers and Activists*, Center for Policy Development, April 2013, http://cpd.or.au/2012/03/post-carbon-pathways, 32-37, 92-95. Still, among most the emphasis is always on don't be pessimistic, one must be optimistic, particularly in public, one absolutely must not talk apocalyptically.

46 See Naomi Oreskes and Erik M. Conway, "The Collapse of Western Civilization: A View from the Future," Daedalus (Winter 2013): 40–58; Jamieson, *Reason in a Dark Time*, chap. 3. For a more equivocal (if not schizophrenic) version of this conclusion, see Paul Gilding, The Great Disruption (New York: Bloomsbury Press, 2011).

47 See Charles Tilly's classic piece, "War Making and State Making as Organized Crime," in *Bringing the State Back In*, edited by Peter B. Evans, Dietrich Rueschemeyer, and Theda Skocpol, 169–91 (Cambridge: Cambridge University Press, 1985).

48 For strong arguments on the need for alternative political economy, see Nick Brooks, Natasha Grist, and Katrina Brown, "Development Futures in the Context of Climate Change: Challenging the Present and Learning from the Past," *Development Policy Review* 27, no. 6 (2009): 741–65, and the literature cited therein.

49 As to what we don't yet have, even in the lab, first and foremost is viable, effective CCS that might—realistically—be brought to scale. See Clive Hamilton, Nor do we have the technology to deal with fresh water issues in that way.

50 See Patrick Heller's chapter, "Kerala: Deepening a Radical Social Democracy," in *Social Democracy in the Global Periphery: Origins, Challenges, Prospects*, edited by Richard Sandbrook, Marc Edelman, Patrick Heller, and Judith Teichman, 65–92 (Cambridge: Cambridge University Press, 2007); and Patrick Heller and T. M. Thomas Isaac, "Decentralization, Democracy and Development: People's Campaign for Decentralized Planning in Kerala," in *Developing Democracy: Institutional Innovations in Empowered Participatory Democracy* edited by A. Fung and E. O. Wright, (London: Verso, 2002).

51 See the discussions of the "social economy of Quebec," and the Mondragon cooperative conglomerate in Spain, in Erik Olin Wright, *Envisioning Real Utopias* (London: Verso, 2010), 204–16, 234–46; discussion of Costa Rica in ; discussions of Seattle, Washington; the Netherlands; and "farmer-managed natural regeneration" (FMNR) in Africa in Mark Hertsgaard, *Hot: Living through the Next Fifty Years on Earth* (Boston: Houghton Mifflin Harcourt, 2011).

52 Mike Davis: "Although forest clearance and export monocultures have played fundamental roles in the transition to a new geological epoch, the prime mover has been the almost exponential increase in the carbon footprints of urban regions in the northern hemisphere. Heating and cooling the urban built environment alone is responsible for an estimated 35 to 45 per cent of current carbon emissions, while urban industries and transportation contribute another 35 to 40 per cent. In a sense, city life is rapidly destroying the ecological niche—Holocene climate stability—which made its evolution into complexity possible." "Who Will Build the Ark," *New Left Review* (2010): 41.

53 There are many relevant (if piecemeal) suggestions, such as small-scale flexible specialization in production, worker and artisan cooperatives, revitalization of family farming and local sourcing of food, decentralized electricity generation via distributed wind and solar technologies, major elaboration of non-fossil-fueled public

transportation, and community organization dedicated to local green education and responsible practices. See, for example, Juliet Schor, *Plenitude* (New York: Penguin, 2010), and the literature cited therein; Bill McKibben, *Deep Economy: The Wealth of Communities and the Durable Future* (New York: Times Books, 2007); Rob Hopkins, *The Transition Handbook: From Oil Dependency to Local Resilience* (White River Junction, VT: Chelsea Green, 2009); David Holmgren, *Future Scenarios: How Communities Can Adapt to Peak Oil and Climate Change* (White River Junction, VT: Chelsea Green, 2009); Shaun Chamberlin, *The Transition Timeline: For a Local, Resilient Future* (White River Junction, VT: Chelsea Green, 2009). At a policy level, as the scientific evidence of approaching catastrophe has become stronger, and as scientists have taken it upon themselves to speak out more strongly, we've seen a spate of books from such authorities offering comprehensive descriptions of necessary radical reforms of policy in the advanced world. James Gustave Speth, *The Bridge at the Edge of the World: Capitalism, the Environment, and Crossing from Crisis to Sustainability* (New Haven, CT: Yale University Press, 2008); David W. Orr, *Down to the Wire: Confronting Climate Collapse* (New York: Oxford University Press, 2009); Lester T. Brown, *Plan B 4.0: Mobilizing to Save Civilization* (New York: W.W. Norton, 2009).

54   To get an idea, look at the content—both the articles and the advertisements—of any recent issue of the high-modernist establishment flagship journal *Foreign Affairs*. You will find never-ending optimistic pumping of high-end modern middle-class professionalism and related educational and policy programs and institutions as the answer to everything and the guarantee of a bright future. This is less rabid and dishonest than what we saw on Wall Street during the recent great bubble, but no less cavalier— and ultimately no less delusional—than those who really believed that the 2004–2007 housing market and Dow were crash-proof.

55   But there are lessons, both positive and negative, to be learned from the practices and experiences of such revolutionary movements, particularly from the Maoist "Yenan Way" of the 1940s; the Cuban revolution before, during, and after the "Special Period"; the Nicaraguan revolution; and the Salvadoran revolutionary struggle. See note 64, below and the accompanying text.

56   Of course, Marx and liberal modernization theorists were right in insisting that Jeffersonian small-producer capitalism of the nineteenth century—proto/early-industrial petty bourgeois radicalism and utopian socialism—was bound to be defeated by capitalist accumulation and industrial concentration. But that doesn't mean that that outcome is irreversible. Something like that outcome was inherent in the capitalism of that time, but that doesn't mean that there is any such thing as "Capitalism" as a transhistorical political economy that must continue to exist in that form—or not at all.

57   For stimulating discussion of underlying theoretical and epistemological issues, see Thomas McCarthy, *Race, Empire, and the Idea of Human Development* (Cambridge: Cambridge University Press, 2009), especially 155–65, 220–29. On general historical background, see Pankaj Mishra, *From the Ruins of Empire: The Revolt Against the West and the Remaking of Asia* (Picador, 2012). On particular countries: Stephen F. Cohen, *Bukharin and the Bolshevik Revolution* (Oxford University Press, 1980); Mark Selden, *The Yenan Way in Revolutionary China* (Cambridge, MA: Harvard University Press,

1971); Richard Sandbrook, Marc Edelman, Patrick Heller, and Judith Teichman, *Social Democracy in the Global Periphery: Origins, Challenges, Prospects* (Cambridge: Cambridge University Press, 2007); Patrick Heller and T. M. Thomas Isaac, "Decentralization, Democracy and Development: People's Campaign for Decentralized Planning in Kerala," in *Developing Democracy: Institutional Innovations in Empowered Participatory Democracy*, edited by A. Fung and E. O. Wright (London: Verso, 2002).

58   We need not go as far in praise as Lawrence Goodwyn, *Democratic Promise: The Populist Moment in America* (New York: Oxford University Press, 1976) or Christopher Lasch, *The True and Only Heaven: Progress and Its Critics* (New York: Norton, 1991). The more recent scholarly work is more balanced, while maintaining a positive judgment: Elizabeth Sanders, *Roots of Reform: Farmers, Workers, and the American State, 1877–1917* (Chicago: University of Chicago Press, 1999); Charles Postel, *The Populist Vision* (Oxford University Press, 2007), vii–viii:

> During the Gilded Age, the corporate elite made exclusive claims on modernity. Captains of finance and industry, supported by economists and political scientists from the universities, held that the particular corporate model they pursued conformed to unalterable laws of progress and development. They derided those who questioned corporate prerogatives as helplessly opposed to progress, bound by tradition, and intractably anti-modern....
>
> At the dawn of the twenty-first century, new structures of corporate prerogatives and control are being presented as the inevitable outcomes of new technologies and the new realities of a global economy. The Populist experience puts into question such claims of inevitability.... The Populist revolt reflected a conflict over divergent paths of modern capitalist development. Such a conclusion is pregnant with possibilities. It suggests that modern society is not a given but is shaped by men and women who pursue alternative visions of what the modern world should be.

For stimulating discussion carrying this theme forward into the progressive era, see Robert D. Johnston, *The Radical Middle Class: Populist Democracy and the Question of Capitalism in Progressive Era Portland, Oregon* (Princeton, NJ: Princeton University Press 2003), especially chap 1, 5, and 22.

59   And see Marc Schneiberg, "What's on the Path? Path Dependence, Organizational Diversity and the Problem of Institutional Change in the U.S. Economy, 1900–1950," *Socio-Economic Review* (2007) 5, 47–80.

60   For a very stimulating argument along these lines, in the context of a discussion of the need to both reassert and "correct" Polanyi, see Nancy Fraser, "Marketization, Social Protection, Emancipation: Toward a Neo-Polanyian Conception of Capitalist Crisis," in *Business As Usual: The Roots of the Global Financial Meltdown*, edited by C. Calhoun and G. Derluguian (New York: NYU Press, 2011).

61   Johnston, *The Radical Middle Class*, 267, referencing Charles F. Sabel and Jonathan Zeitlin, eds., *Worlds of Possibilities: Flexibility and Mass Production in Western Industrialization* (Cambridge: Cambridge University Press, 1997).

62   On property-owning democracy, see Martin O'Neill and Thad Williamson, eds.,

Property-Owning Democracy: Rawls and Beyond (London: Wiley-Blackwell, 2012).

63   One of the main ideologies of the Tea Party movement is right-wing, libertarian producerism. See John Judis, "Tea Minus Zero: The Tea Party Menace Will Not Go Quietly," *The New Republic*, May 5, 2010. Further, there is a virtual renaissance going on in "neo-Jeffersonian" theory and Lincoln studies, as well as in the historiography of Progressivism Two. See, for example, Phillip Longman, "Yeoman's Return: Small-Scale Ownership and the Next Progressive Era," *The New America Foundation*, January 2009: "Finally, because of the long hold and widespread appeal of the yeoman ideal on the American political imagination, a politics that pays honor to this tradition has the potential to bridge the country's cultural divides, just as occurred during the last progressive Era.... The yeoman, even when beat down and betrayed by banks, middlemen, politicians, thin soil, or a bad Internet connection, has a dignity and independence of mind nearly all Americans want to, and should, recognize in themselves." See also John Barry, "Towards a Green Republicanism: Constitutionalism, Political Economy, and the Green State," *The Good Society* 17, no. 2 (2008): "Emphasizing the republican strains native to the political cultures of western liberal democracies could help to create a political environment more conducive to green politics and policy, and allows greens to offer an 'immanent critique' of the current unsustainable development paths being followed by western societies in a language comprehensible to the majority of its citizens." For elaboration, see Barry's recent book, *The Politics of Actually Existing Unsustainability* (New York: Oxford University Press, 2012). For another recent optimistic analysis, see Paul G. Harris, *What's Wrong with Climate Politics and How to Fix It* (Cambridge: Polity Press, 2013).

64   See, in particular, Geoffrey Kurtz's explication of Jean Jaures's conception of a social democratic citizen's army in "An Apprenticeship for Life in Common: Jean Jaures on Social Democracy and the Modern Republic," *New Political Science* 35, no. 1 (2013): 65–83. Also of interest: B. M. Stentiford, *The Richardson Light Guard of Wakefield, Massachusetts: A Town Militia in War and Peace, 1851–1975* (Jefferson, NC: MacFarland, 2013). The development and practice of paramilitary and military units ("guerrilla armies") by idealistic revolutionary movements also provides some important lessons, both positive and negative, regarding the political education and political culture of "popular" armed forces. See, for example, Elisabeth Jean Wood, *Insurgent Collective Action and Civil War in El Salvador* (Cambridge: Cambridge University Press, 2003). The positive accomplishments—and the problems and failures—of the Sandinista police and armed forces during the ten years that Sandinismo was in power in Nicaragua and fighting a guerilla war against forces assisted by the U.S. government, are highly relevant. See William Barnes, "The Past and Future of the Left in Nicaragua and El Salvador: Successes and Failures; Legacy, Prospects, and the Populist Temptation," unpublished manuscript.

65   "Who Will Build the Ark?" *New Left Review* 61 (January/February 2010): 45–46, quoting the UN Human Development Report 2007/2008, 2.

66   This potential is manifest in many of the activists and staff of international humanitarian and environmental civil society—at least in the less technocratic and non-

neo-colonial incarnations of such entities—which is really a very large universe, much more elaborate than most people realize, and carrying a much bigger burden, without which the rest of us would be much more directly confronted with the ramifications of the world's terrible problems.

67 A different version of this paper is published as "Green Social Democracy or Barbarism: Climate Change and the End of High Modernism," in *The Deepening Crisis: Governance Challenges after Neoliberalism*, edited by Craig Calhoun and Georgi Derluguian, Possible Futures, vol. 2, of the Social Science Research Council (New York: New York University Press, June 2011).

Chapter 11. Bringing the End of War to the Global Badlands

1 Aude Fleurant and Sam Perlo-Freeman, "The SIPRI Top 100 Arms-Producing and Military Services Companies, 2013," (Stockholm: Stockholm International Peace Research Institute, 2014).

2 Jeffrey Boutwell and Michael T Klare, "A Scourge of Small Arms" *Scientific American* (June 2000).

3 Nathan P. Gardels, *At Century's End: Great Minds Reflect on Our Times*. (La Jolla, California: ALTI Publishing, 1997).

4 Jonathan Schell, *The Fate of the Earth*. (Stanford, California: Stanford University Press, 2000).

5 Daniel L Byman, "Do Targeted Killings Work?" *Foreign Policy*, (July 14, 2009).

6 Human Security Report Project. *Human Security Report 2009/2010: The Causes of Peace and the Shrinking Costs of War*. (New York: Oxford University Press, 2011).

7 Steven Pinker, *The Better Angels of Our Nature*. (New York: Allen Lane, 2011).

8 Spencer R Weart, *Never at War: Why Democracies Will Not Fight One Another* (New Haven and London: Yale University Press, 1998).

Chapter 12. The White Hats

1 For part of the story of Jomo Gbomo and MEND, see Sebastian Junger, "Blood Oil," *Vanity Fair* (New York, February 2007).

2 Asari Dokubu, "Me, Henry Okah 'Jomo Gbomo,' Judith Asuni and the Niger Del-ta Insurgency," http://saharareporters.com/node/9784/126626 (December 31, 2008).

3 See, for example, Judith Burdin Asuni, "Blood Oil in the Niger Delta," United States Institute of Peace (Washington DC, 2009).

4 "Talking Helmand: The Political Officer's Advice for Armies Campaigning into the Pashtoon Heartland," YouTube video, 1:29:18, uploaded by "CarrCenter," September 24, 2009, www.youtube.com/watch?v=GA7S__Q2olc.

5 See, for example, Mary Kaldor and Shannon D. Beebe, *The Ultimate Weapon Is No Weapon* (New York: Public Affairs, 2010).

6 David Rose, "The Gaza Bombshell," *Vanity Fair*, (New York, April 2008).

7 See *Regaining the Initiative: Palestinian Strategic Options to End the Occupation* (Palestinian Strategy Study Group, August 2008) and Adam Kahane, Chapter 5,

"Stumbling." In *Power and Love a Theory and Practice of Social Change*. (San Francisco: Berrett-Koehler Publishers, 2010).

8   Alastair Crooke, *Resistance: The Essence of the Islamist Revolution*. (London: Pluto Press, 2009).

9   Ron Suskind, "Faith, Certainty and the Presidency of George W. Bush," *The New York Times Magazine* (New York, October 17, 2004).

10 See Shadia Drury, *Leo Strauss and the American Right*, (New York: St. Martin's Press, 1997).

11 Alastair Crooke, "Red Shi'ism, Iran, and the Islamist Revolution," (London: Red Pepper, October 2009).

12 "Statement on Avaaz's Role in Evacuation of Journalists from Syria," Avaaz, August 14, 2012, https://secure.avaaz.org/act/media.php?press_id=379.

13 See, for instance, Gene Sharp and Joshua Paulson. *Waging Nonviolent Struggle: 20th Century Cractice and 21st Century Potential*, (Boston: Extending Horizons Books, 2005). Robert Helvey, *On Strategic Nonviolent Conflict: Thinking About the Fundamentals*, (Boston: Albert Einstein Institute, 2004).

14 See Wael Ghonim, *Revolution 2.0*, (New York: Houghton Mifflin Harcourt, 2012).

15 Drew Westen, *The Political Brain: The Role of Emotion in Deciding the Fate of the Nation*, (New York: Public Affairs, 2007); George Lakoff, *Don't Think of an Elephant!: Know Your Values and Frame the Debate: The Essential Guide for Progressives*, (White River Junction, VT: Chelsea Green Publishing, 2004).

16 See Mary Kaldor, *Global Civil Society: An Answer to War*. (Cambridge, UK: Polity Press, 2003).

Chapter 13. Beyond Survival

1   See Laurence Gonzales, *Deep Survival—Who Lives, Who Dies, and Why?*, (New York: W. W. Norton & Company, 2003).

2   See Don Michael, *On Learning to Plan & Planning to Learn*, (San Francisco: Jossey-Bass Publishers, 1973).

3   See Ian Mitroff, *Why Some Companies Emerge Stronger and Better from a Crisis: Seven Essential Lessons for Surviving Disaster*. (New York: AMACOM, 2005).

4   See Maureen O'Hara and Graham Leicester, *Dancing at the Edge: Competence, Culture and Organization in the 21st Century*, (Axminster: Triarchy, 2012).

Index

C

D

Acknowledgments

Editors' Acknowledgments

This book is a culmination of myriad journeys, inspirations, and ideas. Its contents reflect the work of twenty different authors, writing on subjects as wide-ranging as the nature of state failure to human psychology. They combine to describe a present reality and plausible future that we hope startles, motivates, and helps everyday citizens and our political leaders to resolve some of the most exigent issues faced by humanity. This work would not be possible without the support of innumerable people and institutions, whom the editors and authors thank sincerely and with deep regard.

The editors would first and foremost like to thank Douglas Reil, Leslie Larson, and the entire family at North Atlantic Books, who have supported this project at every stage, and Penguin Random House for helping us distribute this work to a wide audience.

To our coauthors: we are deeply indebted to you. It has been an honor and privilege to work on this project with you, and we look forward to continued collaboration and future publications together.

Andrew Trabulsi would like to sincerely thank: my mother and father, who have supported me in every venture I've ever undertaken, and my sister and brother, Julie and Stephen, who've helped me grow in more ways than I can describe. Thank you as well to: my love, Alexandra Haygood, Nick Leach, Bjorn Cooley, Ting Kelly, Alex Gold, Mick Costigan, Kosuke Hata, Bettina Warburg, Andrew Douglas, Beto Borges, Vasco van Roosmalen, the Paiter-Surui, the Meyer family, Cecily Guest, Jay Ogilvy, Hunter Lovins, Greg Miller, Doug Carmichael, Chris Williams, Deniz Leuenberger, Maureen Taylor, Renn Vara, David Erickson, Edward West, Dori Koll, David Martin, Global Business Network, the Deloitte Center for the Edge, the Long Now Foundation, and the Institute for the Future. Also, a deep thanks to the infinite others who are not mentioned here—friends, colleagues, and strangers—who have inspired me, supported me, and challenged me to explore the world intimately and without fear.

Noah Raford would like to thank: Vinay Gupta, whose conversations planted the seed for this book, David Stevens and Alex Evans, whose early input helped give the project life, Dick O'Neill and John O'Connor, whose sustaining comments on early drafts at the Highlands Forum provided incisive direction, and the many other authors, friends, family members, and colleagues who have helped shape the thinking behind this work. Thank you all.

Finally, the editors and authors would like to thank Napier Collyns, to whom this book is dedicated, whose mentorship, ruthless curiosity, and unremitting support has helped bring this group of writers together, inspired us to carry this project through, and taught many of us how to be better human beings.

Contributor Acknowledgments

William Barnes: Thanks for comments/help on either the earlier version or this version of this paper from: Craig Calhoun, Andrew Blau, Robby Mockler, Andrew Trabulsi, Noah Raford, Jenny Johnston, Erik Olin Wright, Larry Rosenberg, George Scialabba, Jack Spence, Napier Collyns, Bob Horn, Rich Hayes, Dorothy Wall.

Tuesday Reitano: I offer my greatest thanks to my family, Carlo, Giorgio and Valentina, for the constant love, support and patience, and to Mark Shaw for inspiration and advice.

John P. Sullivan: I would like to acknowledge my doctoral advisor Manuel Castells for his tutelage and insights into networks and their impact on the state. His guidance refined my understanding of the complex dynamics of sovereignty and emerging state forms. I would also like to acknowledge the Intelligence Studies Section of the International Studies Association where I have chaired, co-chaired, or participated in panels on this book's theme for over a decade. The collaborative inquiry of that and related efforts are helping to refine our knowledge of networks and the space of flows of the state forms of the future.

Peter Taylor: Thanks to Dr. Kalypso Nicolaidis of St Antony's College, Oxford, for our discussions.

Shlok Vaidya: Many thanks to John Robb for his mentorship, Matt Devost for his patience, and Mark Pfeifle for his insight. Also, India's National Security Guard for listening, and the Railway Protection Force for their assistance.

About the Contributors

Dr. William Barnes holds a PhD in political science from the University of Michigan and a law degree from the University of California, Berkeley. Since 1968, he has taught political science—off and on, hither and yon— while, since 1985, making his living as a trial lawyer in the San Francisco Bay Area. From 1986 to 2006 he worked in, studied, and published extensively on election campaigns and preelection public opinion polling in Nicaragua and El Salvador. He currently teaches part time at UC Berkeley and City College of San Francisco.

Dr. Daniel Biró is currently a lecturer in international studies at the University of South Australia. Daniel holds a PhD in politics and international relations from the Australian National University as well as an MScEcon in strategic studies (Aberystwyth), and a MA in European studies (CEU). The research for his chapter was done as part of—and was included in the final version of—his PhD thesis, to be published as a monograph in 2015 (Ashgate). His current research interest revolves around the issue of marginalization and deviance in international politics, including state failure and the policies of state building, as well as the so-called rogue states.

James Bosworth is a freelance writer and consultant based in Managua, Nicaragua. Most recently, he has written reports on Latin American security, politics, and energy issues; arms trafficking in El Salvador; organized crime in Honduras; and cybersecurity cooperation to combat botnets. His work has been cited in U.S. congressional testimony as well as in the *Economist*, *Wall Street Journal*, *Christian Science Monitor*, and other media outlets. Prior to freelancing, James was associate for communications at the Inter-American Dialogue and director of research at the Rendon Group. James blogs at www.bloggingsbyboz.com, where he provides daily analysis and commentary on Latin American politics and U.S. foreign policy. He has a BA in political science and history from Washington University in St. Louis.

Dr. Nils Gilman is associate chancellor at the University of California, Berkeley. He holds a BA, MA, and PhD in intellectual history from the University of California, Berkeley, and is the author of *Mandarins of the Future: Modernization Theory in Cold War America* (2003) and *Deviant Globalization* (2011), an anthology that explores how globalized black-market economies are challenging traditional state authority. He is also the coeditor of *Humanity*, an international journal of human rights, humanitarianism, and development, published by the University of Pennsylvania Press.

Dr. Jesse Goldhammer is a principal at Doblin, Monitor Deloitte's innovation consultancy, where he develops transformational innovation programs that help clients to solve vexing public and private sector challenges. He is an accomplished innovator, instructor, facilitator, and presenter. Jesse earned a PhD from UC Berkeley in political science. An expert in modern political theory, Jesse has coauthored *Deviant Globalization: Black Market Economy in the 21st Century* (Continuum Publishing, 2011) and written *The Headless Republic* (Cornell University Press, 2005). Dr. Daniel S. Gressang is a strategy and engagement lead for the U.S. Department of Defense and an adjunct professor for the University of Maryland University College. Daniel holds an AB and MA in political science from the University of Alabama, an MS in strategic intelligence from the National Intelligence University, and a PhD in government and politics from the University of Maryland. The views expressed in his contribution are his own and do not reflect the policy or position of the Department of Defense or the United States Government.

Vinay Gupta is a disaster relief, contingency management, and environmental change consultant. He is also the director of the Hexayurt Project, an open-source sustainable-housing initiative and has worked with Rocky Mountain Institute, STAR-TIDES at National Defense University, and UCL Institute for Security and Resilience Studies on a broad range of topics from cybersecurity to renewable-energy investment policy. His first book, *The Future We Deserve,* focuses on mass collaboration as a way to break out of constrained thinking about the future.

Paul Hilder is an organizer and social entrepreneur. He is a board director and cofounder of the British movement 38 Degrees and a cofounder of the global debate website www.opendemocracy.net. He served as campaign director for Avaaz (http://avaaz.org) from its launch until 2010, then as director of campaigns at Oxfam, and most recently as vice president of global campaigns for www.change.org. He has worked on social innovation, development, governance, and conflict resolution internationally, in particular in the Middle East and Europe. He is the author or editor of several publications, including *Contentious Citizens* (Carnegie, 2007).

Graham Leicester is director of the International Futures Forum. He previously ran Scotland's leading think tank, the Scottish Council Founda tion, founded in 1997. From 1984 to 1995 he served as a diplomat in H Diplomatic Service, specializing in China (he speaks Mandarin Chin and the European Union. Between 1995 and 1997 he was senior re fellow with the Constitution Unit at University College London. also worked as a freelance professional cellist, including with Concert Orchestra. He has a strong interest in governance, i and education; is a senior adviser to the British Council on   and has previously worked with OECD, the World Bank other agencies on the themes of governance in a knowledge society and the governance of the long term.

Samuel Logan is the regional manager for Latin America at iJET International, an investigative journalist, and author. He is the director of Southern Pulse | Networked Intelligence, a decentralized, field-based investigations organization, and he has reported on security, energy, politics, economics, organized crime, terrorism, and black markets in Latin America since 1999.

Dr. Noah Raford is a strategist and policy advisor with a focus on foresight and public innovation. He was a senior manager at Monitor / GBN; a senior researcher at the London School of Economics Complexity Programme; a visiting researcher at the Institute for Science, Innovation, and Society at the University of Oxford; and a fellow of the International Futures Forum. Noah received a BA from Brown University, his MSc from the University College London, and his PhD at the Massachusetts Institute of Technology (MIT).

Tuesday Reitano has been working in the field of international development and peacebuilding for the last fifteen years, for ten years in the United Nations, and then as an independent consultant. She currently heads the Secretariat of the Global Initiative against Transnational Organized Crime (www.globalinitaitive.net) a Geneva-based think tank that she helped to found in 2011. Tuesday has worked extensively in fragile states, serving as an advisor to governments and multilateral organizations on issues of governance, justice reform, and post-conflict transition planning. Tuesday specializes in issues relating to transnational organized crime and counterterrorism and has published extensively in both policy and academic journals. She has an MSc in international development, conflict, and security from the University of Leicester, an MBA from McGill University, and an MPA from New York University.

Mark Safranski is a senior analyst at Wikistrat, LLC and is a contributor to *Pragati: The Indian National Interest*. He has an MA in diplomatic history and an MSEd in administration. He is the editor of *The John Boyd Round-table: Debating Science, Strategy, and War* and a contributing author to *Threats in the Age of Obama* and *The Handbook of 5GW*, all published by Nimble Books. Mark is the founder of zenpundit.com, a respected defense, strategy, and foreign policy blog.

Dr. John P. Sullivan is a lieutenant with the Los Angeles Sheriff's Department. He is also a senior fellow at the Stephenson Disaster Management Institute (SDMI) at Louisiana State University, Senior El Centro Fellow at *Small Wars Journal,* and an adjunct researcher on society and global crime at the VORTEX Research Group, Bogotá, Colombia. He is coeditor or coauthor of several books, most recently *Studies in Gangs and Cartels* (Routledge, 2014). He has a PhD from the Open University of Catalonia.

Dr. Peter Taylor received a BA and DPhil from Oxford and then spent thirty years in the London insurance market. After retiring, in 2006, Peter researched into the theory of risk at the Oxford Martin School and helped establish two not-for-profit organizations—the Lighthill Risk Network and then the Oasis Loss Modelling Framework. His publications include "Catastrophes and Insurance" (in *Global Catastrophic Risks,* Oxford University Press, 2008); "The Mismeasure of Risk" (in *The Handbook of Risk Theory,* Springer, 2011); and "Realizing the Value of Uncertainty" (presented at the AonBenfield Hazards Conference, 2013).

Hardin Tibbs is a strategist, futurist, and educator based in Cambridge, England. His consulting work helps organizations understand and adapt to change in the strategic environment. He has worked with leading companies and government agencies in Europe, the United States, Australasia, and South-East Asia on topics ranging from car technology for Nissan to food policy for the U.K. government. His writing about sustainability has been influential, and his work on industrial ecology while a consultant at Arthur D. Little in the late 1980s helped define a new approach to environment and technology. His website is www.hardintibbs.com.

Andrew Trabulsi is a consultant and entrepreneur focusing on technology and economic development policy. Based in San Francisco, his work and research has included technology capacity building with indigenous communities in the Amazon rainforest, community development with the Federal Reserve Bank, innovation consulting with Deloitte LLP, and content development for the Economist Group. Andrew advises public, private, and social-sector clients on issues of strategy, organization, analysis, sustainability, and geopolitics.

Shlok Vaidya is contributing editor for The OODA Loop and is writing a book on the future of India, from which his chapter in this volume is excerpted. He has served as a defense consultant specializing in information operations and as an energy security analyst at a Washington, DC, think tank. Shlok is a frequent contributor to the international press and has conducted extensive field research on infrastructure disruption in India.

Dr. Steven Weber is a professor in the school of information and department of political science at the University of California Berkeley. He is the author of *The Success of Open Source;* coauthor (with Bruce Jentleson) of *End of Arrogance: America in the Global Competition of Ideas;* and coeditor (with Nils Gilman and Jesse Goldhammer) of *Deviant Globalization: Black Market Economy in the 21st Century.*